THE MUNNARI CHRONICLES



# MUNNARI
## ECLIPSED

NOVEL SIX

ML BELLANTE

Munnari Eclipsed

The Munnari Chronicles Series

ML Bellante



BookWise Publishing, Riverton, Utah

www.bookwisepublishing.com

*Producer and Cover/Interior Design:* K Christoffersen

*Cover and Graphics Illustrator*: Hugo Solis

*Cartographer:* Hugo Solis

Library of Congress Control Number: Pending

ISBN 978-1-60645-315-5 Trade Paperback $14.99

ISBN 978-1-60645-316-2 eBook $4.99

Order online at Amazon.com

MunnariChronicles.com

MLBellanteBooks.com

12/20/2022 version

# DEDICATION

*This work is dedicated to family members, friends,*
*and production staff who have been my beta readers.*
*Many thanks for your support and suggestions.*
*They are very much appreciated.*

# TABLE OF CONTENTS

# CHAPTER 1

# A NEW PURPOSE

Maaryah's attacks had become more vicious; it was as though she was venting all of her malevolence toward the Showton, her nemesis, in the punches and kicks she was delivering. Her speed was increasing, and it was all Tondo could do to stay ahead of her combinations, blocking them with the punch mitts he was wearing. Maaryah's hands were wrapped in leather straps even though her fists had become hardened and calloused by her constant practice. Her left slammed into his right punch mitt, and then a right bashed into his left. She followed the two punches with a knee kick that her bondmate managed only partially to deflect, and her knee slammed into his left thigh, causing him to recoil in pain. She continued her combinations as she had been trained, and Tondo's right mitt caught her left uppercut; however, the rising pain in his thigh slowed his reaction to her right cross that skipped over the top of his left mitt and nailed him on the left side of his jaw, dropping him like a rock to the barn floor.

He opened his eyes and focused on two tear-filled golden-amber eyes hovering just above his face. She was saying something, but all he could hear was the ringing in his ears. Slowly, the ringing subsided, and he could hear her voice as if it were in the distance. He blinked, trying to figure out what had just happened and why he was on his back. He began to feel pain on the left side of his face, and he rubbed his jaw with his mitt.

"Tondo, say something; please, answer me!" she cried, her voice in a near panic.

"What happened?" he mumbled as he continued rubbing his jaw.

"I hit you; I hit you hard. I didn't mean to; it just happened. I'm so sorry," she cried.

The cobwebs were beginning to clear from his mind, and he realized what had happened. "Did you just knock me unconscious?"

"Yes. I didn't mean it. I'm sorry, I'm sorry! Are you all right?" She was obviously upset and worried.

"How long was I out?"

"I don't know; maybe as long as it takes to count to fifty or one-hundred," she told him.

He sat up. "Fifty or one-hundred? Oy!" He got to his feet, staggered to a small divitz bale, and plopped down. He looked at her and said, "In all the fights I've ever been in, including battles, I never was knocked out. Now, there I was, flat on my back, punched out by my loving bondmate. You have learned your lessons well; I think a bit too well." He rubbed his jaw again and moved it from side to side, trying to chase away the pain.

"Please forgive me. I didn't mean to hurt you," she said as she kneeled in front of him and removed his punch mitts.

"Oy, knocked out by a woman. If First Sergeant Ames were to learn of this, he'd never let me forget it." Tondo stood up, still a little wobbly, and staggered to the ladder leading to the loft. He slowly climbed it until his head poked above the loft floor. He looked right and then left. When he was satisfied, he descended and staggered back to the divitz bale and flopped onto it.

"Why did you do that?" Maaryah asked as she sat next to him.

"I was just checking to see if Numo and Sofi were up there. I don't want any witnesses to my shame," he told her with a chuckle.

She gave him a push, "Stop it! You're okay."

"That was a pretty good punch. I don't think anyone has ever hit me that hard."

"I'm sorry. I just got carried away. It seems all I want to do is attack, ever since I felt good enough to get out of bed."

Over five detzamars—more than two-hundred days—had passed since the assassins attacked the estate. She'd spent over two detzamars in bed, another detz housebound but ambulatory, and the last two detzamars exercising and training. At first, she became winded very quickly, but that had passed, and she was nearly back to her earlier form prior to the attack. Although her inner healing power had hastened her recovery, it did nothing to relieve the sleep-terrors she suffered several times a wernt. Tondo would awaken her and hold her tightly, caressing her head until she could relax and attempt to go back to sleep.

"Tondo," she said.

"Yes?" he responded.

"I can't do this anymore."

“You can quit training anytime you wish. I thought you wanted to train.” He was a bit mystified by her statement.

“That’s not what I mean. I found myself at the cliffs again yesterday. I just wanted to lean forward and fall, but I stopped myself when I thought of the pain it would cause you.” Shock filled his face as he stared into her eyes, wondering if he’d heard her correctly. “Yes, it’s true, and it’s not the first time since the attack. I miss our children.” She covered her face with her hands and began sobbing. He took her in his arms and held her tightly.

“So do I, my love, so do I,” he commiserated as he caressed her head.

“I just can’t do this anymore,” she repeated.

“What is it you can’t do?”

“I can’t stay here and count divitz bales. Counting bales was my purpose before we had children. Loving and nurturing our children was my purpose when they came. I need a new purpose in life. That vestang killed our son and took our daughter. I want Maari back! The Showton and his assassins must pay for what they’ve done. We have to put an end to their evil before others suffer like we are. When Foreman Nestor whipped me, I burned with anger and revenge. There was nothing I could do about it as a slave. I’m not a slave anymore, and I will do something about this!” She paused and took a deep breath before continuing. “I want your blessing.”

“My blessing for what?”

“I must join the fight and end this pestilence. I’ll either lose my mind or take the plunge if I don’t,” she admitted.

“What do you have in mind?”

"The Te Femma warrior faction needs recruits. I want to join them and fight against the Showton. I want to kill him just as I killed the Slayers."

Her words hit Tondo hard. He knew emotions had been building in her ever since she learned of the loss of their two children; however, he never guessed it would lead to this. He wanted to change her mind, but where would it take them if he did? He knew exactly how she felt, and he also knew he would exact his vengeance, claim his pound of flesh. Could he in good conscience deny her the same outlet? No.

"Are you sure that's what you want? The sisterhood will never accept you. You'll always be an outsider in their eyes," he warned.

"I don't care! I just want to fight. I once wondered how men could go into battle over and over. Now I know," she told him as blistering vengeance consumed her.

He paused as she waited with searching eyes. He recalled his many previous battles on this world and his homeworld. He thought of the horror and threat he had faced. Worry and fret for her safety fell over him like a dark shroud. He couldn't bring himself to utter the words of his approval. All he could do was nod as deep sorrow overcame him. She returned a smile, kissed him on the cheek, and walked out of the back of the barn, moving to the archery range. He remained seated on the bale as a tear ran over the dampness of her kiss, for he knew the Showton had killed her innocence as assuredly as his assassin had killed their son. The scar on her soul was as tangible as Foreman Nestor's scar on her back. The attack had changed her, and never again would their lives be the same. He wondered if they would recognize each other when this horrible war was over. It was a heartrending realization, yet there was no going back. He didn't want this; she didn't want this; but this is what they had, and there was no way of escaping its reality.

Later that day, Tondo sent an army messenger to summon the recently promoted Sutrum Sestardus Harmon, the senior non-officer for the entire army and Maaryah's father. The messenger was also to contact Haro, the sword and armor-smith, who was still overseeing the construction of the two huge cannons Tondo had ordered built.

Idop and Fayeetez had returned to their posts near the Ancient City a couple of detzamars earlier. An entire troop of mounted Tondo Brothers had been summoned to the estate. Never again would he relax his vigilance for the safety of his residence. The Showton had shown his utter ruthlessness and a willingness to make this fight personal, so Tondo would respond in kind. There was little he could do now other than prepare, but when he retook Te Femma, and swore he would free the city, his offensive would pummel the Showton's forces until his nemesis was defeated, captured, and executed. There was no room in Tondo's heart for mercy this time. This was now a personal battle, and it would be a fight to the death. His blistering hatred of their nemesis assured him he could not lose.

Tondo had spread the false rumor that his bondmate, the ameera, had been killed during the attack. He had personally asked each estate resident and his close friends to keep his secret. He feared that if the Showton got word that not only had his attack failed to kill the main target—himself—but also had failed to kill his bondmate, another attack might be attempted. King Teg-ar-mos and Queen Ootyiah were aware of his ploy and concern; however, Queen Ezora and Rana Fardinza were kept in the dark.

The queen of Te Femma had been growing more and more frustrated by the day. Not only was she angry at Tondo's delay and seeming lack of urgency in freeing her city, but she had also been living off the feral king's generosity, which irritated her to no end. She had little faith in Tondo's new weapons, the big guns he was developing. She was certain nothing could bring down the Te Femma city wall, and his delay was a waste of time. When his feral army arrived at her beloved city, she knew the sisterhood would rise and retake the city themselves. Little could she imagine the cruelty and repression the Showton and his minions were capable of, nor the horror her subjects were suffering.

Tondo and Sutrum Sestardus Harmon were sitting in the manor house living room with worried expressions, their eyes rolled up, looking at the ceiling.

After a few moments of quiet, Maaryah's angry voice echoed down the stairway, "Don't you dare put your hands there!" After another few quiet moments, she grouched, "I've warned you once already! If you touch me like that again, I'll strangle you with that cord!"

A few more moments passed as Tondo and Harmon continued to stare at the ceiling, occasionally glancing toward one another with worried expressions.

"That's it!" Maaryah yelled, "I'll crush you like a creeper!" The two men heard rustling sounds and then a thump.

"Master Tondo, help me!" Haro called out in panic. Tondo looked at Harmon, slowly got out of his chair, and deliberately marched up the stairs. When he entered the bedchamber, he found poor Haro shoved against the wall with Maaryah's right hand at his throat, pinning him in place. She was wearing a short, utilitarian tunic.

"I warned you not to touch me that way," Maaryah's tone expressed anger and frustration.

Haro's eyes were full of fear as the tall woman held him by the neck. His eyes glanced to the side, and he saw Tondo, "Praise the great god! Master Tondo, help me!"

Tondo stopped and examined the scene, and after a short delay, he asked, "Maaryah, what are you doing?"

"This little creeper kept touching me in private places. I warned him to stop, but he didn't listen. Now, I'm going to squeeze his neck until his eyes pop," she carped.

"Please, lady Maaryah, I must take these measurements," Haro pleaded; a thick cord with markings was draped around his neck and both ends hung in front of him.

"Maaryah, let him go," Tondo said calmly. Maaryah looked his way and reluctantly released her grip on Haro's neck, but she remained in front of him, her left hand pushing against Haro's shoulder, keeping him pinned against the wall.

"I refuse to put up with this indignity another instant," she growled emphatically.

"Now, remember, you agreed to this," Tondo reminded her.

"I didn't realize he'd be putting his hands all over me."

"My love, he has to take these measurements if the armor is to fit properly. You don't want it to pinch and bite tender places, do you?" Tondo asked as he suppressed a laugh.

"Why can't I just use Te Femma armor?" she wondered. She gave Haro an evil stare, released him, and walked to Tondo.

"There is no Te Femma armor, at least not until the city is freed. Anyway, I want you in the best armor possible, and Haro makes the best. Remember, the armor he crafted for me saved my life more than once. I want nothing less for you," Tondo counseled.

"Does he have to keep touching me? I hate that."

"I don't mean nothing by it, lady Maaryah. I have to make sure the measurements are correct. Please don't be angry with me," Haro pleaded.

"Maaryah, let him finish his work; it will only take a short time," Tondo told her. He could see she was not convinced by his or Haro's pleas, but she submitted. She moved to the center of the room and put her hands on her hips.

"Go ahead, Haro, you can proceed," Tondo encouraged. With some trepidation, Haro moved toward her. Unexpectedly, her orange aura ignited, and Haro jumped back. "Maaryah, that's enough of that!" Tondo scolded. A darker expression of disgust filled her countenance. She growled her angst, pushed down her aura, and it extinguished. Tondo nodded to Haro, who nervously continued his work, grateful that Tondo remained in the room until he finished his task.

A few days later, as dawn was breaking, Maaryah and Harmon departed the estate on mounts with neither notice nor fanfare. As they reached the knoll overlooking the estate grounds, they took a short side trip to a grove of oak-like trees where a small grave had been placed. A flat stone covered it, engraved with the words 'Harmon—beloved son of Tondo and Maaryah.' She dismounted. Maaryah kneeled and brushed away some recently fallen leaves. She gently touched the stone as her tears began to flow, spilling onto the stone marker. Her father silently watched as she expressed her unending love for her baby boy, yearning to cuddle him in her arms once again. Reluctantly she remounted, and they continued their journey.

Several days later, Harmon and Maaryah arrived at the Teg-ar-mos Brigade post. They turned their samarans over to the army's stable attendant. The two walked the remaining distance to the Te Femma warrior faction encampment on the post, Harmon leading the way and Maaryah trailing behind, carrying a small bag of personal items over her shoulder. When they reached the warrior faction headquarters, Harmon asked an aide where the faction commander was, and he was told she had gone to the recently constructed training building. Harmon and Maaryah walked to it, and Harmon entered while Maaryah waited outside.

"Sutrum Sestardus Harmon, what brings you here; come to inspect our new training building?" Megatus Nedenna asked, her voice echoing in the large, empty room. She recognized him because he had been in many of the meetings. she and her senior lieutenants had participated in with Sutrum Megatus Idop, the recently promoted army commander. She knew Harmon's main priority was looking out for the welfare of the soldiers in the army.

"I'm glad to see it's finished, zerr. It will be much better when the tables and benches arrive," he told her, his voice also echoing in the empty room. "However, I didn't come here to see the building. There's a new recruit outside who wishes to join your faction, and I'm sure she's tough enough to become one of your sisters."

"Bring her in, and we'll see," Nedenna told him, a scowl replacing her smile.

"Maaryah!" Harmon called. Maaryah walked through the doorway and set her bag on the floor near the door. She then proceeded to where the others were standing. "This is Maaryah. Maaryah, this is Megatus Nedenna, commander of the Te Femma warrior faction, and these are her subcommanders, Neva Megatus Deveena and Neva Megatus Zuni." Maaryah simply nodded, not wanting to display any knowledge of military protocol at this time. Harmon smiled wryly and continued, "Obviously, she doesn't know anything about army procedure. I'm sure you can change that."

"Where did she come from?" Zuni asked.

"She's from one of the outlying estates, and she says she's tired of watching divitz grow," Harmon told her.

"Oy? Divitz! All right, sutrum sestardus, I'll handle it from here. You're dismissed," Nedenna said. Harmon saluted and walked out, not giving his daughter a second look. Maaryah felt alone and isolated as she stood before the three taller women. They seemed to be examining her, attempting to determine her worth. "Have you had any training in defending yourself?" Nedenna asked.

"I've had some," Maaryah answered.

"Is that a slave mark?" Deveena wondered, pointing to her forehead.

"Yes, I was once a slave."

"Oy, that's just wonderful. Not only is she a sub, but she's also another slave. Just what we need," Deveena grumbled sarcastically.

"Do you really think you're tough enough to join the Te Femma warriors?" Zuni asked.

"Yes, I can take care of myself if I have to, and I can handle anything a sister can," Maaryah answered.

"Ha, you've heard of the sisterhood. I think she should be tested before we let her in. She seems too short," Deveena grumbled. Maaryah was very tall for a woman from the kingdom, but all three Te Femman commanders were taller.

"Yes," Nedenna agreed. "Zuni, fetch Sestardi Dori. She'll help us determine whether this one is worth our time."

Zuni left the building, and while they waited, Nedenna walked around Maaryah a few times, scanning her frame from head to foot. "You appear to be healthy and strong. Are you of sound mind and body?"

"Yes," was Maaryah's simple reply.

Zuni returned, followed by another woman. She was tall, stocky, and tough-looking. Zuni handed Nedenna a couple of long leather straps. Nedenna passed them to Maaryah. "Do you know what these are for?" she asked. Maaryah nodded and started wrapping her fists. The other woman did the same. When both women had finished, Nedenna said, "I expect you to defend yourself the best you can. Sestardi Dori is quite skilled, so don't feel discouraged if she knocks you down. I expect you to get up and keep fighting until I say stop. Any questions?" Maaryah shook her head and got into a defensive stance. Nedenna stepped away as Dori approached, banging her wrapped fists together with the glow of delight in her eyes.

"Hoy, little sub, let's see what you're made of," Dori huffed as she advanced. Maaryah stood her ground as she watched Dori prepare to launch a right-hand punch. Dori's arm swung toward Maaryah in a wild haymaker. Maaryah ducked, and Dori's swing passed over her head. Maaryah stepped forward, quickly hitting Dori in the forehead with a stunning left jab. The sestardi's head snapped back, and then Maaryah launched a right cross, pushing off with her trailing right foot and putting the weight of her body behind the punch. Her fist slammed into the side of Dori's jaw, and the sestardi dropped, ending up spread-eagle on the wooden floor.

Maaryah hovered over her until it was apparent the sestardi wasn't getting up anytime soon; then, she walked over to Nedenna and asked, "Is there anything more to this test?"

The three officers looked at each other and then at Dori with expressions of disbelief. After some delay, Nedenna said, "That's all."

"Easy test," Maaryah told her as she began removing the leather straps from her hands. Nedenna turned and walked out of the building, her two subordinates following.

Maaryah was confused. The three officers had just walked out, leaving her with no idea what she was to do next. She went to her bag of personal things and pulled out a waterskin and a towel. She moistened the towel and returned to the unconscious Dori. She began wiping the sestardi's face.

Dori soon began moving, then she groaned, "What happened?"

"I hit you, and you went down," Maaryah told her.

Dori sat up and began rubbing the side of her jaw. "Lucky punch," she growled.

"Would you like to try again?" Maaryah asked, her voice firm and self-assured.

Dori looked at her and smiled, "I like your confidence, little sub." She began to stand, and Maaryah helped by steadying her.

"What's a sub, and why do you and the officers call me that?"

"A sub is a woman who lets a man control her; she's subservient to her feral masters, as all you outsider women are," Dori told her.

"Outsider? Is that someone who's not from Te Femma?" Maaryah asked, acting like a dumb recruit.

"Yes. Where did you learn to fight like that?" Dori wondered.

"A family member is a soldier, and he trained me."

"A feral taught you, ha? He must be a tough one. Most of these ferals are worthless trash, not worth my spit."

"I take it an outsider male is a feral."

"Ha; crude, unkempt, smelly. I don't know how you subs tolerate 'em," Dori grumbled.

"Stop calling me a sub, or I'll punch you in the face again," Maaryah told her angrily. She already hated the term. It reminded her of the days when she was referred to as slave.

Dori gave her an angry glare, then her expression softened, and she smiled. "I think you're gonna be all right, little one. You're not like those undersized subs who tried to join the warrior faction before."

"What happened to them?" Maaryah wondered.

"They either failed the test or got chased away by the sisters," Dori explained. "But I don't think you'll run."

"The sisters? Who are they?"

"Follow me; I'll introduce you," Dori said with a wry smile. Maaryah had a feeling this introduction was not going to be a friendly one.

Sestardi Dori walked into the barracks where several women were waiting. "Apto, what took so long? Are we going to have training today, or are we just going to sit here?" one of the women asked in an angry tone.

"Stop calling me apto. As long as we're in the Feral's army, you'll refer to me as sestardi. Is that understood?" The other woman nodded. "Good. The officers introduced me to a new recruit. Maaryah, come here," Dori called. Maaryah entered and looked around, her bag over her shoulder. The other women gave her cold stares.

"She's a sub, isn't she?" one asked with disgust.

"She's a wretched slave, too," another noted.

Dori nodded. "Maaryah, you can take this cot," the sestardi told her as she pointed to the empty kip nearest the door. Maaryah walked over to the bunk and dropped her bag on it. The woman sitting on the closest berth got up, walked to Maaryah's cot, grabbed her bag, and tossed it through the open doorway.

"I won't have no stinking sub sleeping next to me. We're all Stontza here, and not only are you not Stontza, you're a worthless sub-slave. Take your cot outside. You can sleep under the stars where I can't smell you," she growled.

Maaryah walked through the doorway and retrieved her bag. She reentered and dropped it on her assigned bed once more. The antagonistic sister reached for it again, and when she did, Maaryah shoved her hard, and the sister lost her balance and fell over her own bunk, ending up on the floor. She got up and stormed toward Maaryah.

Sestardi Dori intervened, stepping between the two. "Today, we're going to practice unarmed fighting. You two will be the first to show me what ya got," Dori ordered. "All right, everybody to the Stontza Circle. Move it!"

The sisters dashed out; Maaryah waited for the others to exit, and then she followed at a trot until she reached a large circle outlined by small white rocks. Maaryah's opponent stood near its center, grinning and slamming her leather-wrapped fists together. Maaryah also entered the ring and waited. Dori handed Maaryah leather straps and waited while she wrapped her fists. The two women faced each other, and

Dori signaled a start. The Te Femman went down in a flash after Maaryah hit her with a triple combination of punches. Her opponent was helped out of the circle. Another quickly took her place, and Dori signaled another start. It wasn't long before the second Te Femman was assisted from the ring. Each Te Femma sister took her best shot at the newcomer one after the other, but in every encounter, Maaryah's opponent was defeated by punches, kicks, or throws.

By the end of the exercise, no one had been able to defeat the shorter sub. Maaryah was exhausted, sweaty, scraped, and bruised but undefeated. Not only had Tondo taught her how to fight, but he had also increased her endurance by conducting training sessions from time to time that went on for segment after segment, concluding with a long-distance run. She hated those sessions, but now she fully understood and appreciated their purpose.

The women filed back to their barracks and prepared to take their daily baths in the wash-building, a room containing several large barrels of warm water set partially into the ground. The others waited, and Maaryah was permitted to choose a barrel first. She disrobed and climbed into the nearest one. The other women were astonished when they saw her scars. They looked at each other, wondering what had happened to her.

Maaryah relaxed as she soaked in the warm water, her aches and pains slowly subsiding. She wondered what she had gotten herself into. Not only had she fought the sestardi, but she also had to fight every other woman in her barracks of two ranks less one—eleven additional sisters altogether. As she leaned back in the soothing waters and pondered, she realized Dori had just done her a favor. She had defeated everyone in the two ranks assigned to her barracks and had gained their respect. Maybe, they would never accept her as one of their own, but if she earned their respect, that would be good enough for her.

# CHAPTER 2

# OPENING PANDORA'S BOX

Tondo and Haro remained at the estate until Hermanez arrived, then they sailed to the Ancient City's dock. Tondo gave him Maaryah's blue sword as they parted ways and told him to finish her armor as quickly as possible. It was a tall order because nearly all of Haro's time had been taken up by the construction of the two massive guns. Nevertheless, once the famed weaponsmith had shown Pendor how to build them, the blacksmith could handle it on his own, of course, with the assistance of many other army laborers assigned to the task by Tondo. Haro immediately began work on Maaryah's armor, but he would stop to inspect the progress on the guns several times a wernt.

Maaryah had been with the Te Femma warrior faction for more than two detzamars—over eighty days—and she was proving her worth daily. The sisters still referred to her as 'the sub,' but they had gained increasing respect for her. She worked hard, didn't complain no matter what the assignment, and learned quickly. Sestardi Dori noticed that Maaryah had a sharp mind and could solve problems quickly. The sisters would turn to the sub for a solution whenever the ranks had to resolve some training puzzle. Maaryah would organize her group, and they quickly solved the problem.

Dori wondered how a sub could assume leadership the way this recruit did. There was a mystery in her past that the shorter outsider was keeping to herself. However, the sestardi was a pragmatist, more interested in getting through the day successfully than anything else. As long as Maaryah kept doing what she was doing, Dori saw no need to question the mystery.

Neva Megatus Zuni had just summoned Sestardi Dori into her office for a meeting. "Sestardi, Megatus Nedenna just met with the one-eyed commander, and he says it's time we start following the feral army's organization. You have two ranks that need rank leaders—neva sestardies. Who do you recommend?" Zuni asked.

"Zerr, Areena. She's been in the Stontza the longest and always does a good job with her assignments," Dori told her.

"Good. You and I agree. And the other rank?" Zuni asked.

Dori took a deep breath and then said, "Maaryah."

"The sub! You can't be serious." Zuni was staring at the sestardi with cold eyes.

"Yes, zerr, I'm serious. The sub is the best warrior in the brick. If I didn't know better, I'd say she was an officer," Dori told her.

"How can a slave be a leader? She's spent all her miserable life doing what she's been told to do. Anyway, the sisters won't take orders from her." It was apparent that Zuni was displeased with the sestardi's choice.

"I don't know noth'n 'bout slaves, but I can tell you this: the sisters already do what she says, zerr. It's really something to behold. I wish I had more like her," Dori admitted.

"If I approve her promotion, it will be up to you to see that things work out. Let me warn you, Megatus Nedenna isn't going to like it, so you better make sure she's as good as a sister, or you will suffer the consequences. Do you still want her as a rank leader?"

"Yes, zerr," the sestardi replied firmly.

"All right then, call a formation of the ranks, and I'll present the two with their promotions," Zuni ordered. Dori saluted and exited the office.

A few days after Maaryah received her neva sestardi stripe, Megatus Nedenna was informed that Sutrum Megatus Idop would arrive in two days to inspect the small Te Femma faction. The women worked hard to make things look their best, but two days wasn't much warning.

When Idop arrived, the entire warrior faction was in formation, all three hundred or so. He rode in on his samaran, his white ensign flowing in the breeze close behind. He dismounted and strode to Nedenna. She saluted, and he returned it.

"Megatus, I will inspect your troops. Come with me," he told her.

The two marched to Zuni's side of the formation, and Idop moved down each rank, inspecting the women's equipment and asking a question here or there. Eventually, he reached Maaryah.

"You're kind of short to be in this faction," he said to her with a sly smile. She almost laughed because he was shorter than everyone around him. "What's your name?" he asked.

"Neva Sestardi Maaryah, zerr," she answered.

"Hoy, Neva Sestardi Maaryah, what do you think of your training?"

"Zerr, physical training, military protocol, and team-building exercises are excellent."

"What about combat training?" he asked.

"Zerr, combat training is all wrong for us. We are being trained to fight like men. The sisters have a more fluid style that suits their strengths better," Maaryah expounded. She could see Nedenna's eyes and expression grow angry.

"Sutrum Megatus Idop, Neva Sestardi Maaryah is an outsider, and she hasn't yet learned when to keep her mouth shut. She doesn't speak for the sisterhood. I suggest you ignore her remarks," Nedenna said, her voice strained and cold.

"You have enough confidence in her to make her a rank leader," he said. "Neva sestardi, do you think I should present this issue to the ameer?"

Maaryah's knees almost buckled. Idop had just put her in a dreadful position. As she had stated, the truth of the matter was that the sisters detested the style of combat drills they were required to learn. Yet, if she affirmed her statement, Megatus Nedenna would be outraged. She decided to go with the truth as she saw it and let the consequences fall where they may.

"Yes, zerr, I do," she replied firmly.

Idop smiled and took a step to the side, facing the next warrior in the rank. Nedenna also stepped to the side, taking her position directly in front of Maaryah. Her face was red with anger, and her eyes were throwing daggers at the shorter neva sestardi. After a brief delay, mercifully, Idop moved on with Nedenna following.

Two segments later, Sutrum Megatus Idop and his contingent departed the Te Femma warrior faction area. Hardly had their dust settled before Zuni, Dori, and Maaryah were summoned to faction headquarters. The three entered Nedenna's office and saluted. Their senior commander was sitting behind her desk, glaring at the three.

"Never have I been so humiliated by a member of my command. I knew the sub would be trouble, but I allowed her promotion because you two assured me she had shown herself up to the task. Obviously, you were in error. What do you have to say for yourselves?" Nedenna was livid.

"Zerr," Zuni began, "Maaryah only shared our own sentiments. You and I have discussed this issue in the past."

"It's my responsibility to present our concerns to the Feral, not a neva sestardi. If the one-eyed feral passes along what she told him and I get summoned to explain, I and the entire city faction will be embarrassed. It's bad enough to be under feral command; now, to have to explain the comments of a low-ranking sub is beyond reason," Nedenna's face was turning red again. "Sestardi, I understand you recommended her promotion. I expected better judgment from you." Nedenna paused, allowing Dori to respond.

"Zerr, if given the same choice, I would make the same recommendation. Maaryah is my best warrior," Dori said with confidence.

Nedenna's angry demeanor turned harder. "Even after her stupid comments, you two still support her. Unbelievable! Both of you are Munnoga-touched." Nedenna's indignant glare turned to Maaryah, "She needs to learn when to keep her thoughts to herself. Put her in charge of the privy detail, and keep her there until I feel she's learned how to keep her mouth shut. You two will be on the privy detail if the sub does anything else that stupid. Now, get out of here!" The three saluted their commander and exited her office.

The privy detail was the most detested duty in the faction and was rotated daily. Nedenna's order placed Maaryah in charge of that hated task until further notice. The assigned sisters spent all day cleaning and preparing privies—latrines—for the entire warrior faction's three-hundred or so members. After the privies were cleaned, the detail prepared the baths. This duty was not what Maaryah had in mind when joining the faction. It reminded her of a lowly slave assignment. At the end of every day, she had to endure the derisive remarks of her barracks mates. She could take their jibes, but she was losing their respect, and that she couldn't bear. She wondered if she could ever recover. She felt like a failure and cursed Idop for putting her in such a detestable situation.

Tondo had just cut a new order for the Te Femma warrior faction and had dismissed the T´ezpont commander. An aide entered and informed him that a temple priest had requested a meeting with him. He was told the priest seemed upset. "Bring him in," Tondo said. A short, thin man dressed in blue robes walked into his makeshift office in the corner of a warehouse on the Teg-ar-mos Brigade post. This was where Tondo's huge guns were being constructed.

"Ameer, thank you for taking the time from your busy schedule to meet with me. I am Sutro Adept Inverso, temple alchemist," the priest said in introduction.

"Master Inverso, how may I help you?" Tondo asked.

"Ameer, it has come to my attention that you are using an explosive powder. May I examine it?"

"Certainly," Tondo told him. He stood and exited the warehouse with the priest following close behind. He walked into an isolated small wooden building encased in several rows of sandbags. The building was too small for both men to enter, so the priest waited outside. Tondo soon returned with a handful of dark powder. He held his hand out and poured the powder into the priest's cupped hands. Inverso sniffed it and then looked up with a worried and concerned expression.

"Where did you get this?" the priest asked in near panic.

"I had it made right here," Tondo told him, surprised by the priest's terrified expression.

"Are you responsible for its mixture?" Inverso asked.

Tondo felt he was being interrogated. "Yes, why do you ask?"

The priest walked to a nearby trash fire and dropped the powder into it. It ignited with a rush of sound and white smoke. The priest looked stunned. "Ameer, you cannot use this. It is against temple code. It's too dangerous," the priest warned.

"Don't worry, Master Inverso, I've seen to its safekeeping."

"That's not what I mean. If you use this terrible power, you will answer to the unnamed god for the death and destruction it unleashes," the priest was nearly frantic. "How did you gain the knowledge to make it? Did one of the priests teach you?"

"Master Inverso, no priest showed me how to make it. The Caver people in the wasteland taught me. They use it to dig their tunnels. What's this about a temple code?"

"Ameer, the priests have known about this powder for hundreds of spans. The ancient ones warned us never to reveal its components and mixture, for the day its secret becomes known, the prophecies warn, devastation will follow. I beg you to destroy what you've already made and make no more."

Tondo was not about to change his plans. "Master Inverso, I have a city to retake, and I must free the people suffering under a murdering tyrant's foot. This powder will allow me to do it."

"That is no excuse for defying temple code. You leave me no choice. I must report this to the Sutro Seer," Inverso declared.

"Do what you must, master, and I will do what I must," Tondo affirmed.

Maaryah was knee-deep in a trench being dug for the disposal of bodily waste well off the post. She'd been on the privy detail for over two wernts—more than twenty days—and she was growing more frustrated every day. She did not expect this when she chose to join the Te Femma warrior faction. She wanted to train and prepare for battles against the Showton's armies, but all she was doing now was overseeing the digging of holes in the ground and the disposal of human waste. She may as well return to the estate and count divitz bales because she felt she was accomplishing nothing of substance here.

As Maaryah and the others were engaged in their odious duty, a detachment of four men riding samarans passed them. They had purple streamers on their helms, indicating they were assigned to Ameer Tondo's Headquarters Troop. Maaryah intently watched as they continued on, moving out of sight when they passed into the Te Femma encampment.

Maaryah returned to her repugnant assignment. When the trench was completed, the waste was dumped from a half-barrel, and its contents splashed onto one of the sisters. She growled her fury. If one wasn't careful, they could be splattered with waste; a very disgusting mishap, and the main reason the assignment was so hated. It was wise to keep one's mouth tightly shut when pouring the barrels into the trench.

Undoubtedly, Maaryah thought, that was why Nedenna assigned me to this loathsome duty.

After all the half-barrels were emptied, freshwater from another barrel was used to wash down the waste barrels, and a white powder was scattered over them. They were placed back into the wagon, and the privy detail headed back to the Te Femma area, where they returned the cleaned waste barrels, and then they moved to the next privy and repeated the process.

As Maaryah prepared her detail to go to the next latrine, Sestardi Dori approached. "Neva Sestardi Maaryah, clean yourself and put on clean clothes. You are to prepare for a meeting with Megatus Nedenna," she told her.

"Sestardi, what's this meeting about?" Maaryah wondered.

"I don't know, but you, me, and Neva Megatus Zuni have been summoned. You done anything lately to get us in trouble?" Dori laughed.

"Nothing I can think of, sestardi, unless the megatus doesn't like the job we've been doing with the officers' privy and bath," she replied jokingly.

"Hoy, hurry, and get ready. We don't want to keep her waiting. We could all end up on the privy detail," she said with a chuckle.

The three women entered Nedenna's office and saluted their commander. After returning their salutes, she spoke in a flinty tone, "Earlier today, I received an order from the Feral. It appears Sutrum Megatus Idop did indeed pass along what Neva Sestardi Maaryah told him. The Feral has ordered me to cease combat training immediately," Nedenna was staring at Maaryah the entire time she was telling them this news. Nedenna paused, and the other three wondered what was coming next. Nedenna continued, "Why that feral would value the words of a lowly non-officer escape me. In any case, he has ordered me to select twenty potential officers to be sent to the officer training school called T´ezpont. He has made arrangements for an accelerated program that will last three detzamars—one-hundred and twenty days. A training day will last eleven segments, and there will be a half-day of rest on Du-Zet. The Feral has ordered me to take this training, and I am also ordering you three to take it. Zuni, I want you to select seven more from your command. I expect the seven names on my desk by the end of the day. Neva Megatus Deveena will also attend, and she will choose nine from her command. The Feral says that after our training is completed, he wants us to train the sisters using our own combat tactics. He will then inspect our progress. Every time I think I have that feral figured out, he does something that surprises me. Maaryah, are all ferals like that?"

"No, zerr. Ameer Tondo has a reputation for being unpredictable," Maaryah offered.

"Indeed he is, and it's a well-deserved reputation. Maaryah, you got lucky this time, but don't press your luck. Do you understand what I'm saying?" Nedenna's voice was cold and stern.

"Yes, zerr!" Maaryah quickly responded.

"All right then, you're all dismissed." The three saluted and filed out.

When they got outside, Zuni stopped and faced the other two. "Maaryah, I'm going to keep my eye on you. Megatus Nedenna is right; you got lucky. I will say this, though, good job! I'm glad you spoke up; someone needed to," she turned and walked to her HQ.

It was Dori's turn to address the outsider, "I never expected nor wanted to become an officer. Now, I got you to blame for that. I should kick you in the arse," she said jokingly.

"You're welcome to try anytime, sestardi," Maaryah shot back with a laugh.

"Welcome back, Master Inverso. Have you made your report to the Sutro Seer?" Tondo asked.

"Yes, I have, and he has instructed me to inform you to cease making the powder. His Eminence knows its power and its danger, and he refuses to allow its manufacture by non-priests."

Tondo was about to stand and demand a meeting with the Sutro Seer himself, but he stopped and calmed a little as he thought about the priest's careful wording and tepid countenance. "Tell me, Master Inverso, will the priests provide me with what I require?" Tondo asked with a smile. He watched as Inverso's expression changed from moderate defiance to embarrassed submission. *He looks like a child who's been caught with his hand in the cookie jar,* Tondo thought.

"The Sutro Seer requires that I see your needs are met, but I implore you not to unleash this power on an innocent world," Inverso pleaded.

"It can't be helped. The world is no longer innocent, at least not as long as the Showton continues expanding his wickedness. I would prefer the powder not be used, as well, but I can think of no other way to save the people of Te Femma," he admitted.

The master's expression turned sad. "How much of the powder do you require?"

"I think ten wagon loads will be sufficient; for now, that is," Tondo told him as he watched the priest's expression change from sadness to horror and his shoulders slumped noticeably.

Inverso quickly regained his composure. "I'll personally see that it's done. May the great god forgive you for what you are doing," Inverso told him. Tondo didn't respond, for he already knew he was opening Pandora's box.

# CHAPTER 3

# ANOTHER FRONT

Every morning, just as the p´atezas cleared the horizon, and every evening just as it sank, the residents of the City of Women were required to show their proper respect to the Showton. He would sit on the queen's throne at the top of the palace stairs and glory in the people's forced exaltation. Ten rotting heads remained on their platforms in front of the throne, two charred bodies in metal cages rested on the center landing halfway down the stairs, along with the rotting corpse of the Showton's hamstrung example. When he was satisfied by the people's enforced respect, he would return to the palace, passing the rotting body of Arbon Marna still nailed to the palace door. It seemed everywhere one turned in Te Femma, death greeted them. It was nearly a daily ritual for some unfortunate to be executed for a disrespectful attitude, gesture, or remark.

Young males old enough to fight were conscripted into the Showton's service and sent to one of his armies in a distant land. They were deemed to be of little use because of how they had been raised in the Te Femma culture, but that mattered little. The Showton needed warm bodies to fill the ranks of his far-flung armies, and that's all he got from Te Femma.

A span had passed since the city was taken, and the army of the United Kingdom had not returned. By now, the Showton was fully aware of the depth of the treaty dispute between the king of the United Kingdom and the queen of Te Femma, who had cowardly abandoned her subjects. It appeared to the Showton and his top advisors that there would be no help for Te Femma coming from the kingdom a second time. This made the Showton smile, for he knew, as long as the cities remained separate and alone, he could easily pluck off each one like ripe fruit from a tree.

He surmised that overthrowing the United Kingdom would be challenging, but he was in no hurry. He would consolidate his victories, strip bare the resources of the conquered, and bide his time. He would concentrate his forces and launch one final campaign when all was ready. It would result in the destruction of the only real threat he had faced so far, the Army of the United Kingdom and the power behind it, the fortunate man who had avoided his manslayers by pure luck. Nevertheless, the Showton knew that this blue-eyed rascal was suffering. His woman and infant were dead, and his young daughter was taken. Every time the Showton thought of this miserable man and his miserable life, it made him smile. He had to be a coward for not immediately marching forward and engaging. There was nothing to concern himself about this wretch. In time, the United Kingdom would fall, and this faintheart would follow the others of his family in death.

"Master, we have received a message from the Hanteeva Army. Haptane Hanteeva says two cities have allied, and they have combined their forces. They are coming to break his siege on Perdona, the city he has surrounded," an attendant told the Sutro Showton.

"How many in Hanteeva's army?" the Showton asked.

"As of last count, the typical army muster, about fifteen-thousand, master."

"How many here in Te Femma?" he questioned.

"Also fifteen-thousand foot, plus an additional three-thousand mounted warriors, the ones you brought with you, master," the attendant told him.

"Good! I will take the three-thousand and help Hanteeva. Attendant, how many war orders have I issued?"

"One-hundred, master," came the attendant's response.

"This is War Order 101: Order the Invincibles to join me at Perdona. I'm certain that Fifteen-thousand can easily hold this city. I doubt the United Kingdom will do anything now," the Showton surmised.

"What do you want us to do with the Tondo girl, my master?" the attendant asked.

"Take her and the old woman to my city. I will lodge there for the cold season. See that the child isn't harmed. I plan to train her for use in the future."

# CHAPTER 4

# BLOOD BADGE

Officer training was rigorous, and by the time the Te Femma class had reached the halfway point in their fast-paced program, all the women were tired, stressed, and irritated, but that was all part of the accelerated course. The trainers took copious notes and reviewed their findings every wernt with the T´ezpont commander, Sutro Megato Wetzen. He would then summarize their findings and present the results to Megatus Nedenna. It was then up to her to ensure the trainees remained on track. The trainers expected a few of the officer candidates to quit or be washed out for failure to perform satisfactorily. Still, Nedenna made it her personal goal to ensure every sister, including the sub, Maaryah, completed their training successfully. So far, she hadn't lost even one.

The trainers had divided the class into two groups, those under Neva Megatus Deveena's command and those under Neva Megatus Zuni's. The two groups competed against each other, and each group's aggregate score was posted for all to see on every Du-Zet. It added to the stress and provided some friendly competition; however, there were occasions when this friendly competition wasn't very amicable. In one instance, during hand-to-hand combat training, the drill sestardi had chosen Deveena and Maaryah as opponents. Deveena always held a grudge against the outsider, beginning on the day Maaryah joined the warrior faction. Both had been looking forward to this confrontation, and both were expecting to win. The sestardi lost control of the situation almost immediately as his training session turned into a real fight between the two. His pleas to stop the contest fell on deaf ears. Dori grabbed his arm, pulling him away, warning the little feral to get out of the way before he was trampled.

Maaryah was fast, and Deveena was just as quick. Maaryah was strong, and Deveena was just as powerful. Maaryah knew many moves, taught to her by Tondo. Deveena knew many different movements, learned during her many spans in the Stontza. One or the other was thrown down more than once during the match. Deveena wore her hair short with tight Dutch-like braid bands from hairline to crown; the sides of her head were shaved, just like all the other sisters in the faction wore theirs. Maaryah, on the other hand, had kept her long braid, which was coiled and pinned tightly against her head. Zuni and Dori had warned her several times that her braid would get her into trouble someday, but she ignored their counsel. Her braid was her only link to her cherished little girl, Maari, and she was loath to cut it off; however, Deveena didn't know about Maaryah's personal tragedy, nor would she have cared. Her goal was to put the sub in her place and teach her that she would never measure up to a sister once and for all.

Each time the two women came into contact, Deveena attacked Maaryah's pinned braid, eventually loosening it until it was hanging down the center of her back. The fight continued with neither opponent gaining the upper hand until Deveena made a move in which she over-extended herself just a bit and was off balance. Maaryah seized the opportunity and stepped into her, throwing Deveena over her hip and back just as Tondo had taught her. She knew that when Deveena hit the ground, she would quickly put her in an arm bar, ending the contest. As Deveena was flipped over Maaryah's back, her hand clutched Maaryah's braid, and when she hit the ground, she gave it a yank, pulling Maaryah down by the head. Deveena then rolled on top of Maaryah and pinned her sub opponent's arms with her legs, her forearm across Maaryah's throat, and her right hand still clutching Maaryah's braid. The match was over, and Deveena had prevailed.

The arrogant Te Femman was justified in her claim that Maaryah was only an inferior sub and always would be. Maaryah was mortified by her defeat. Of all the sisters she wanted to defeat in the class, Deveena was at the top of the list. She ached to teach her a lesson in humility, and she had failed. The trainer was grateful neither woman was seriously injured and quickly terminated hand-to-hand combat training for the day.

After the match, Zuni's team returned to their barracks for some rest and free time. Maaryah handed Dori her personal dagger and told her to cut off her braid. Dori obliged her and didn't understand Maaryah's tears. The plait was put with the rest of her things, and she was seen holding it from time to time, lost in a tear-inducing memory.

The class was quickly approaching graduation day. All twenty-one women had passed, and preparations were being made for the presentation of rank. Usually, Idop made the presentations, and occasionally Tondo would do it. However, he was reluctant to participate because a ritual called Blood Badge had been instituted, starting right after the first class had graduated. Each graduate was given the rank insignia of neva megato, a zanth-colored bar pin. The pin had two short spikes on its back that held the symbol in place with clasps. It was a hassle to pin in place, so the presenting officer simply positioned the badge on the recipient's chest and hammered it in place with a fist. The spikes penetrated clothing and flesh. The men considered the two tiny scars a sign of honor for their accomplishment. Tondo didn't care much for the ritual, but the men approved, and it increased their feeling of brotherhood, so he allowed it to continue as long as it didn't get out of hand.

By the time graduation approached for the women, Idop was away, inspecting the Second Brigade posted near the city of Terratia. Because Maaryah was in the graduating class, Tondo decided it would be best if he didn't attend because he wasn't sure he could contain his emotions. The responsibility for making the rank presentations fell to the T′ezpont commander, Sutro Megato Wetzen.

The day before the presentations were to be made, Wetzen went to Tondo's headquarters. When he entered the office, Tondo could see worry on his face. "How can I help you, sutro megato?" Tondo asked.

"Zerr, are you sure you wouldn't prefer to make the rank presentations tomorrow? The Te Femmans are proud and may consider it a slight if a senior officer doesn't present the badges," Wetzen explained.

"Yes, I've considered that. I've decided they'll just have to accept it." Tondo noticed that Wetzen looked even more uncomfortable after his statement. "Wetzen, what's the problem?"

"The blood badge, zerr. What should I do?" Wetzen asked, his voice expressing concern.

"Hoy, yes, that. I suggest you simply hand them their badge of rank. Performing the ritual with these graduates wouldn't be a good idea," Tondo advised.

"Thank you, zerr," Wetzen said in relief.

"You're dismissed," Tondo said, and after Wetzen had left, he began to chuckle as he thought about Wetzen's quandary. Had he pounded the blood badge into a sister's chest, she probably would have pounded him into the turf.

# CHAPTER 5

# WALKING ON AIR

After graduation and promotion—the three senior officers were not promoted—the new junior officers were assigned their commands. Each neva megato was given two or three ranks of six warriors each. The unit was referred to as a neva-brick, so it would not be confused with a standard brick that was more than three times its size. Maaryah was placed in command of Dori's two Stontza ranks. Zuni felt it better to move Dori rather than Maaryah. The sisters in Maaryah's barracks had already accepted her as a leader, even though she was only a sub.

The sisters preferred fighting style was done in teams of three warriors. This fact worked well with the army's standard six-warrior rank formation because each sister faction rank consisted of two Te Femman three-warrior teams. After a full detzamar had passed since the women graduated from T′ezpont, Ameer Tondo sent word that he would be inspecting the Te Femma warrior faction. First, he wanted to see a demonstration of the sisters' fighting techniques and tactics. Second, he had to determine how the new faction, which was no larger than a troop of between two-hundred-fifty and three hundred warriors, would fit into the army's structure.

Tondo informed Megatus Nedenna that he would spend an entire afternoon with her faction, taking a last-meal with her and her two senior officers. This was the first time Nedenna would host a feral, and it bothered her to no end. She had a low opinion of outsider males to begin with, and her time spent in the feral world so far had not changed her thinking; she considered them uncouth and mundane. Now, she had to entertain one for several segments, including the last meal. She counseled with her two senior officers on what to do because, as usual, she wanted her command to be impressive in all regards. She had no doubt that the sisters were ready to show their combat skills, but she was stymied about what entertainment would be appropriate for a feral during last-meal.

"I've heard these ferals enjoy half-naked sub dancers carousing around their table while they eat. The thought of it makes me ill. Do you have any suggestions we can live with?" Nedenna asked. Deveena and Zuni looked at each other and then back to their commander, neither saying a word. Nedenna continued, "I want to impress the Feral while he's here, so what should I do?"

Deveena had an idea, "Ask the sub. She's lived in the feral world and knows what they want." Deveena watched as Nedenna silently pondered her words. "If the Feral isn't satisfied, you can put the blame on her," she added.

Nedenna smiled, "Yes, that will do. Zuni, bring her here. Before you do, tell me what you've learned about her. I had the opportunity to observe her at T′ezpont, and she doesn't act like any slave I've ever seen. She seems almost aristocratic." Nedenna's statement caused Deveena to laugh out loud.

"There's not much I can tell you, zerr; she doesn't talk about her past. The sisters tell me she has many scars, some look like weapon wounds, and she suffers sleep-terrors often. They also tell me she carries the marks of childbirth," Zuni told her.

"Childbirth! What's she doing here?" Deveena wondered.

"Yes, that's very odd," Nedenna commented, "but she is an outsider, after all."

"That shouldn't make any difference," Deveena angrily grumbled. "Only a worthless sub would abandon her child?"

"Have you learned where she's from? I remember Sutrum Sestardus Harmon telling us she came from one of the kingdom's outlying estates. Do you know which one?" Nedenna wondered.

"Shc told Dori she was born a slave on the Oetan Estate, and that's where she grew to adulthood. I guess she was freed when the king ended slavery in his kingdom," Zuni offered.

"She's not like any sub I've ever seen. I want you to find out all you can about her. Now, bring her here, and we'll get her suggestions for pleasing the Feral," Nedenna told Zuni.

"Maaryah, I've summoned you here to get your ideas on how to entertain the Feral. He's coming to inspect the faction, and he'll take last-meal with the senior officers. You know the feral world better than we do. What do you suggest?" Nedenna asked.

Maaryah's eyes darted from Nedenna to Deveena and then to Zuni. The sisters called all outsider males ferals, but she knew exactly who 'the Feral' was. She'd heard him called that ever since she'd joined the warrior faction. The term always offended her, but she had become calloused to its use.

"Zerr, what do you mean?" Maaryah wondered.

"I've heard ferals like to watch half-naked dancing girls while they eat. Is that true?" Nedenna asked.

"Yes, most do," Maaryah responded.

"May the great mother spare us!" Deveena exclaimed.

"So, you're suggesting we find some dancing subs for Ameer Tondo's pleasure?" Nedenna asked, her face expressing her disgust.

"No, zerr, I'm not. I've heard that Ameer Tondo doesn't appreciate such things, especially when he's with the army," Maaryah told her.

"So, then, what do you recommend we do?" Zuni asked.

"Zerr, have him join you in the mezz, that's all."

"That's it? What if he's expecting something more . . . more vulgar and debased?" Deveena asked, expressing little confidence in Maaryah's insight.

"Zerr, I was asked for my recommendation, and I gave it. Not all outsider men are the same," Maaryah shot back, her tone hard and cold.

Deveena turned to Nedenna and said, "If the Feral is disappointed, we'll blame her and expel her from the faction. That should appease him."

"Deveena, you overstep your authority!" Zuni grumbled. "Maaryah is my responsibility, and I will handle it if it comes to that."

"Alright, Maaryah, you're dismissed," Nedenna told her. Maaryah saluted and departed.

"I don't trust a word she said. You'll end up being embarrassed, again," Deveena warned her commander.

"Maaryah is wise, megatus; I'd take her advice if I were you. At the very least, we'd be spared the indignity of watching a bunch of scantily clad subs sashaying around our table," Zuni said with a chuckle.

"Agreed. We'll do it her way, but if she's wrong . . . " Nedenna didn't complete her threat.

Tondo had been closely observing the sisters' maneuvers as they engaged in mock combat. Their three warrior teams worked amazingly well together. Their mode and tactics were fluid and quick; their assaults and ripostes were stinging and threatening. He could see they would be difficult to counter by any standard army formation he could imagine. The problem he now had was integrating them into the army. Their unique style of motion and movement would not mesh well with the male foot brigades. He could think of only one solution.

"Megatus Nedenna, I am very impressed by the skill of your warriors. I have never seen such a well-trained unit. The only problem I have is how to meld your command with the male ranks; however, every army needs a reserve, a unit of the best warriors held back and then committed at the critical moment. When your city's faction reaches its full numbers, that's what I'll do." He watched as Nedenna's eyes widened, revealing her delight, but her stolid expression never changed. Tondo looked into the sky and noticed the p´atezas hanging just above the horizon. "Megatus, when do we eat? I'm hungry."

"Whenever you're ready, ameer. Follow me to the mezz," Nedenna told him.

Nedenna guided Tondo to the mess hall with Deveena and Zuni close behind. They were the first to enter the building and sat at a table in the area reserved for officers. Four orderlies quickly set wooden trays full of food in front of each officer, and they began to eat. The other sisters soon filed in and were served portions of food as they moved down the line. From time to time, a junior officer entered, moved to the officer area, and was served by an orderly. Tondo watched the mezz door intently, trying not to be obvious, but when Maaryah entered, he almost jumped to his feet. He was shocked to see her hair was cut short and braided in the typical Te Femma style, but she looked as beautiful as ever. She moved past his table without even glancing in his direction. When he realized his eyes were following her, he quickly averted his gaze. She found her usual table near the back corner of the hall. Dori soon joined her; she was the only sister who regularly shared a meal with the sub. Maaryah was served her tray of food and began eating; all the time, her eyes were fixed on Tondo's back.

"Megatus, this has been an enlightening afternoon for me. Your warriors are very impressive. Do you think they're ready for battle?" Tondo asked.

"Yes, zerr, we are," Nedenna answered with confidence.

"The army will be moving out soon to begin the second Te Femma campaign. Some of my senior officers think your small warrior faction should remain here, serving as a home guard," Tondo told her.

"This is not our home!" Zuni exclaimed.

"Ameer, you can't leave us here. We must help free our city," Nedenna was almost pleading.

"It would be a disgrace to be left behind; the ultimate insult," Deveena growled.

Tondo leaned back in his chair and spread the fingers of his hands on the table. "My sentiments, as well," he told them. "However, your faction is too small to be an independent command. I will place you under the leadership of one of the other brigade commanders. It's either that or leave you here." Tondo knew Nedenna and her senior lieutenants would object to being placed under the command of yet another feral. Still, he also knew the alternative he presented would be utterly unacceptable to them.

Deveena's face turned red, and her eyes were cold and angry. Zuni stared at his hands, noticing the unique band on his finger, her expression impassive. After a pause, Nedenna responded, "Given the two options, I'll take the former. Whose brigade do you have in mind?"

"Stonewall . . . I mean Nestess; he commands the Teg-ar-mos Brigade," Tondo told her.

"That's the brigade you defeated the two other cities with, isn't it?" Nedenna asked.

"It's the very first brigade in the army, and it has a proud history. You'll be expected to live up to its standards," Tondo said with a sly grin, and he watched as Nedenna almost responded with a curse, but she held her tongue. "Nestess will meet with you tomorrow, so be prepared. I don't want to hear of any trouble between you two because you'll be left behind if I do. Is that understood?"

"Yes, zerr," Nedenna stiffly replied.

"Good. Now, let me commend you for your temperance and good judgment," he told her.

"Zerr, I don't understand. What are you referring to?" Nedenna wondered.

"In the past, new brigade commanders always tried to impress me with lavish last-meals and dancing girls. I had to set them straight. I don't tolerate such foolishness in this army. I'm glad that at least one commander has more sense than that. I'm very impressed with you and your warriors. Now, all we need do is free your city and grow your brigade. I'll take my leave now. Good luck to you in our upcoming campaign." Tondo got up, and so did the women at his table. Nedenna's eyes fell upon Maaryah, still sitting at her corner table, and the Te Femman commander smiled at her. Tondo marched out of the mezz alone and was gone. Maaryah watched him leave, aching to call out his name.

A few days later, on Du-Zet, four ferals delivered something to Maaryah's billet. Later that day, another feral arrived at her quarters and remained there for a couple of segments before departing. Word travels fast in a small army encampment, and it wasn't long before Zuni heard that Maaryah was entertaining ferals privately in her quarters. Zuni was outraged and went storming into Maaryah's billet.

"Maaryah, have you been seeing ferals in here?" she demanded to know.

"I've had some male visitors today, but they simply made deliveries and left."

"I've been told that a little feral was here for two segments. What was he delivering for that long?"

"Armor," Maaryah simply replied.

"Armor? Let me see it," Zuni demanded. Maaryah walked to an armor stand in the corner of the room and removed a cloth covering. A suit of exquisite blue scale mail was revealed, along with a sheathed sword of unusual design. Zuni went to the stand and closely examined the armor. She pulled the sword partially from its scabbard and examined its blue blade. "These are well crafted. How can a slave pay for these things?" she growled.

"The armorsmith is a friend of mine," she replied.

"A friend, is he? What's his name, and why was he here for two segments?" Zuni demanded.

"His name is Haro, and we were slaves together on the same estate. He had to make some final adjustments so the armor would fit properly, and that's why he was here that long," Maaryah explained.

"I've heard of this Haro. So, you two were slaves on the same estate. Was that the Oetan Estate?" Zuni asked.

"Yes, zerr," Maaryah answered.

"I've wondered about you ever since you came here, and I've checked into the things you've said about your past, which isn't much. But the mystery is beginning to unravel. Oetan was disgraced by his king, wasn't he?"

"Yes, zerr," Maaryah responded nervously.

"His estate became the Tondo Estate, didn't it?"

"Yes, zerr," Maaryah said meekly.

"Show me your hands," Zuni ordered. Maaryah held her hands in front of herself, and Zuni grabbed her left wrist. "I've seen an unusual finger band like this before, but I couldn't remember where. The other day, I saw it again. The Feral has one just like it. Quite a coincidence, wouldn't you say?" Maaryah didn't answer. "Now, it has become clear to me. You're his spy!"

"I'm not a spy!" Maaryah firmly replied.

"Then what are you, one of his pleasure-girls?"

"No!" Maaryah nearly shouted.

"I've heard that these ferals can have as many concubines as they want. Are you one of his second-rate greevayrs?"

"Ameer Tondo doesn't have any concubines," Maaryah told her.

"Then what are you?"

Zuni had her cornered. Only an outright lie could save her now, and that she wouldn't do; she couldn't lie to the one who had always been her advocate. She took a deep breath. "He's my bondmate," Maaryah admitted in a worried tone.

"You must take me for a fool. It's common knowledge his greevayr, his bondmate as you put it, was killed when assassins attacked his estate last span."

"I survived the attack, but I was severely wounded," Maaryah pulled down the neck of her tunic, exposing the scar of the metren's exit wound. "The assassin's metren went through my back and chest, and then it pierced my infant son's heart. They took my young daughter with them when they left," Maaryah was nearly in tears.

Zuni was shocked by Maaryah's admission. "Why would the ameer claim you were killed?"

"He didn't want the assassins to try again."

"It is said the Feral's bondmate saved Queen Ootyiah's life during the Night of the Slayers and was wounded," Zuni said with searching eyes. Maaryah raised the left sleeve of her tunic, exposing the scar on her upper arm. Zuni shook her head, "May the great mother preserve us. You are who you claim to be. If you're his bondmate, that means you share his title and royal rank," Zuni quickly realized.

"I share his title. The king bestowed the royal rank of rezus on me separately for my service to him and the kingdom during the Munnari War and for saving the queen's life."

"I must report this to Megatus Nedenna," Zuni said.

"Please, Zuni, don't. She'll demand I leave the warrior faction, I'm sure."

"You claim you're not a spy for the Feral. Then why are you here?"

"I've joined the faction to seek vengeance upon those who killed my son and took my daughter. I will do all I can to put an end to the Showton's evil, and I'll get my daughter back," Maaryah told her.

Zuni smiled, "Hoy, now, that's something I can fully understand; however, if I don't tell my commanding officer about you, I'll be conspiring in the same deception you've been engaged in. I won't do that."

"Please, I must stay with the sisters' faction. I can't serve in a male unit. If you reveal my secret, Deveena will demand I be thrown out; you know she will."

"You should have considered that before you perpetrated this fraud," Zuni told her. She turned and was about to leave when she noticed something odd in another corner of the room. It was a perfectly round stone, bigger than a person's head, and heavy enough to cause the floorboards to sag. "By the great mother's smile, what's that?"

"It's a gunstone," Maaryah told her. Her voice was subdued, and her countenance was depressed.

"Gunstone? What's it for?"

"Others like it will be flung out of the gunz Tondo is making," Maaryah explained, her spirit sinking.

"Gunz, gunstones, what are they?" Zuni wondered.

"They will open your city's wall."

"Impossible! Why is this one here?" Zuni wondered.

"Tondo wants me to exercise with it."

"Exercise? How much does it weigh?"

"About four stones."

"Four stones! All right, neva megato, show me how you exercise with something that heavy," Zuni demanded.

"Zerr, I'd rather not."

"I don't care what you'd rather do. Show me how you exercise with that heavy thing. That's an order!" Maaryah closed her eyes and took a deep breath. "I'm still waiting!" Zuni grouched in an irritated tone.

Maaryah raised her left hand to quiet her commander; her eyes were still closed. Zuni watched the gunstone begin to move by itself, almost imperceptibly at first, but its movement soon became clearly evident. It started to rise off the floor and continued rising until it was head high. Maaryah opened her eyes as the gunstone moved toward them. Zuni took a step back as Maaryah positioned the stone between them, her face showing the strain of the effort. Zuni gasped, breaking Maaryah's concentration, and the gunstone dropped, crashing through the floorboards, coming to rest in the dirt, half of the enormous round stone protruding above the level of the floor. Maaryah looked at Zuni, who was gawking with an open mouth.

"You're a sorceress!" was all Zuni could say.

"No, it's the inner-power of the temple priests. Tondo awoke my power many spans ago," Maaryah explained.

Zuni was clearly amazed by what she had just witnessed. She had heard about Tondo's seemingly magical abilities but found it hard to believe. Now, she had seen for herself, with her own eyes, something impossible, yet there was the evidence at her feet. She silently stared at Maaryah for a long time. She finally turned and exited the billet. Maaryah prepared herself to be called before Nedenna and expelled from the Te Femma warrior faction. She despaired.

The segments slowly passed, and Maaryah nervously waited for the summons, not even going to the mezz for last-meal because she had no appetite. A Zuni aide arrived at dusk and told her to report to her commander's office. She expected to be greeted by Zuni, Nedenna, and a smirking Deveena; however, when she entered the HQ, her commanding officer was the only one there.

"Zerr, Neva Megato Maaryah reports as ordered," Maaryah said as she saluted.

Zuni was sitting behind her desk and returned Maaryah's salute. "Maaryah, I have spent all afternoon pondering your situation. You're my best officer, and I'd hate to lose you, especially now that I've seen what you can do. We'll be in battle soon, and I need you. I've decided to keep your secret, but if anyone finds out who you really are, it will be the end for both of us."

A huge smile filled Maaryah's face. "Thank you, zerr, thank you. You won't regret your decision."

"I already do. Now, get out of here and have the hole in your billet's floor repaired, but don't let anyone learn what caused it," Zuni ordered.

"Yes, zerr; thank you, zerr," Maaryah saluted and quickly exited. She felt as if she were walking on air as she returned to her quarters.

# CHAPTER 6

# THUNDER ON A CLEAR DAY

The two large blue guns Tondo had commissioned were finally completed.

They were huge; a grown man could rest inside a blue barrel. Pendor had estimated their weight at more than one-hundred-and-fifty stones. Each was nearly as long as three men were tall. They were so heavy and massive that they could not be fired from their carriages. A robust wooden frame was built to position the guns, and this frame had limited adjustability. Once aimed, the guns could only fire in the same general direction until the entire structure was moved; an operation that could take several segments. Once emplaced, these monsters could only fire in one direction, giving them a single primary purpose: the destruction of city walls.

Over the past span, Tondo had his men build a replica of the wall protecting the city of *Anterra*; the wall was one radett long and just as high and thick as the city wall. The big guns were positioned about four rads from the wall. Tondo's gun crews had charged one of the massive weapons and loaded it with a gunstone. A long fuse was lit, and the onlookers took cover behind sandbags, for no one was sure if the gun would explode under the incredible pressure generated by the priests' black powder. Tondo, Idop, and Fayeetez watched through a framed open space in their sandbag bunker. Haro and Pendor did the same from another bunker nearby.

After a long, heart-pounding delay, the chamber ignited with a loud whoosh, expelling smoke and fire. The main charge ignited, the gun jumped, and the ground shook as flame, smoke, and gunstone belched from the gun's muzzle. The entire area was covered in thick white smoke, obscuring the weapon and blocking the view of the target.

Everyone remained in their bunkers, stunned by the massive explosion they had seen, heard, and felt. Only Tondo seemed unaffected by the horror that was unleashed. He climbed out of his bunker and walked toward the gun; others soon followed. Haro and Pendor dashed to the monstrous weapon and closely inspected it. It didn't take long before their worried expressions turned to joy as they embraced and hugged each other, patting their backs. The gun had survived its first firing without damage. The smoke was clearing, and as it did, all eyes looked downrange to see the gunstone's effect on the wall. Tondo began jogging towards it, and the others followed him at a run.

The gunstone had hit the wall right of center, halfway up. It had crashed through the stone blocks, causing many higher blocks to tumble out of place, several falling to the ground. After a quick inspection, everyone returned to the guns and finished preparations for the second gun's firing. The first gun was swabbed with oil to cool it down before another firing.

After a half-segment, the second gun was ready, and a match was put to its fuse. The gun roared, the ground shook, and smoke again covered the area. When it had cleared, everyone could see that the wall had been hit to the left of center and a little lower than the first shot. Many more stone blocks were either destroyed or toppled. An immense opening in the wall had been created about two men's height above the ground.

After more than a segment, the first gun roared again, and another section of the wall was breached. The other monstrous weapon soon fired also, blasting open a huge hole, clearly breaching the wall, allowing many observers to step through the rubble and pass to the other side. The wall had been breached with only four firings of the guns. The senior observers gathered around Tondo, congratulating him for this amazing achievement. Tondo accepted their praise in silence. It was obvious he was upset.

"Tondo, what's the matter? You should be celebrating. What you've accomplished is unbelievable. We will easily defeat the Showton's defenders at Te Femma," Idop said, thrilled by the power of Tondo's creation.

"Ameer, why the sad face?" Fayeetez wondered.

"I see more than just a few destroyed blocks of stone. In a couple of detzamars, you will witness the true horror I've unleashed here today. A man from my homeland once helped create a weapon of devastating power. Now, I fully understand his lamentation when he quoted from an ancient text, 'I am become Death, the destroyer of worlds.'" Tondo walked away from the others and sought private introspection.

The sisters were taking midday meal in the mezz when the building shook, and a roar, the likes of which no one had ever heard before, rumbled through the camp, echoing off buildings and distant hills.

"By the great mother's stare, what happened?" Dori exclaimed.

Zuni quickly joined them. "Maaryah, what was that?" she wondered.

"Tondo's gunz must be ready," she guessed. Zuni looked at her with eyes wide.

"What's a gunz?" Dori asked.

"They're weapons that will allow us to free Te Femma. We'll be moving to your city soon."

Zuni nodded, but Dori had a puzzled expression. "How do you know that?"

"All you have to do is talk to the right feral. It's common knowledge," Maaryah told her as she attempted to recover from appearing to know too much.

"You been talking to ferals? I thought you had more self-respect than that," Dori told her with a critical eye.

"I've lived all my life in the feral world. Some of these men are all right."

"Little sister, you and I need to have a talk about proper relationships," Dori told her with a laugh. Zuni simply smiled. Before they finished their meal, the second gun roared, shaking ground and building, causing a stack of wooden trays to come crashing down, scattering across the mess hall floor. The chatter in the mezz increased in volume as everyone wondered what the fear-inducing roar could be.

Queen Ezora and Rana Fardinza dashed onto the palace courtyard and joined the king and his counselors.

"King Teg-ar-mos, what was that rumble?" the queen asked.

"It sounded like thunder, but it's a clear day. How can that be?" the rana wondered. The king looked perplexed.

"Your Highness," a counselor began, "could it be Ameer Tondo's new weapon? I think the sound came from the army's garrison way over there," he said as he pointed.

"It's being built at the brigade post, but that's two marches away. It doesn't seem possible, but it is the Messenger's weapon, inspired by deity, after all. Inform Megatus Titus that I will be leaving for the Teg-ar-mos Brigade in the morning. I want to arrive there before nightfall, so we'll be riding hard all day." It wasn't long before another rumble was heard. Everyone looked into the sky but saw no clouds. Before they left the courtyard, two more thundering booms were heard. Everyone was now confident the sounds were coming from the army post far in the distance.

When the p´atezas was low in the sky, the King's Contingent rode onto the Teg-ar-mos Brigade post. The king was told that Tondo was with the big guns, and an army aide guided him there. Tondo was overseeing the movement of the massive cannons from their firing frames to their four-wheeled carriages. Numo had arrived a few days earlier with the estate's ten younger thrice, which would pull one of the guns. He and the thrice waited nearby. Sire Yotendo was also called upon to provide another ten of the three-horned beasts for the second gun. The king approached, dismounted, and walked over to Tondo.

"Easy boys, this thing will smash you flat. Take your time. I don't want anyone hurt," Tondo warned. He then noticed the king, "Your Highness, I wasn't expecting you. My apologies," he said as he knocked the dust off his clothing with his Stetson-like hat. "Men, pay attention! Keep your eyes on Little Boy, not the king," he shouted. "Sorry, Your Highness, this gun weighs more than one-hundred-and-fifty stones, so we must be careful."

"Little Boy? Is that what you're calling this weapon?" the king asked.

"Yes, zerr. This one is Little Boy, and that one is Fat Man."

"Your Highness," Idop began with a bow, "Tondo has a penchant for giving his creatures names. Now, he's giving names to weapons, too."

"Fat Man makes sense, I guess, but Little Boy? I don't see anything little about that monster," the king noted.

"The names have reference to a couple of weapons from my homeland. I'll explain their meaning, but I don't have time right now."

"All right, ameer, I'm looking forward to it. Now, show me what these big things can do. We could hear them all the way to the palace."

Tondo explained how the test firings were conducted, showed him a stack of gunstones, and walked him to the demolished wall. He couldn't help but notice the king's worried expression.

"You say only four gunstones did this?" the king asked in wonder.

"Yes, Your Highness. No city wall can withstand them. Te Femma will be ours soon," Idop proudly proclaimed.

The king's expression darkened, "Does the Showton have weapons like these?"

"There's been no evidence he does," Tondo said. "There are ways to defeat these guns, Your Highness. You have to stop them from being set up," he said, attempting to ease the king's mind.

"Ha. When you reach Te Femma, the first thing I want you to do is seize the salt mines and restore salt shipments. The kingdom is beginning to run low," the king said.

"That won't be a problem," Idop told him.

"When will you move on Te Femma?" the king asked.

"We're ready to go. I'll send out orders to all the brigades in the morning. Fayeetez already has a mounted troop on the East Road," Tondo said.

The king nodded his approval, then added, "I have agreed to let Queen Ezora join you on the journey. You'll need to secure her safety."

"Sounds like a job for the Te Femma warrior faction," Idop interjected.

# CHAPTER 7

# THE SOUL OF THE KINGDOM

Tondo had just adjourned the council of senior officers, and the men formed small groups to discuss various topics brought up during the meeting, particularly marching order. Tondo noticed Megatus Nedenna standing alone off to the side, so he went to her. "Megatus, as mentioned in the meeting, your warrior faction will have responsibility for the queen's safety."

"Yes, zerr, it will be an honor. Thank you," Nedenna told him.

"You'll be an independent command for that assignment. When we approach Te Femma, you'll be placed under Nestess's command. I'm planning to have his brigade lead the main assault."

"Zerr, we would like to be at the front. The sisters must be the first to enter the city," she requested.

"Nestess will handle the details, and I expect you to abide by his orders."

"Yes, zerr," Nedenna said in an annoyed tone.

Tondo moved on, and as he passed one of the groups, he heard someone ask another, "Did you hear what happened yesterday in the city? There was a death-match in the amphitheater, and people paid coin to see it."

Tondo stopped and joined the group, "Did you say there was a death-match in the amphitheater?" he asked.

"Yes, zerr. I've never heard of such a thing. People paid good coin to watch. The baron must have made a stone of bhat because I hear thousands of people witnessed it; gentry, commoners, and freed-men," one of the men explained. Baron Torvenza controlled all entertainment in the old kingdom, and he was working diligently to spread his control throughout the entire United Kingdom.

Tondo was appalled at gladiatorial matches being held as a public event. He was the one who had proposed the amphitheater be used for entertainment purposes, but this was not what he had in mind. The thought of citizens enjoying spectacles in which men slaughtered one another for the pleasure of others was abhorrent to him. He remembered the accounts he'd read of such things during the Roman Empire, where literally thousands were killed over many days of such games. He would not stand for it, and he immediately mounted his samaran and headed for the king's palace.

King Teg-ar-mos and Queen Ootyiah were entertaining Queen Ezora in the evening after an enjoyable last-meal and a private performance featuring Zedona on the gartz vant. The entertainers had departed, and the three sovereigns were discussing the upcoming Te Femma campaign when Tondo burst into the room unannounced and obviously angry.

A startled king asked, "Ameer Tondo, you appear upset.

What is the problem?"

"Did you condone the use of the amphitheater for public death-matches?" Tondo asked in a heated tone.

"I neither condoned nor objected," the king told him, a bit surprised by the question.

"Have you considered where this may lead?" Tondo asked, still obviously upset.

"Lead to what? Death-matches have been held for hundreds of spans," the king reminded him.

"A disgusting fact! It's bad enough such barbaric events are held in private settings, but now, allowing public killings for the pleasure of common citizens cannot be allowed. I demand you put an end to it!"

The king hadn't seen Tondo this upset since he'd learned about the fall of Te Femma. The king leaned back in his chair and quickly glanced at Queen Ezora before speaking, "Ameer, this is not the time nor the place to discuss this issue."

"Unfortunately, the matter has just come to my attention, and it must be dealt with immediately before the entire kingdom is infected by its wickedness," Tondo's voice still reflecting his anger and frustration.

"You make it sound like a disease. What difference does it make if the sport continues?" the king wondered.

"It's a corrupting influence upon the heart of man. The value of life is diminished, and it breeds cruelty. I've struggled to lift the kingdom from such decadence. Allowing the slaughter of others for pleasure extinguishes not only life but crushes the good seed within the heart of those who find enjoyment in it. You cannot allow it to continue. I demand you put an end to it this instant!"

"Ameer, you overstep your authority," the king growled. Queen Ezora and Queen Ootyiah were becoming uncomfortable witnesses to the confrontation.

"When it comes to matters for the soul of the kingdom, I speak as the Messenger. Remember the Sutro Seer's counsel, 'You are to oversee a more righteous kingdom.' It is the great god's command. I cannot support nor can I sustain a people who allow and revel in such butchery," Tondo's voice was cold and hard.

"Do you mean you cannot support or sustain me? You have sworn an oath to do so," the king angrily reprimanded.

"If this barbaric practice is allowed to continue, I will immediately leave the kingdom and never return," Tondo threatened.

His threat startled Queen Ezora. "Ameer Tondo, you must free my city. You must protect the kingdom. We depend on you."

"Guards!" the king yelled. Two guards quickly entered the room. "Fetch Baron Torvenza. Tell him I need to see him immediately." The guards promptly exited, and the king turned to Tondo, "Ameer, please pull up a chair and sit. We will resolve this issue tonight." Tondo nodded, found a chair, and sat. Queen Ootyiah became a calming influence as she shifted the discussion to more pleasurable topics while they waited for the baron's arrival.

Baron Torvenza, a taller than average and stately-looking man, entered the room escorted by two king's counselors. It was obvious he was worried.

"Your Highness," he said with a bow.

The baron nervously waited, his eyes darting from face to face. "Baron, you already know Ameer Tondo and Queen Ootyiah. May I introduce Queen Ezora of Te Femma, the City of Women." The baron bowed to the queen. "Counselor, provide the baron with a chair," the king ordered, and a chair was moved to the group of other royals. "Baron, please sit." Torvenza nervously took his seat. King Teg-ar-mos continued, "The reason I've summoned you here is to discuss deathmatches in the kingdom. Ameer Tondo objects and demands they be ended."

"I will not tolerate such a practice any longer. Using the amphitheater for such displays and charging people a fee to watch will end immediately." It was apparent Tondo was not offering a suggestion; he was making a demand.

Anger flashed in the baron's eyes, "Your Highness, it was the ameer's proposal that the amphitheater be used for entertainment. And I might add, it has proven to be very profitable, and it provides Your Highness a substantial sum from the tax these performances render."

Tondo was outraged by the baron's comments. "My recommendation was for uplifting entertainment; however, you've corrupted my suggestion and turned it into something evil and wicked. Glorying and profiting in death is despicable, and it will end right now!"

The baron turned to the king, "Your Highness, deathmatches have been held for many, many spans. Before, only a very few could enjoy these exciting performances. After the ameer's suggestion, all of the kingdom's citizens can enjoy the sport."

“Enjoy; performances; sport; are you listening closely, Your Highness? Do you want your subjects reveling in death? As I have said, I cannot support a kingdom that does, and I doubt the great god will, either,” Tondo was emphatic. He turned to Queen Ezora, “Your Highness, does Te Femma engage in such practices?” He already knew what her answer would be.

“No, never has my city permitted such atrocities. It’s bad enough to execute criminals, but to make sport of death is vile and uncivilized,” she said.

The king looked at Queen Ootyiah, and she nodded her agreement. “Baron Torvenza, I must concur. I order you to end death-matches immediately.”

“Your Highness, please reconsider,” the baron pleaded.

“No, Ameer Tondo is right. Death for sport is no longer acceptable,” the king said.

“What about other blood-sports?” the baron asked. The king looked to Tondo.

“All blood-sport is debased; however, as long as it doesn’t lead to death or gruesome injuries, I will not object,” Tondo told him.

“My death-fighters, what am I to do with them?” the baron asked.

“Tell them they have a place in the army if they wish,” Tondo suggested.

“These men are treated like the great performers they are, and they earn hundreds of bhat each span. They’ll never be satisfied with the piddly pay a soldier earns,” the baron said.

"They'll also have a better chance of survival in the army than in a death-match. Remind them of that fact," Tondo declared. The baron frowned but said nothing.

"Baron, you're dismissed," the king said. After Torvenza was gone, the king turned to Tondo, "Ameer, I knew we could solve this problem. I hope you're satisfied."

"Yes, I'll be returning to the army in the morning. I have a city to liberate," Tondo said with a bow. He spent the night at his city house and was on the road back to the Teg-ar-mos Brigade post before the p´atezas had cleared the horizon.

As it turned out, none of the baron's death-fighters were interested in joining the army. They preferred the higher standard of living, notoriety, and the thrill of the fight death-matches offered. Baron Torvenza officially ended all public and private death-matches as the king decreed; however, it was rumored that these matches continued in clandestine gatherings, for which the audiences paid a hefty untaxed fee to watch.

# CHAPTER 8

# A BLOODY HORROR

During the move along the road to Te Femma, Neva Megato Maaryah's neva-brick was assigned several days of duty as the queen's guards. The responsibility rotated regularly, and each time her neva-brick performed its assignment, Maaryah worried that she would be discovered by either the queen or the rana. Fortunately for Maaryah, the helms she and the other guards wore made identifying the individual encased in them difficult. Maaryah was even addressed by the queen a couple of times during her unit's stint of duty, but the queen was never the wiser as to whom she was speaking.

Fayeetez's cavalry led the advance to Te Femma. He sent scouts ahead to reconnoiter and send back reports. When the scouts reported that the salt mines were lightly defended, Fayeetez took it upon himself to launch an assault that reclaimed them for the queen and the United Kingdom. The attack was quick and deadly. The enemy guards were cut down by charging, mounted troopers before they knew they were under threat.

Many sisters from the city had been forced to mine salt and were treated worse than slaves. Poorly fed and overworked, many had died, only to be replaced by others from the city. The emaciated freed sisters expressed their undying gratitude to their liberators, and never once were the men referred to as ferals.

After the dust had settled, the victims treated, and the Showton's surviving guards placed in bindings, Fayeetez sent his written report to the ameer and army commander Idop, several days behind the army's lead elements.

"Your Highness," Tondo said to Queen Ezora as he handed her a small pouch, "I have received a report from Megatus Fayeetez, commander of the mounted troops. Acting on his own initiative, he has retaken the salt mines." The queen opened the pouch and poured salt into her other hand. Her countenance lit up, and a huge smile replaced her dour expression.

"Ameer Tondo, this is marvelous news!" she exclaimed.

"Fayeetez says his men have freed over one-hundred sisters who were forced to work in the mines. He regrets to inform us, they've been brutalized, starved, and they've told him, nearly a hundred others were worked to death," Tondo reported.

"I want those Showton monsters executed," the queen demanded.

"I sympathize, but vengeance must be tempered with justice. The guards will be assumed innocent of any wrong-doing until proven guilty in a proper and fair hearing. I expect any charges against them or others in the Showton's service to be substantiated by two or more honest and reliable witnesses."

"The very fact that these horrible things have been done is grounds enough to convict them all," Rana Fradinza said.

"True enough, but I expect a formal tribunal to be held for anyone charged with a crime. I will allow your city officials to conduct these proceedings; however, I will see that my officers monitor them to ensure fairness. Will you agree to that?" he asked. The queen's dour expression returned, and she nodded her reluctant acceptance.

"Ameer, after the Munnari War, what did you and the king do with those who fought against you?" the rana asked.

"Prince Men-dre-dor, the barons, and the lords were required to swear an oath of allegiance to King Teg-ar-mos. After that, everyone was allowed to go home," Tondo explained.

"That seems too generous," the queen observed.

"Anterra was never under direct threat, and the enemy's armies didn't commit atrocities. The two evil kings ordered the execution of ten innocent priests and paid the ultimate price during the battle for their wickedness. Also, the invaders suffered over twenty-thousand casualties, including nearly five-thousand killed. That was punishment enough," Tondo told them. He continued, "I realize the situation in Te Femma is different, and I suspect the city's residents have suffered greatly under the Showton's cruelty. My homeland has a term for such wicked behavior, and it's called 'crimes against the people.' Those who are found guilty are executed or incarcerated for many spans."

"All right, after the city is liberated, I will see that all those who have committed crimes against the people, as you put it, are given a fair review, and then they'll be executed." Upon hearing the queen's statement, Tondo only responded with a sour expression.

As the army's foot soldiers continued toward the City of Women, wagon after wagon passed by them, going in the opposite direction. Each wagon was full of salt taken from a vast mountain of salt the Showton's men had stockpiled.

By the time Tondo and Idop reached the city, it had been sealed tight by the Showton's defenders. The two senior kingdom commanders, arrayed in full battle gear, stepped forward, accompanied by several armed warriors with shields, one carrying the United Kingdom flag. The party stopped about two stones' throw from the main city gates and waited. A short, stocky man soon appeared on the stone parapet above the gates, the flag of the Showton held by a warrior at his side.

Tondo took a step forward and began speaking loudly, "I am Ameer Tondo, representing King Teg-ar-mos, ruler of the United Kingdom, and Queen Ty-fen-Ezora, ruler of Te Femma. The city is surrounded, and you are significantly outnumbered. It would be a wise and honorable choice to surrender and save the lives of your men."

The man on the wall replied, "I am Haptane Tort´arden in the service of the Sutro Showton, and I rule this city in his stead. You will never overcome these walls; if you lay siege to the city, you will only cause its citizens to suffer. Now, return to your United Kingdom and tell that cowardly dethroned queen she no longer rules here," the Showton commander demanded.

"The queen has returned to reclaim her throne and free her subjects," Tondo shouted, his voice echoing off the stones.

"She has no subjects; they now serve the Sutro Showton," Tort´arden yelled back. He then gave an order that Tondo couldn't clearly understand but became evident when several rockmen stood and hurled their rocks. Tondo quickly stepped back as his warriors raised their shields, and the stones bounced off them harmlessly. On Tondo's command, the shields were lowered, and the ameer and Idop returned the volley of rocks with two well-placed arrows, both hitting the haptane in the chest. He fell backward and wasn't seen again. Another volley of stones followed, and Tondo's warriors again deflected them with their shields. The shields quickly parted just long enough for two more arrows to be launched and find their marks amongst the rockmen. The hail of stones ended abruptly, and Tondo's party quickly withdrew.

The two senior commanders went to the queen for a short conference. "Your Highness, the sisters are now undoubtedly aware of your return," Tondo said.

"They will rise up and cast off that filthy feral scum in the city; I know they will," the queen replied with conviction.

"While we wait, I'll see to the preparation of the gunz. They will arrive by the end of the day," Idop said.

It took all of the next day for the guns to be positioned, set up, and mounted in their firing frames. They were placed about four rads from the city's main gates. Rockmen flung stones toward the gun crews from time to time, requiring the teams to add large wooden shields to the firing frames for protection. Idop moved several archers closer to the wall, protected from the slingers' rocks by several warriors with shields. Each time the rockmen flung their stones, the archers responded with arrows. After a couple of segments of skirmishing, the rockmen stopped their harassment of the gun crews, having gotten the worst of the exchanges.

When the p´atezas was setting, Idop reported to Tondo and Queen Ezora. "Your Highness, ameer, the gunz are in place and ready to be used," he declared.

"Tomorrow, as soon as it's light, we'll begin the assault," Tondo said.

"The Teg-ar-mos Brigade, reinforced with the Te Femma warriors, will lead the attack. The Second Brigade will follow. The other brigades will hold their positions, keeping the city sealed inside the ring. Fayeetez and his mounted troopers are patrolling the surrounding area," Idop informed the ameer and queen.

"I don't understand why the sisters haven't risen up. I expected them to have attacked by now. Why haven't they?" Queen Ezora wondered.

"Your Highness," the rana said, "I'm sure they will attack when the main assault begins." Tondo had learned that every able-bodied sister in the Te Femma queendom had received basic Stontza training and was expected to help defend their city if and when called to serve. Tondo wondered if the sisters had any fight left in them after being under the Showton's foot for nearly two spans, although he kept these thoughts to himself.

"Megatus Nestess," Megatus Nedenna began, "it is the responsibility and duty of the Te Femma warrior faction to be the first into the city if the wall is opened." Nestess, the commander of the Teg-ar-mos Brigade, was holding his final battle planning session before the assault, and Nedenna was already objecting to his order of battle.

"I want Megato Debruntz's troop in first, followed by Megato Abrenta's troop. I expect them to push the defenders back . . . "

Nedenna interrupted, "This is an outrage!" she declared.

Nestess gave her a cold and threatening stare, and she ended her protest. "As I was saying before being interrupted, I expect Debruntz and Abrenta to push back the defenders. Megatus Nedenna, your troop-sized warrior faction will then enter the breach and fight your way to the palace. It's your assignment to take and hold it. Since you are familiar with the city, you'll know the fastest way to get there. Megato T´ezdeezo will follow you with his troop and provide additional support."

"Thank you, Nestess, and I apologize for interrupting," Nedenna told him.

"Megatus Nedenna, please remember, we're on the same side here, and we all have the same goal: to free your people," Nestess told her. Nedenna didn't respond, but her expression softened.

Tondo had conferred with Haro and Pendor, and it was decided to use double shot in the first firings of the guns; two gunstones were loaded into each gun. Tondo wanted to begin the assault with shock and awe by demolishing the two massive gates of the city's main entrance with the guns' first blasts. His primary purpose for this was to stir fear in the hearts of the Showton defenders by immediately showing them how hopeless their situation was.

"Ameer Tondo!" Megato Frunden, the commander of the gun crews, shouted, "The gunz are ready!" Tondo nodded.

"Megato, you may ignite the charges!" Idop shouted to the gunz commander. The shields protecting the gun crews from the Showton's rockmen were raised, and a burning match touched a gun fuse. The colossal cannon's chamber ignited with a roar as flame and smoke belched from Little Boy. As they flew toward their target, the two huge gunstones seemed to tumble in slow motion. An instant later, Fat Man belched fire and smoke as two more gunstones tumbled through the air. All four stones slammed into the heavy wooden gates, shattering them to pieces, sending deadly wooden and grave-tum shards in all directions.

Tondo raised his farseer as the gentle morning breeze pushed away the smoke and dust. "Excellent work, megato!" he yelled, "The gates are down. Now, begin work on the wall."

Queen Ezora and Rana Fardinza could not believe what they had just witnessed. The mind-numbing horror of the terrific explosions coming from the guns terrified them, and then to see the effects the gunstones had on their invincible gates was stunning. They stared at Tondo in disbelief. They concluded that only a god could wield such horrific power.

It took the gun crews more than a segment to ready the guns for another firing. This time, each imposing weapon was loaded with a single gunstone. Tondo didn't want to press his luck and lose one or both guns. The monstrous weapons roared again, and the ground shook. When the smoke cleared, parts of the wall on either side of the demolished gates had been hit and were crumbling. The gun crews swabbed the guns with oil to cool them and prepared to load them for another firing. The teams worked furiously for a segment and a half. When they were ready, two more enormous gunstones plowed into the wall and demolished another section.

The bombardment lasted all day and continued through the night. By morning, a considerable section of the wall was down, and it was time to launch the assault. Tondo could see Showton taskmasters whipping unwilling and terrified city residents as the thralls finished constructing a wooden barricade where the massive gates had once stood. It was evident to the Showton defenders that this would be where the kingdom army was likely to assault first. As Nestess's men and Te Femmans formed up, a large formation of Showton warriors could be seen assembling behind the barricade.

Tondo glared at the gathering enemy formation and grumbled, "The fools!" He then turned and shouted to the gun commander, "Megato Frunden, load the guns with grapeshot and fire when ready." After charging the weapons, the gun crews placed several cloth bags into the barrel of each gun. The bags contained a multitude of two-inch diameter gunstones. In effect, the guns would now act like giant shotguns. The two-inch stones would have little impact on the wall itself, but they would devastate man and beast.

The Showton's warriors were well-positioned to turn back the forthcoming assault. When the two guns fired again, grapeshot fanned out of their muzzles and tore into the barricade, sending devastating wooden shards and stone balls, tearing into the flesh of the entire Showton formation. Where a barrier and several hundred men once stood, there was now only a red stain on the displaced stones and the shattered wooden obstacles. Tondo raised the farseer to his eye and examined the scene. He could clearly see the carnage the grapeshot had caused; body parts and gore were splattered everywhere in the breach.

"Sutrum Megatus Idop," Tondo called, "Order the assault to begin." Idop gave the order, and the hornman standing beside him sounded the Advance to Battle. Five-thousand men and three-hundred women moved forward at a steady and unrelenting pace. When they reached the fallen blocks, their formations broke apart as kingdom warriors scrambled over the stones and into the city. Tondo was watching through his farseer, and he saw a warrior clad in blue armor clamber over and through the large bloody blocks, quickly disappearing into the city. He lowered his farseer as worry and dread clutched at his heart.

Even with the knowledge Tondo had shared with her long ago about the power of the guns, Maaryah was shocked by their jarring intensity. For a day and a night, the guns had pounded the city wall, and with each detonation, the ground shook, and the force of the explosion could be felt in the air, rattling a person's chest. The sisters under her command grew nervous and worried by the Feral's awful weapons. Even though Maaryah was unnerved by the gunz chest-thumping roar, she had to calm her warriors and remind them that the fire-belching engines of battle were on their side. She assured them that the gunz would guarantee victory. Her steady and commanding demeanor eased the sisters' worry and fear.

When Nestess's brigade formed up, and the enemy was seen preparing to make a defense at the breach, bolstered by a hastily constructed barricade, excitement and apprehension filled each warrior's heart, male and female alike. Unexpectedly, the great guns unleashed their terror one more time and literally blew away the waiting Showton defenders. The horn sounded, the order was given, and the formations quickly advanced. The two male units were the first to charge through the breach in the wall, finishing off the stunned and shaken survivors of the guns' final blasts.

When Nedenna's warriors reached the breach, they were appalled and nearly overwhelmed by the horror unleashed by the gun's grapeshot. Arms, legs, guts, and other body parts lay in great heaps of gore, and as the sisters advanced, they became surrounded by the horrific scene, their sandaled feet splashing through the carnage of blood and flesh in places. Tondo had warned Maaryah about the devastation the guns would unleash, but the reality was much more horrifying than she had ever imagined. She forced herself forward, trying not to look at the mangled bodies of her enemy. She pushed her two ranks through the fallen, bloody stone blocks and quickly reformed inside the city with the other neva-bricks. Zuni then led her formations on a dash to the palace. The Showton defenders were already demoralized, putting up scant resistance, and any who did were quickly cut down by the sister's three-warrior teams. In what seemed an instant, they were at the palace's steps. Deveena's neva-bricks dashed up the stone stairs and battled their way into the royal residence as Zuni's neva-bricks, supported by T′ezdeezo's men, secured the outside of the building.

Nestess's men flooded into the city and dashed to the side gates, throwing them open after slaying any defenders who dared try to stop them. Elements of the other brigades then began pouring into the city. The Showton's men retreated deeper into the city and began to reform with the hope of organizing a last line of defense. At this moment, the sisters within the walls rose up, grabbed long-hidden weapons, and tore into the ones who had tormented them for nearly two spans.

After a little more than two segments of slaughter, the battle was over, and the city was taken. Many surviving Showton warriors attempted to hide but to no avail. If a city sister found a cowering Showton feral, she cut him down without mercy. The enemy soldiers soon sought refuge by surrendering to the male warriors of the United Kingdom, begging them to spare their lives and not turn them over to the crazed Te Femmans.

A steady flow of messengers from the brigade commanders reported to Idop, keeping him apprised of the progress of the assault. Tondo, Queen Ezora, and Rana Fardinza stood nearby, listening as each report came in. When a sister dashed up to Idop, all eyes and ears were on her.

"Sutrum Megatus Idop," the messenger began, "Megatus Nedenna wishes to report that the palace has been taken."

"Return and tell her to conduct a room-by-room search for any Showton warriors. When that is done, report back to me," Idop ordered.

"Yes, zerr!" the messenger replied. She then saluted and dashed back into the city.

"Your Highness, when do you wish to enter the city?" Idop asked.

"As soon as possible," the queen replied.

"Before she does, I will personally inspect the city and determine the risk," Tondo told them. He quickly strode to his war-samaran, held by an orderly nearby, mounted, and promptly rode off toward a side gate with several Tondo Brothers and aides accompanying him.

Idop also mounted and went to the breach in the wall to inspect the guns' butchery. As he scanned the remains of the bloody horror, his stomach turned, and he nearly vomited. His awe of the guns instantly changed as a wave of revulsion hit him. He thought of Tondo and his goodness, yet the man was capable of unleashing such a bloody horror.

*Indeed,* Idop thought, *only one sent by the gods could hold such extremes of the heart.*

After a couple of segments, Tondo returned and approached the queen on his mount. "Your Highness, the slaughter of the enemy is worse than I expected. The streets are crammed with dead and dying Showton warriors. I have ordered their removal, but it will take some time, probably a day or two. I recommend you delay your entrance into the city until that's done," Tondo suggested.

"Ameer Tondo, I have waited for two spans to return to my city. I will not wait one day longer. I must see my people, and they must see me," the queen firmly told him.

Tondo nodded, "Very well, Your Highness." He signaled an aide, and the man rode up to him. "The queen will be entering the city in two segments. I want a path cleared from the remnants of the main gates to the palace. See that it's done," he ordered. The aide saluted and galloped into the city.

Word quickly spread that Queen Ezora would soon enter and return to the palace. Nedenna's sisters hastily opened the palace armory and issued Stontza halberds to each warrior. A line of sisters was positioned on either side of the stairs leading to the palace grounds. There wasn't time for the sisters to clean and polish their gear. They took their positions and waited, wearing the soiled and bloody kit they had stormed the city in; only the halberds were clean and unbloodied. Maaryah formed her two ranks at the center landing of the palace stairs, near the cage containing the charred remains of two unfortunate victims of the Showton's cruelty.

A red p´atezas was low in the afternoon sky when word was received of the queen's imminent approach. Nedenna's warriors prepared themselves for the queen's arrival as sisters from all over the city gathered in front of the palace and along the street she would be taking. It wasn't long before shouts and cheers were heard at the city's far end, where the demolished main gates once stood. As the cheers grew louder, Maaryah could see the queen riding atop the howdah of the army's command raster, in full view of all onlookers. Following closely behind the raster, mounted on war-samarans, came Tondo and Idop. Rana Fardinza, also riding a samaran, followed them. Maaryah's pride in hers and her bondmate's achievement swelled in her bosom.

The raster stopped near the foot of the stairs. A ladder was put in place, and Tondo and Idop helped the queen as she descended from the howdah. A constant chorus of cheers emanated from the vast throng; nearly every sister had tears of joy running down her cheeks. The return of their queen meant the end of their long-suffering.

Megatus Nedenna ordered her command, "Ready, salute!" The sisters raised their halberds in front of themselves vertically and held them there.

The queen slowly climbed the stairs with Megatus Nedenna following at her left, one step behind, and Rana Fardinza, one step back on the right. Tondo and Idop followed them. When the queen neared the central landing, she looked at the rotting corpse lying on a stone step and asked, "Who is this?"

"Your Highness, I've been told it's Betra, an innocent who would not prostrate herself before the Showton. He had her hamstrung as an example to the others," Nedenna told her.

"And who are they in the cages?" the queen asked as she pointed to the central landing.

"Your guards, Minta and Pentina, Your Highness," Nedenna said. A faint gasp escaped Maaryah's mouth before she could restrain herself, catching Tondo's attention. It was then he noticed the shorter sister in blue armor standing at attention and holding her halberd in salute. Although his expression did not change, a wave of relief passed over him, for he now knew his precious Maaryah had survived the bloody assault apparently unscathed.

The queen continued up the stairs and paused when she saw the ten rotting heads on platforms resting above the last step. "What kind of corrupt individual revels in such slaughter?" the queen wondered. She continued toward the palace. When she noticed the remains of another victim nailed to one of the palace doors, she asked, "Who is this?"

"Arbon Marna," Nedenna replied.

"This is beyond belief! The Showton is not a feral; he's a monster. Megatus, see that all these victims are removed with as much honor and dignity as can be mustered. I will hold a memorial for them and all the other victims of the Showton's depravity," the queen declared, and then she entered the palace.

# CHAPTER 9

# RETRIBUTION

Queen Ezora summoned Tondo and Idop to the Throne Room as darkness fell. They found her sitting on her throne, placed atop a platform. As they entered, the queen stood and quickly went to them, greeting them near the center of the room. She held out her hands to Tondo, and he took hers in his.

"Ameer Tondo, We would be remiss if We didn't personally thank you for what you have done for the city, the sisterhood, and Us. We doubted it could be done, but you were correct. We believe you must be sent by the deities."

"Your Highness, all I can tell you is this: I was sent by the king," he told her with a roguish smile.

The queen returned his smile and said, "Of course." She turned to Idop, "Sutrum Megatus, your warriors were magnificent." She stepped back and faced the two as her countenance became stern. "We have been receiving reports from Our subjects concerning the Showton's abuses. We want you to hear what they suffered during Our absence. Please, take a seat and learn for yourselves," the queen said as she pointed to a pair of empty chairs next to the royal platform stairs. She turned and climbed to her throne. "Bring in the next attester," she called.

For the next two and a half segments, sister after sister testified of the horrible treatment they and their families suffered while under the control of the Showton's forces. Stories of murder, torture, sexual assault, and general depravity were expressed. Tondo's heart was touched as he heard mothers lamenting the death of a child or the forced conscription of a son or broesayr into a faraway Showton army. He personally knew their pains, heartbreak, and suffering. It seemed the Showton's ferals took great pleasure in forcing the genteel males to engage in blood-sport matches, some ending in the death of one of the forced participants. The sisters' testimony was an awful exposition, and both Tondo and Idop were relieved when the queen called for a recess near the midnight segment. She then met privately with the two men in her study.

"Ameer Tondo, after listening to what the sisters described, do you still insist on hearings being held for these degenerate ferals?" she asked.

"Believe me, Your Highness, I fully sympathize with the feelings your subjects expressed this evening, especially after what the Showton did to my family; however, I cannot condone mass executions based on general assumptions. The United Kingdom must maintain a higher moral code. Life is precious and must be treated with great respect because it cannot be restored once it is taken away. As I have said, I expect a formal process to be conducted for each Showton follower charged with a crime against the people," Tondo reiterated. By Idop's sour expression, he could tell that his second-in-command disagreed, but he remained silent.

The queen's countenance reflected her disapproval. "I will do as you ask, but I consider it a waste of time and city resources."

Over the next half-span, tribunals were conducted for every one of the survivors in the Showton's army. Three city magistrates oversaw the proceedings in each case, and Tondo sent three officers of equal rank to witness the process. Of the Showton's fifteen-thousand troops, about five-thousand had been killed during the assault or died of their wounds in succeeding days. Nearly every officer was convicted of crimes against the people and received sentences of forced servitude in the salt mines for periods ranging from five to twenty spans. Many were sentenced to death and executed for particularly horrendous crimes. More than half of the non-officers were also convicted of crimes against the people and received sentences similar to those of their officers. Regular Showton soldiers, mostly forced conscripts, were given some leniency as the magistrates tended to accept the ferals' pleas that they were only following orders and could not refuse their superior's commands; however, many feral soldiers also received sentences of death for exceptional cruelty or wanton depravity. Most sisters were satisfied that justice had prevailed when all was said and done. Nevertheless, many sisters still would have preferred all Showton ferals to be put to death.

Tondo was appalled by what he had learned, so he refused to allow any of the Showton's men into the United Kingdom army. He felt that even those not found guilty of a serious offense had been tainted by the actions of their peers. He preferred seeing them held as prisoners of war, and so they were.

# CHAPTER 10

# EXCEEDING THE QUOTA

The day after the city was liberated, the Stontza was re-formed, and the call went out requesting recruits for both a reformed Stontza and the Te Femma warrior faction. Nedenna was stunned when she saw the number of sisters queued up to volunteer for service in her growing band of warriors; there were literally hundreds on the first day, and more came in succeeding wernts. The final number volunteering to join the faction was nearly eight-thousand sisters, exceeding the quota stipulated in the treaty. When the recruits were asked why the sudden willingness to serve in the Feral's army, the overwhelming response was vengeance. The Showton's cruelty had started a fire that would burn in the hearts of the women until the Showton himself was immolated by the sisters' ire, and the world purged of his dross.

Eight-thousand recruits were more than the warrior faction could handle all at once. Training began with the first one-thousand who'd signed up. After the first group completed their training, a second one-thousand recruits were trained, and so it went through several iterations. Training only took a couple of detzamars, about eighty days, because most recruits already had some Stontza training.

Maaryah's neva-brick of only twelve soon became an entire brick of thirty warriors. Most of the newly recruited sisters balked at the idea of serving under a sub, but she quickly put an end to their prejudices by offering to train anyone willing to step into a Stontza Circle with her. She suggested that any sister considering a challenge first consult with the veteran sisters. As it turned out, only one exceptionally tall sister took her offer and quickly regretted it as the rest of the brick watched.

As the warrior faction grew, promotions were fast in coming for the T´ezpont graduates. It wasn't long before Maaryah became a troop commander in charge of more than three-hundred warriors. Shortly after receiving her new assignment, she was promoted to megato. When the warrior faction reached eight-thousand, the three senior commanders, Nedenna, Deveena, and Zuni, decided to organize the faction into eight one-thousand warrior wings. The proposal was submitted to the queen for her approval, which was quickly forthcoming. The three senior Te Femma commanders now needed to select eight wing commanders who would hold the rank of sutro megato. It was decided that four wings would be under the command of Deveena and the other four under the leadership of Zuni.

"Deveena, have you decided who your four wing commanders will be?" Nedenna asked.

"Four solid Stontza sisters, Hertora, Mindetta, Ratorni, and Pet´uri. They performed well during the storming of the palace, leading their neva-bricks from the front," Deveena told her.

"Good. I've known them all for a long time. I know they're quite capable. Zuni, have you chosen your wing commanders?" Nedenna asked.

"Yes. Dori has become an excellent officer. The sisters trust her, and she is very diligent," Zuni told her.

"Dori was an excellent apto in the Stontza; I agree, she has become an outstanding officer. Who else have you selected as wing commanders?" Nedenna asked.

"Pratina and Nitori, both Stontza and both from Dori's brick."

"Good sisters. And your final choice?" Nedenna wondered.

Zuni took a deep breath, then answered, "Maaryah."

"Maaryah!" Deveena spewed, "She isn't Stontza; she's a sub, not a sister; and what's worse, she's slave-stock. You can't be serious."

"She's the best officer in my command. The sisters trust her judgment and follow her orders. She's tough, and she's smart. I want her as a wing commander," Zuni said, her voice expressing irritation.

"Every time we discuss faction leadership, you always bring up that sub's name. I'm beginning to think you two have a special relationship," Deveena charged with a wicked smile.

Zuni clutched the grip of the sword at her side and pulled it partway out of its scabbard. "How dare you challenge my decision! I demand satisfaction!" she growled.

"I don't have time for this foolishness. Deveena, you're out of line; now, apologize; that's an order," Nedenna commanded.

"All right, I'm sorry I struck a nerve," Deveena said with a snide chuckle. Zuni pushed her sword fully back into its scabbard with a loud snap.

"Maaryah did well during the assault," Nedenna said. "She has a good grasp of tactics, and she reacts well to changing situations. I think she'll make a good wing commander."

"She shouldn't even be here. She's an outsider and can't represent our city," Deveena told them. "She's not worthy of leading the privy detail."

"Maaryah's under my command, and I want her as a wing commander," Zuni said in a firm and angry tone.

"Just keep her away from me," Deveena fired back.

The following day, a faction formation was held, and the eight new wing commanders were presented their badge of rank, the three zanth bars of a sutro megato.

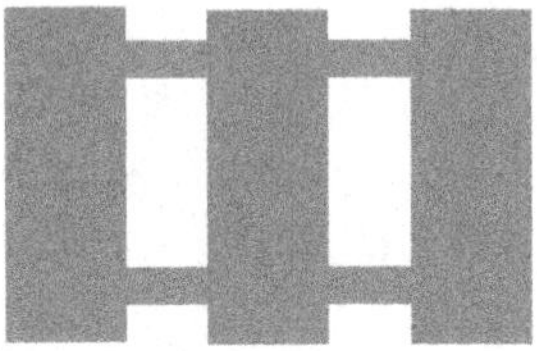

In less than five detzamars, the fledgling Te Femma warrior faction had grown to become the largest unit in the army. The warrior faction became fully activated in a special ceremony before the queen and other city dignitaries, and its banners unfurled, making it officially the Te Femma Brigade. Tondo made it the army's prestigious reserve force as he had promised long before. Its unique size and organization would serve well in that assignment. As Tondo saw it, the brigade could be committed to battle as an entire force of eight thousand warriors. With its new command structure, Tondo realized it could be broken down into its two subcommands of four-thousand each, or even into its constituent eight wings. These elements could be committed as independent commands. That's how Tondo and Idop saw it; however, Megatus Nedenna wasn't a bit pleased with the idea of dividing her brigade.

# CHAPTER 11

# HEARTRENDING TORTURE

Half a span had passed since the city was retaken, the Te Femma Brigade was now fully formed, and the Showton prisoners dealt with. Tondo had the male units moved to the far northeastern border of the Te Femma realm. This served two purposes. First, it advanced most of the army forward and in a position to begin the next campaign. Second, it substantially reduced the number of friendly ferals in and around the city. Something that greatly pleased the queen.

It was at this time, and under the insistent and badgering encouragement of the ameer, Queen Ezora issued a decree granting the Te Femma slaves their freedom. The edict was not announced publicly, for the queen knew it would result in additional turmoil. The sisters had reluctantly accepted the queen's previous order to grant the slaves their time. Now, the slaves were free, their time truly becoming their own forever.

As Tondo was preparing his next campaign plan, Fayeetez rushed into the ameer's headquarters. Tondo hadn't seen his cavalry commander for some time because he'd been with his mounted troops performing long-range reconnaissance.

"Sutro Megatus," Tondo began, "it's good to see you again." Fayeetez had received a well-deserved promotion shortly after Te Femma was liberated.

"Ameer, I have returned to give my report in person. The enemy is moving towards us. I've seen two large formations approaching from the southeast. I've also received reports that two more equally large formations are approaching from the southwest," Fayeetez reported.

"How many warriors in these units?" Tondo asked.

"Zerr, each formation consists of two armies of about fifteen thousand each. That's about sixty-thousand altogether," Fayeetez estimated, then he added, "I've ordered the mounted brigades to threaten their advance but not engage. If we move the army quickly, we may be able to attack the two groups separately before they can combine forces."

"Very good, Fayeetez. Your threats may force them to halt and prepare for battle, slowing their movements. If we act quickly, we can take advantage of that." Tondo turned to an aide, "Notify the brigade commanders that there will be a council of war when the p´atezas sets. I want them all in attendance. Tell Sutrum Megatus Idop I want to meet with him as soon as he's available." The aide saluted, held a short meeting with other staff aides, and then several quickly departed. Tondo turned back to Fayeetez, "What about tanter units? Have you seen any mounted formations?"

"Yes, zerr, each foot column is accompanied by several hundred men mounted on tanters. I've advised my commanders to avoid direct contact. We've been running them around in circles, as Harmon suggested. Eventually, their mounts tire. So far, I've held off attacking, but I think, when their mounts are exhausted, it would be a good time to strike. Quick, sharp thrusts, and then equally quick withdrawals," Fayeetez told him.

"Excellent. Death by a thousand cuts," Tondo said, causing Fayeetez to smile. "Describe the terrain you've seen. Is there a suitable place to engage the enemy that gives us the advantage?" Fayeetez began describing what he had seen.

Megatus Nedenna, commander of the newly formed Te Femma Brigade, stationed a short distance from the city, had just received orders from Sutrum Megatus Idop to have her brigade rejoin the army. She called a meeting of senior commanders: Deveena, Zuni, and the eight wing sutro megatoes.

"The brigade has been ordered to rejoin the feral army now that we're fully formed. I've been told by Idop that he's planning to attack a Showton force, but he must wait until our brigade joins them. He expects us to arrive in five days. I want to get there in three. Can your commands travel a march and a half per day?" Nedenna asked.

"My command can do it easily," Deveena quickly responded.

"Yes, my sisters can do it," Zuni said.

"The sisters can do it," Maaryah agreed, "but the big challenge will be the wagon teams. They won't be able to keep up," she warned.

"They can catch up later," Deveena said in an annoyed tone.

It was apparent to Maaryah that her commanders had no concept of moving such a large force over long distances. "The wagons carry food and water, as well as cooking gear. We'll need to see that the sisters are well fed each day if we're to move that far that fast," Maaryah told the others.

"Give the sisters three days' rations and forget the wagons," Deveena said, annoyed by Maaryah's warnings.

"That's added weight to an already heavy load; unless you want the sisters to leave their armor and weapons in the wagons," Maaryah said sarcastically.

"No!" Nedenna exclaimed. "The brigade will arrive fully prepared to go into battle, if necessary. This is our chance to show the rest of the Feral's army our superior abilities. Does anyone have a solution?"

"The problem is the wagons; they're too slow. How can we lose the wagons?" Zuni wondered.

Maaryah waited a few moments to see if anyone else would speak up. No one did. Finally, she said, "Let's not worry about the wagons at all. Let them arrive later. We need pack animals to carry enough field rations for each warrior in the brigade. I'm sure the queen can arrange that."

"That's pretty presumptuous, you pathetic sub. After what the Showton's ferals took from us, there's little left to draw upon. There's few pack animals remaining, and their owners won't part with them," Deveena chastened. Maaryah glared at her but didn't respond.

"Yes, pack animals would do it. I'll meet with the queen later today. We only need the animals for a wernt, and then they'll be returned. I'm sure Her Highness can arrange it," Nedenna said.

"How many days rations?" Deveena wondered. "We only need three, and that would reduce the number of pack animals required."

"I suppose you're right," Maaryah quipped. "The brigade can go without food while we wait for our wagons to arrive, or maybe you were planning to beg the ferals for their food?"

"Beg the ferals; outrageous! You're a mutinous sub!" Deveena shouted. "I'm filing charges against you."

"Deveena, she's right," Nedenna said. "We may need ten days' rations." The meeting was adjourned, and the officers went their separate ways. Maaryah was becoming frustrated with these meetings because she and Deveena always got into a dispute. She chuckled to herself as she remembered how the tanters would butt heads from time to time while they were at the estate. That's how she felt about herself and Deveena; constantly butting heads. The subcommander's constant badgering was becoming exasperating, but Maaryah wasn't going to back off, especially when she knew she was in the right.

Later that afternoon, a herd of samaran pack animals arrived at the brigade area; the owners had happily loaned their animals and considered it their contribution to the Showton's defeat. The following morning, the brigade was up and moving just as a red p´atezas broke the horizon. Nedenna led with Deveena at her side, both riding samarans. Deveena's four wings followed. A mounted Zuni led her four commands, with Maaryah's wing bringing up the rear of the combat elements. The pack animals followed, creating a massive cloud of dust as they plodded along, occasionally breaking into an amble as the samarans and their handlers struggled to keep up with the fast-moving women warriors.

As planned, it took three days for the brigade to arrive at the army's bivouac area. The women marched in, their heads held high, and very proud of their accomplishment. Tondo and Idop were very impressed when informed of the brigade's earlier-than-expected arrival; however, several male warriors lined the road and gawked as the women passed. Most men watched silently, but one particularly obnoxious feral taunted the women as they passed while his companions howled in laughter at his needling remarks.

"Look, boys, the pleasure brigade has finally arrived! We won't need campfires to keep our feet warm tonight!" he bellowed. And so it went as the women marched past. When Maaryah's wing approached, she immediately became aware of the man's harassment, and she wasn't going to tolerate it.

"Standard-bearer, pass me the flag!" she ordered. Each wing in the brigade carried a banner identifying the unit represented by its color. Maaryah had chosen orange for her wing, which caused others to wince and wonder why she had chosen what they considered such an awful color. She never explained her reasoning. The banner was passed, and she brought it to her left side, holding the banner's pole close to her body and kept in place by her left arm and hand. As her wing approached the insulting feral standing at their left, she grasped the upper section of the flagpole with her right hand, and as she passed the offensive male, she pulled down on the pole with her right hand while holding the pole's center with her left. The long rod pivoted, and its butt flipped up, catching the invidious offender right between the legs. He grabbed his groin and fell to his knees, moaning in pain. Maaryah quickly straightened the flagpole, not even breaking stride. A few chuckles could be heard coming from the sisters' ranks. The feral observers were howling with laughter as their companion fell to his face in the dirt.

"Standard-bearer, prepare to receive the flag!" Maaryah ordered. She passed the flag to the standard-bearer, her duty now completed.

Two of Idop's aides met Megatus Nedenna and directed her and the brigade to their assigned encampment location. Maaryah's wing was directed to its area, and they established their camp. They would be sleeping under the stars for the next several days as they did during the march, their tents arriving with the wagons. The sisters received their cold rations and rested, fully satisfied with their accomplishment.

As dusk approached after the brigade's arrival, a short feral army officer accompanied by two subordinates stormed into Maaryah's area.

"Zerr," one of Maaryah's aides began, "an angry feral wishes to speak with the commander of the orange banner. He seems very upset."

"Upset?" Maaryah wondered.

"Yes, zerr. The little feral claims a woman attacked and injured one of his men."

Maaryah smiled, crossed her arms over her chest, and said, "Bring him here." The aide saluted, returned to the waiting ferals, and escorted them to Maaryah. The senior, unmarked freeborn feral stood in front of her, looking up, for she was a full head taller than he was. He was staring at the slave mark on her forehead, and after a few moments, his angry look grew more stern.

"I am Dant´un. One of the women attacked my man with a pole. I've been told he'll be out of action for several days. I want the attacker scourged," he demanded.

Maaryah noticed the two zanth bars on his chest, indicating his rank was megato, a troop commander. "Tell me, megato, what was your man doing when he was attacked?" Maaryah asked.

"He was simply observing the women marching in," Dant´un told her.

"Who told you that?"

"That's what he and the others with him said."

"Ha, is that so? It seems they failed to mention the disparaging and insulting remarks he was making."

"Do you have any witnesses to that?" Dant´un asked in a perturbed tone.

"Only eight-thousand or so. He was quite thorough in his verbal abuse toward warrior, non-officer, and officer alike," Maaryah said with a smile.

"Nevertheless, I want to know the attacker's name," he demanded.

"Maaryah is her name, megato," she answered.

"I want her scourged!" he demanded.

"That's not going to happen."

"If you won't do anything about it, I will. I demand to see her. Bring her here."

"I'm Maaryah, and I'm the one who dropped your man. He deserved what he got. You should thank me for not bringing formal charges against him for disrespecting officers and non-officers. I could also file a formal complaint against his superiors because of his poor training," she said defiantly.

"Who's the commander of this unit?" Dant´un growled.

"I am!" Maaryah answered with an angry tone. She lowered her arms, revealing the three zanth bars of rank on her chest.

Dant´un just stared at her rank badge and said nothing, quickly realizing he was treading on weak-ground. "Now, megato, do you wish to continue with your complaint?" she asked, her voice hard and cold.

"No," he simply replied.

"No, what?" she challenged.

"No, zerr."

"Good. I suggest you explain to your men that they keep their disrespectful remarks to themselves if they know what's good for them. Do you understand?"

"Yes, zerr."

"Now, Megato Dant´un, do you make it a practice of scourging your men?"

"No, zerr."

"Then why would you want to scourge a sister?" Dant´un didn't respond, but he and his fellow feral officers looked nervous. "Dant´un, I'm going to remember your name, and if I ever hear that you made such a threat again, I'll see that Ameer Tondo learns your name, as well. I'm sure you know how he feels about such practices." Dant´un became even more nervous. After a long, stern glare at the short feral, Maaryah snapped, "You're dismissed," The three men saluted, performed a sharp About-Face, and quickly departed. Maaryah watched as they moved away, a satisfied smile slowly creeping across her face.

Late the next day, Tondo called another council of war with his brigade commanders. He included the Te Femma

Brigade subcommanders Deveena and Zuni and the brigade's eight wing commanders. When Tondo told Idop this the day before, Idop smiled and took the opportunity to razz him for including Maaryah in the council. Tondo tried to explain why he had invited so many Te Femma commanders, but Idop wouldn't hear it. He was convinced the ameer wanted to be near his bondmate. Tondo offered only a feeble defense because he wasn't sure he needed all the women at the meeting. Still, he kept saying the Te Femma Brigade was the army's reserve force and could be committed into battle as a whole unit or divided and committed as subcommands or wings. Nevertheless, he was looking forward to seeing his beloved Maaryah.

A sand table was placed in the tent's center representing the terrain and battle formations. The officers crowded around it as Tondo explained his plan. "The enemy is approaching in two main groups. Each body appears to be thirty-thousand warriors, mostly foot soldiers; however, each group has a few tanter units with them. Fayeetez's men have been harassing both formations, and they have slowed their advance. I don't want the two groups to merge. My plan is to attack the eastern body before it can join the other one. We'll then turn and attack the western force. Fayeetez says this table represents the terrain and is the best place to take on the east column. It's a two-day march from here. When we get there, I want your brigades in battlefront formation with the Te Femma Brigade and archers at the rear. The entire line will move forward and engage the enemy line. Shortly after contact is made and battle initiated, Idop will slowly pull back the center. The flanks will remain fixed or continue to advance, if possible. I doubt this enemy has ever faced archers before, so I will order them to start shooting their arrows into the enemy's rear ranks when the time is right. As the battle develops, I will order our reserve to move and seal the enemy's fate. I want them crushed. Otherwise, we'll be outnumbered the next time we engage. Any questions?"

"Ameer Tondo," a familiar voice came from behind the officers crowding around the table; it was Maaryah's. "Will you commit the reserve as a brigade, or will it be committed in smaller commands?"

"I can't say at this time. It depends on how the battle develops. The important thing is to deny the enemy an opportunity to withdraw. Once the trap is sprung, we've got him," Tondo said as he raised his right hand and closed it into a fist. A few more questions were asked and answered, and then the officers were dismissed.

Tondo tried to catch Maaryah before she left, but she quickly exited the tent and was gone. By this time, the p´atezas had set, and it was night. He took a deep breath and stared into the darkness. His beloved Maaryah was so near, yet she was so far away. He yearned to touch her, to hold her, but he dared not. It was heartrending torture.

"Maaryah!" Zuni called. She stopped and waited for her commander to catch up.

"You sure left the war council in a hurry. Why the rush?"

"I need to prepare my wing. We'll be moving into battle soon."

"Maaryah, I've known you long enough to see you're upset. What is it?"

She looked at the stars, then to Zuni, and took a deep breath. "I couldn't stand it any longer."

"Couldn't stand what?"

"To be so near to him, yet unable to touch him."

Zuni smiled, "I see; I've never considered how difficult this must be for you. You love him dearly, don't you?"

"I do, with all my heart. I want this war to end so we can be together again. I think he's the most wonderful man under the stars. My joy was full until the Showton crushed our happiness," Maaryah shared, her voice breaking with sadness.

"I must admit, I've never met a feral like him. At first, I thought he was just another blustering outsider like all the rest, but the more I learn about him, the more I respect him. It's as though there is an aura of authority surrounding that outsider," Zuni confided.

"You don't know the half of it," Maaryah replied absentmindedly.

Zuni looked at her quizzically, then asked, "I've heard some of the feral commanders say that he surrounds himself with burning red fire when he becomes angry. Are you telling me that's true?" Maaryah silently nodded, causing Zuni's eyes to widen. "If he glows red, does that mean you do, too? After all, you have the same powers as he does, right?"

Maaryah nodded again and said, "Orange, my aura is orange."

Zuni was shocked, causing her to ponder for a moment before speaking again. "I know you've been angry many times. Why have I never seen it?"

"Just like my love for Tondo, I must keep my anger under control to protect my secret," Maaryah explained.

"So, that's why you chose that awful color for your banner," Zuni realized.

"Yes," Maaryah told her with a laugh.

"Maaryah, I'm glad you trust me enough to share these things with me. Just like the Feral, the more I learn about you, the more I respect you."

Maaryah smiled even though Zuni's reference to her bond-mate as 'the Feral' offended her; she kept the offense to herself. After a short pause, she said, "He's so near, yet he's so far away. I want to hold him and be held by him, but I dare not. It's heart-rending torture."

# CHAPTER 12

# RECALLED

Tondo had an excellent view of the battlefield from his perch atop Myron's raster. The opposing armies had aligned and faced each other, separated by three or four arrow flights. The Showton's force appeared to be thirty-thousand warriors, just as Fayeetez had said. An enemy unit of about three-hundred troopers mounted on tanters had been positioned on Tondo's left. The rest of the enemy army was on foot and stretched across his front, overlapping his line on both ends. His four foot brigades were positioned in the center with two mounted units of two-thousand five-hundred on either flank. He had placed the Te Femma Brigade behind the main line on his right. The archers were put in the center to the left of the sisters. Tondo placed his command raster behind the center-right of his foot soldiers and to the side of his archers' expected line of fire, the Te Femma Brigade to his right rear.

It was approaching the midday segment, and it was a hot, cloudless day. A gentle breeze blew from the north, cooling the men and blowing toward the Showton's force. A Showton horn blared, echoing across the field of battle, and the enemy began their advance. Tondo gave an order, his hornman sounded Advance, and the United Kingdom army quickly moved forward, the foot soldiers banging their shields with the shafts of their assembled metrenas with each step. As Tondo's men advanced, they kicked up dust, and the breeze pushed it into the faces of his enemy. Although annoying, it didn't slow their relentless progression one bit. When within range, Tondo's men let fly their metrenas, and then they charged with a shout. The two lines collided in a roar of angry voices and clanging metal. Neither side made any gains at first, but soon, Tondo's two center brigades slowly fell back. The ameer smiled, for Idop had started pulling the enemy in, letting them think they were winning, arming the trap that would be their undoing.

As Tondo watched, the enemy cavalry, numbering only in the hundreds, started a dash around his army's left flank. His main concern was dealing with these troopers, and since they were now committed, he breathed easier. As the ememy's mounted formation skirted his flank, Tondo, seemingly ignoring the enemy's mounted threat, gave an order to his hornman, who quickly sounded a command. Both of his mounted brigades broke from their positions on the flanks and, ignoring the tanter unit on the left, began a charge around the enemy in a dual pincer movement.

"Megatus Nedenna!" Deveena shouted over the roar of battle, "A large formation of mounted enemy is moving around the army's left. What's the Feral thinking? He's a fool! We'll be attacked from the rear. You must do something before it turns into a disaster."

Nedenna thought for a moment, and then she yelled an order, "Brigade, Turn About!" Her command was repeated through the brigade. She dug her heels into her mount's sides and dashed to Maaryah's wing, which had been at the rear of the Te Femma formation, but now was at the front. "Maaryah, at the quick pace, advance and halt those mounted warriors before they cause mischief," Nedenna commanded.

"Zerr, have you received Tondo's orders?" Maaryah asked in a shout.

"There isn't time! I must act now, or all is lost," Nedenna yelled back.

"Zerr, Ameer Tondo knows what he's doing; wait for his command."

"Obey my order! And no more delays!" Nedenna yelled.

"By your command, megatus," Maaryah said reluctantly. "Follow me!" she shouted to her wing. The order was repeated down the line, and the entire formation quickly trotted across the rear of the kingdom army, followed by the rest of the brigade, moving diagonally behind the army's front line. The enemy's mounted troopers wheeled wide and refused to engage the superior numbers of the Te Femma Brigade's ranks, bristling with sharp halberd top spikes.

"Zerr," the hornman shouted, "the women are moving to the rear!" Tondo spun around and uttered a curse under his breath as he watched the Te Femma Brigade moving towards the advancing tanters, who quickly broke away, leaving the sisters with no target and well out of position for the next phase of his plan. Tondo faced the front again and brought his farseer to his eye. "Hornman, sound Mounted Recall. Our troopers will be slaughtered without foot support." He then shouted down to an aide, "Tell Idop, the plan is broken, and he's to advance his brigades." The aide saluted and dashed off. "Nedenna, what in the names of the Five Shadows are you thinking?" he said to no one in particular.

The battle raged for a few segments before the Showton's army began a slow and orderly withdrawal. By the time night arrived, the action was suspended with neither side able to declare victory.

Tondo called a meeting with his army's commander after nightfall. "I think we should relieve her of command," Idop said.

"I would if I could, but only the queen can do that; remember, it's her brigade. Unfortunately, we have to live with whomever she places in command," Tondo growled in frustration.

"You must demand the queen replace her," Idop grouched.

"I'll take it under advisement," Tondo grumbled.

"Does Nedenna realize what she's done?" Idop wondered, his anger clearly etched on his face.

"If she doesn't, she soon will. I'm going to make it abundantly clear to her."

Nedenna, Deveena, Zuni, and the eight wing commanders had been summoned to the ameer's headquarters, a grand two-story stone building located in a large town near the location where the battle took place.

"Maaryah, what's he going to do?" Zuni quietly asked in a worried tone.

"I don't know, but I've never felt him so enraged before. We're in serious trouble."

"How do you know that?" Zuni asked.

"I can feel it by my inner-power. He's angry and worried."

"Worried? Why?"

"I don't know, but I'm sure we'll soon learn," Maaryah said as she watched one of Tondo's aides approaching Nedenna.

"Megatus, Ameer Tondo will see you and your senior officers now," the aide coldly stated. Nedenna followed the aide, and her officers filed in behind her, Maaryah at the rear.

It didn't take an inner-power to see that Tondo and Idop were furious; their angry glares said all. Nedenna stopped a few steps in front of her two superior officers, Deveena and Zuni, a step behind her, and the eight wing commanders in a line behind them.

"Megatus Nedenna reports as ordered, zerr," she said with a salute. Tondo returned her salute and stepped in front of her, forcing down his rising anger. Idop remained in place as he scanned the formation behind her, his wrathful unpatched eye moving from face to face. Tondo's cold blue eyes examined Nedenna from head to foot and then rested on her nervous eyes with a withering look that bore into her soul, causing her to shudder for an instant.

"Megatus, your actions ruined our chance to destroy the Showton's force. What do you have to say for yourself?" Tondo snarled, his tone cold and hard, the veins in his neck showing.

"Zerr, I felt my action was the right thing to do given the developing situation," she replied, her voice revealing her stress.

"And what might that be?" Tondo spat back.

"The Showton's mounted unit was about to attack the army's rear. Since my brigade was the only one not already engaged, I had to act to save the army," she explained.

"How many large-scale, open-terrain battles have you commanded?" Tondo asked, his voice gruff and challenging.

"None; only city defense, zerr," she replied meekly.

"So, with all that experience, you knew exactly what needed to be done, did you?" Tondo asked sarcastically. His face was turning red, and Maaryah could detect the struggle he was having in keeping his aura down.

"It was clear to us all something had to be done . . . immediately, so I acted," Nedenna explained.

"Did you receive any counsel from your senior officers?" Tondo asked, still struggling to keep his aura under control.

Nedenna turned her head slightly to the right and caught sight of Deveena standing behind and to her side. She quickly turned her face toward Tondo again and replied, "I assume full responsibility for the brigade's actions."

"As well you should!" Tondo nearly shouted. He looked past Nedenna and studied the officers behind her. "Didn't any of your senior brigade leaders advise you to wait for my orders?" Tondo gruffly barked. No one replied for several uncomfortably long moments.

Nedenna finally answered, "Zerr, Sutro Megato Maaryah advised me to wait for your orders." Tondo looked at Maaryah, and his angry expression relaxed just a bit. Maaryah could detect the beginnings of a smile at the corner of his mouth, but it didn't last long. His eyes grew hard and angry again as they shifted back to Nedenna.

"At least one of your officers has some intelligence. Because you moved your brigade into the line of fire, I was unable to order the archers to cut down the enemy's mounted troops, and they were allowed to move away undamaged. Because your brigade was out of position, I could not order it to advance and block the Showton army's retreat, and it was allowed to escape.

Because of your unsound decision, the enemy withdrew in good order, and it will unite with the other Showton column advancing on us. Not only has your poor judgment endangered this army, but you have also endangered your home city. I must order the army to withdraw to a more defensible position, and we must prepare to confront a force that will significantly outnumber us. All this because you didn't follow orders and acted on your own misguided judgment. What do you have to say for yourself now?" Tondo was growing angrier and angrier.

Nedenna said nothing. What could she say? Her unwise actions had been utterly in error, exposing her lack of battle savvy and inexperience.

Tondo's anger reached the boiling point, and he lost control. His aura ignited, and it washed over Nedenna and the others. Several women gasped, and Nedenna grimaced in pain, but she did not move, her eyes nearly shut and her body stiff. Tondo moved back a couple of steps, easing the bite of his aura as he attempted to regain control. Slowly, it began to fade.

He looked past Nedenna and ordered, "All of you are dismissed. Megatus, you will remain here for . . . for additional training." The women quickly filed out and prepared to return to their units, for the enemy was still nearby and a threat.

Before Maaryah left the deserted township, she entered a two-story building at the edge of town and climbed the stairs, moving to a balcony with a clear view of the nearby battlefield. To her surprise, Zuni was already there. Maaryah stepped to her side, and they stood in silence, watching the two armies' distant campfires glowing in the darkness.

"What do you think will happen in the morning?" Zuni finally asked.

"The enemy will either attempt to hold us here or withdraw and merge with the other Showton force coming from the south-west. I guess Tondo will pull us back before we're trapped."

"How do you know all this?" Zuni wondered.

"Tondo would challenge Idop with military situations at the estate. Tondo was training him, and I would observe. It wasn't long before he included me in the training."

Zuni smiled and shook her head, "So, you've not only learned fighting skills from the Feral, but you've also been trained in strategy by him. No wonder you always seem to be a step ahead of the rest of us." Maaryah didn't respond but only grimaced at Zuni's absentminded use of the term 'the Feral' for her bond-mate. "What will happen to Nedenna; to us?" Zuni wondered.

"By the time Tondo and Idop are finished with her, she'll feel like she was trampled by two thrice. I doubt she'll make the same mistake a second time. As far as the rest of us, we'll be expected to carry-on; however, the men in the army know what has happened, and the brigade will be blamed for the trouble we've caused, and rightly so," Maaryah advised.

"Will she ever be trusted again; will the brigade?" Zuni asked.

"Nedenna will have to earn Tondo's and Idop's confidence again. We'll all have to regain the army's respect," Maaryah lamented.

"You mean the ferals'—all the other men's trust—don't you?" Zuni wondered. Maaryah nodded, and Zuni closed her eyes and dropped her chin onto her chest. She uttered a muffled profanity.

Maaryah and Zuni stood quietly pondering for several long moments until they heard a sound coming from below the balcony they were standing on. In the dim glow of the moons, Maaryah could barely see Deveena's features. She was carrying a creature under her arm, and after taking a few steps, she released it, tossing it into the air. The large bird-like beast unfolded and flapped its wings, flying off in a westerly direction toward the city of Te Femma. Deveena watched the winged creature disappear into the darkness, and then she mounted her samaran and ambled toward the battlefield and the glowing campfires.

"Was that a nightflier Deveena released?" Maaryah asked, her voice revealing her building anger.

"Yes, the queen told us to use them to send important messages to the palace and keep her informed of the army's location and status," Zuni replied without emotion.

"Does Deveena write the messages?" Maaryah wondered.

"Ha, by order of the queen. Deveena thinks she's fooling Nedenna and me, but we know she is the queen's eyes and ears in the brigade," Zuni told her. Maaryah didn't respond, but her expression turned hard and cold. She'd had enough of spies. The estate spy, Doros, had caused much mischief for her and her bondmate. Now, she had to deal with another one. Only this time, she knew who it was. Her angst toward the annoying subcommander increased substantially, causing her aura to ignite, forcing Zuni to step away quickly and gawk in wonder.

As the p´atezas's morning rays touched the gartz window of the royal bedchamber, Queen Ezora arose, washed her hands and face, and dressed herself, not having yet chosen a new lady-in-waiting. In the quiet of the morning, she paused and thought how lonely it was without the fellowship of her beloved saber-cat protectors. A new pair was being trained, but it would take much time because training giant felines was dangerous work.

The queen's moment of solitude was interrupted as Rana Fardinza entered. "Your Highness, we received a report last night from Deveena," the rana said.

"Nightflier?" the queen wondered.

"Yes, Your Highness."

"What does she say?" the queen asked.

"A battle was fought, and the Feral's army must retreat in order to defend the city."

"What? The Feral was defeated! Is the city in danger?"

"It isn't clear what the city's situation is, Your Highness, but it can't be good."

"I will declare a day of prayer and sacrifice seeking the great mother's protection! Now tell me, what happened?" the queen wondered.

"It appears Nedenna acted unwisely, and her actions ruined the Feral's plan."

"Give me the details," the queen demanded, her tone angry, revealing her frustration.

"I'm sorry, Your Highness, but that's all the report says."

"This appears to be a disaster. In the brigade's first engagement, Nedenna proves to be incompetent. This cannot stand. I must speak to her myself. Have her recalled," the queen ordered. Rana Fardinza bowed and exited the queen's bedchamber.

Three riders approached Maaryah. She could immediately see they were from the queen. One carried the insignia of an arbon, an advisor to the queen. The other two were elite guards. They rode up to Maaryah and halted.

"You there, I am Arbon T´uepornee on official business from Queen Ezora. Where is Megatus Nedenna?"

"Follow me," Maaryah told her. The arbon and her two guards dismounted and handed the reins of their mounts to nearby orderlies. They followed Maaryah to a small farmhouse.

"Arbon, that is brigade headquarters. Megatus Nedenna's standard is uncased, so she's inside," Maaryah said, pointing to the building. "Would you like me to announce your arrival?"

"That will not be necessary," the arbon said. She then walked to the two sentries standing on either side of the door. The sentries saluted, and the arbon entered. Her two elite guards waited outside. Maaryah returned to her wing and, about a segment later, watched as Nedenna rode by, escorted by the arbon and the two elite guards. It was easy to see that Nedenna was worried.

"Megatus Nedenna," the queen began, "We understand there has been a battle. Tell Us about it."

Nedenna explained what had happened in great detail. She included her error, for Zuni had informed her that Deveena was seen releasing a nightflier, undoubtedly telling the queen of her trouble with the Feral.

"So, Nedenna, in your very first battle with the full brigade, you've brought shame upon the name of Te Femma?" the queen accused. Nedenna hung her head and nodded. "What has the Feral to say about all this?"

"He is angry with me; he and Sutrum Megatus Idop. They've expressed their . . . their displeasure, Your Highness."

"Yes, and We can see why. We understand the city may be in danger. Now, you've earned Our displeasure, as well. We're surprised the Feral hasn't demanded your dismissal," the queen turned introspective for a moment. "Maybe it's Our fault for placing you in a position you weren't suited for," Nedenna raised her head and looked at the queen with sad eyes for a moment; she hung her head again.

"Your Highness," Rana Fardinza began, "Nedenna was an excellent Stontza commander, and her defense of the city kept the Showton's army at bay, allowing the Feral to break the siege."

"Yes, We haven't forgotten. Nedenna, you have served the city and Us well until now," the queen took a deep breath and paused. Nedenna straightened her back and lifted her head, awaiting the queen's ruling concerning her fate. The queen's face brightened, and she continued, "We are pleased to learn you are with child. It must be a happy time for you and your broesayr." Nedenna's expression changed from worry to surprise.

"Your Highness, I'm not . . . "

Rana Fardinza quickly interrupted, "Nedenna, it is fortunate you are with child. You will be honorably relieved of command and advanced to the royal rank of toepaur, just as past Stontza commanders have been under similar circumstances. This will allow you to raise your child in the traditions of the city and advise the queen on military and city security matters. You'll also receive a comfortable stipend for your position. Were you not with child, you could be disgraced."

Nedenna hung her head once more. "Thank you, Your Highness. You are most generous," she said with sadness.

"Now, Nedenna, spend time with your broesayr. Bring your baby to Us when the time comes so We may hold the child," the queen said with a smile.

"Nedenna," Rana Fardinza began, "who do you recommend assume leadership of the brigade, Deveena or Zuni?"

Nedenna looked up with sad eyes and responded, "Neither."

"What?" the queen said in surprise.

"Your Highness, the best officer in the brigade is Sutro Megato Maaryah, commander of the Eighth Wing," Nedenna said.

The queen looked at Rana Fardinza with questioning eyes, "We are not familiar with this sister." She watched as the rana shook her head, indicating she was also unfamiliar with the person. "Where's she from, the city or one of the provinces?"

"She's not from Te Femma. She's an outsider," Nedenna told the Queen.

"A sub!" the queen and rana exclaimed together.

"Are you suggesting the brigade be commanded by a lowly sub?" the rana asked in astonishment.

"If you want the best, she's the one," Nedenna told her.

"Where did she come from?" the queen asked.

"She came from one of the estates in the United Kingdom," Nedenna answered.

"Describe her. Is she short and frail like most subs?" the queen wondered.

"She's shorter than the sisters but much taller than other outsiders, including ferals. She has earned the sisters' respect. Her hair is black, and she carries a slave mark of the kingdom," Nedenna said.

The queen looked at Fardinza again, and the rana asked Nedenna, "What color are her eyes?"

"Amber, I believe," Nedenna answered. The queen and rana looked at each other once more, and surprise was etched on their faces.

"Did you say she carries a kingdom slave mark?" the queen asked. Nedenna nodded. "Thank you, primatza, you are dismissed," the queen said. Nedenna gave the queen a Te Femma salute, turned around, and quickly marched out.

"Rana, what do you think? Could this mystery person be the ameera?" the queen asked.

"Ameer Tondo reported she was killed by the assassins who attacked his estate. So this Maaryah couldn't be the ameera, unless . . . "

"Ha, unless the Feral wanted everyone to believe she had been killed for some reason. If it is her, what would she be doing in Our brigade?" The queen shook her head, perplexed by all this unexpected news. "Nevertheless," she continued, "we can't have an outsider commanding the brigade. It's either Deveena or Zuni. Assemble the toepaurs and arbons; we must act quickly," the queen ordered.

# CHAPTER 13

# ROYAL WITNESSES

For the past couple of wernts, the army retreated towards Te Femma. Fayeetez had found good ground, and Tondo moved the army to it in preparation for its upcoming encounter with the Showton's combined force. Deveena was in temporary command of the brigade. Fortunately, Maaryah's and Deveena's paths had not crossed during that time; however, Maaryah had just been summoned to brigade headquarters, so she prepared herself for another uncomfortable confrontation. The image of the two tanters butting heads flashed in her memory. She was ushered into the command tent, where she saw that Zuni and Dori had arrived before her. Deveena was standing next to Arbon T´uepornee.

"The arbon has an announcement to make," Deveena said with a smile.

T´uepornee began to speak, "Megatus Nedenna is with child, and she has been relieved of command as tradition requires. She will soon be advanced to the royal rank of toepaur. The queen has decreed that Neva Megatus Deveena be promoted to megatus and assume command of the Te Femma Brigade."

"Thank you, arbon, you are dismissed," Deveena brusquely ordered. The arbon quickly exited, obviously surprised by Deveena's curt dismissal. A cruel smile filled Deveena's face as an aide pinned the two four-pointed zanth diamonds badge of rank to the front of her military tunic. She was now officially the new commander of the brigade. Maaryah knew trouble was coming, and in a heartbeat, it did.

"It's quite surprising to learn Nedenna is with child, isn't it?" Deveena mused. "She must have found more free time than we supposed. Nevertheless, the queen has made her ruling, and it's now up to me to see that things are put right after Nedenna's disgraceful performance in the last battle. The first thing I must do is get the brigade's command structure in proper order. Nedenna was too liberal in promoting outsiders to important leadership positions," she said while glaring at Maaryah. "I'm putting an end to that practice, but first, I need to clean out the clutter." Deveena's glare changed to a wicked smile. "Maaryah, I promote you to neva megatus." Maaryah stared back at her new brigade commander in shock. That was the last thing she expected to hear from her antagonist. Deveena picked up a small pouch lying on her desk and tossed it to Maaryah. She caught it, wondering what Deveena was planning. "Now, Neva Megatus Sub, you have the rank to make an Honor Challenge to your commander, which, as you've seen, is me. Do you know what that is?" Maaryah nodded. "Good. You've got the salt. Now, make the challenge. You have two witnesses," Deveena told her as she looked from Maaryah to Zuni and then to Dori.

"Zerr, I have no intention of making an Honor Challenge," Maaryah told her.

"Coward!" Deveena shouted. She then relaxed a bit, and her wicked smile returned. "I order you to make the challenge," she told Maaryah.

"Deveena, you can't do that!" Zuni exclaimed.

"It's Megatus Deveena now, is that understood?" Deveena barked as her glare fell on Zuni. "This is now my brigade, and I can give any order I please. This worthless sub needs to be severely chastised and expunged from our ranks. That, I intend to do." Her angry stare turned again to Maaryah, "If you don't make the challenge, you will be the highest-ranking officer ever to lead the privy detail, and that's all you'll be allowed to do in my brigade."

The memory of that loathsome assignment soured Maaryah, and she'd had enough of Deveena's badgering. She quickly recollected what Tondo had told her about how Nedenna conducted her Honor Challenge to him, but she'd forgotten the details. She poured a handful of salt from the pouch into her right hand and flung it at Deveena, standing a fair distance away. Only a little salt actually hit Deveena, mostly landing on her lower legs and feet.

"Just like a worthless sub, you can't even conduct a proper challenge. I will enjoy putting you in your place, just like I did at T´ezpont," Deveena spewed. She turned to Zuni and Dori, "You two saw her throw the salt. The challenge is valid. I will notify the queen. Now, leave me."

"Your Highness," Rana Fardinza said, "Sutro Megatoes Hertora and Mindetta have a message for you from Megatus Deveena."

"What is it?" the queen asked.

"They say they're under orders to deliver it to you personally, Your Highness."

"Very well, present them," the queen ordered.

The two sisters were summoned, and they marched into the Throne Room in perfect step. They halted two strides short of the queen's platform, and each dropped to her right knee in genuflection. "Your Highness," Sutro Megato Hertora began, "we bring a message from Megatus Deveena."

"Yes, so We've been told. What is it?" the queen asked.

"An Honor Challenge has been made. Neva Megatus Maaryah challenges Megatus Deveena for command of the brigade. Salt has been thrown, and the challenge accepted. The antagonists request you send two witnesses to the challenge. It will take place on the day you specify," Hertora explained.

The queen looked to Rana Fardinza in surprise, who was obviously as shocked as the queen. "Is this challenger, Maaryah, the outsider We've heard about?" the queen asked the two officers.

"Yes, Neva Megatus Maaryah is an outsider, Your Highness. She is not one of the sisters. She is from the United Kingdom." Mindetta replied.

"You may stand," the queen said, and then her eyes lowered as she pondered the situation. After a long pause, she looked at the two officers. "Inform Megatus Deveena and the challenger that We will personally witness the challenge. You may take your leave with that message."

"Your Highness!" the two officers said in unison as they slapped their left shoulders with their right hands in salute. They smartly turned about and marched out of the room.

After the two officers had left, the queen turned to Fardinza and said, "I must meet this Maaryah and learn what she is scheming. I don't like this unexpected turn of events. I don't like it at all!"

The brigade's senior commanders had assembled in the abandoned town's great hall, which had served as the provincial governor's seat of office. Deveena stood in front of the formation, with Zuni behind her at the right and Maaryah at the left. The eight wing commanders were in a line behind them; the recently promoted Sutro Megato Areena having been assigned to replace Maaryah as the Eighth Wing commander. All eleven officers were wearing Te Femma armor and helms.

The door to the hall opened, and two queen's elite guards entered, taking positions on either side of the doorway. Queen Ezora soon followed the guards and stepped into the hall, Rana Fardinza behind her. Megatus Deveena dropped to one knee and bowed; all the other officers did the same. The queen advanced until she stood in front of the kneeling brigade commander.

"Megatus Deveena," the queen said, "I have come to learn for myself the nature of this Honor Challenge."

"I am at your service, Your Highness. What can I do for you?" Deveena asked, her head bowed, and her voice somewhat muffled due to the helm.

"For now, nothing," the queen told her. She then walked to Zuni and stood in front of her. "Neva Megatus Zuni," she said.

"Yes, Your Highness. I await your command," Zuni said, her head bowed.

"Very well," the queen responded. She then moved in front of Maaryah and looked down, her emerald-green eyes stern and cold.

"You must be Neva Megatus Maaryah, the outsider."

"Yes, Your Highness," Maaryah said, her head bowed like the others.

"Is it true? Have you initiated an Honor Challenge for command of the brigade?"

"Reluctantly, Your Highness, I have," Maaryah replied, her head still bowed.

"Reluctantly, you say? Explain yourself," the queen demanded.

"I was ordered to make the challenge by Megatus Deveena."

"Megatus, is this true?" the queen asked in surprise.

"Yes, Your Highness. Nedenna advanced the outsider above her station. I want the sub out of the brigade. She doesn't belong with the sisters; she never has. It's my personal duty to see that this slave-stock officer is chastened, physically punished, and as the loser of the challenge, expelled and barred from ever holding a brigade position again," Deveena responded with an angry tone.

"I see. It disappoints me to learn this. I expect my senior commanders to resolve their differences without coming to such an unfortunate impasse. Isn't there a way to resolve this short of an Honor Challenge?" the queen asked.

"No, Your Highness. The outsider must go. Not only is she a sub, but she also carries a kingdom slave mark. She is unworthy to lead the sisters or represent our city." Deveena spat the words.

A disappointed expression fell over the queen's face. She looked down at Maaryah, "A kingdom slave mark, is it? Remove your helm," she ordered. Maaryah did as the queen commanded, but her head remained in a low bow. "Look at me; I want to see your face," the queen ordered. Maaryah did as the queen commanded. The queen instantly recognized her and looked to the rana, who had a broad smile on her face. "It seems the reports of your death were in error. Why would the ameer say you were killed?" the queen wondered.

"I almost died from my wounds, Your Highness. He feared the assassins would try again, and he wanted to protect me and the other estate residents from another attack. That's why," Maaryah explained.

"Ameera Tondo," the queen spoke loud enough for all to hear, "you must stand. Royalty never kneels to royalty. The rest of you may stand, as well." Deveena quickly stood and turned around, glaring at Maaryah. The queen continued, "Ameera, you could not have kept your secret this long. Others must have learned who you are. Name them," the queen ordered.

Maaryah remained silent, but after a short, uncomfortable pause, Zuni spoke up, "I knew, Your Highness."

"And you told no one?" the queen asked in surprise.

Maaryah came to Zuni's defense, "Your Highness, I begged her to keep my secret. I feared I would be expelled from the brigade."

An angry Deveena interrupted, "So, all this time, you've been the Feral's spy, and Zuni has been your accomplice." She faced Zuni, "I'm surprised and disappointed in you. You're a reprehensible traitor! On those grounds, you are expelled, and you will be banished. You no longer have a place in my brigade."

"This is my brigade, and don't you forget it, Megatus Deveena! I will determine who's to be expelled or banished," the queen shot back. "Ameera, why have you joined the Te Femma Brigade? Are you a spy?"

"The Showton killed my son and took my daughter. I couldn't wait at the estate; I had to join the fight to bring him down and find Maari. That's why I joined the brigade, and it's the only reason," Maaryah told her.

The queen eyed Maaryah closely for several long moments before responding. "I believe you," the queen finally said. "Ameera, will you withdraw your challenge?" the queen asked.

"I will if Megatus Deveena withdraws her order," Maaryah replied.

"Deveena, will you withdraw your order?" the queen asked in an angry tone.

"Only by your command, Your Highness," Deveena growled.

The queen glared at her, only now fully realizing her new brigade commander's disdain for the ameera. She quickly realized she couldn't have such contention between the brigade's senior officers. If this strife continued, the queen discerned, it would affect the brigade's cohesiveness and weaken it at a time when the city's very survival was at stake.

The queen took a deep breath, "No, it's not my order. I can see the challenge must go forth. Unfortunately, I will be the ultimate loser in this affair. Here we stand, on the verge of a battle that may seal the fate of our city, and I'm about to lose another brigade commander or two subcommanders. This is intolerable!"

"Your Highness, you must provide two witnesses," the rana reminded the queen.

"Yes, yes, of course. I will be my own witness, and after the second witness is notified, I will provide you with the day the challenge will take place," the queen announced.

"Ha, Rana Fardinza, it is good to see you again," Tondo said in greeting, "I've only just now been informed of the queen's arrival. Otherwise, I would have greeted her myself. What brings Queen Ezora to the army? Is she worried about the defense of her realm?"

"Ameer, Her Highness will be attending an Honor Challenge for command of the Te Femma Brigade. She requests you be her second witness," the rana told him with a wry smile, a smile that mystified Tondo.

"I don't approve of Honor Challenges. I would rather not be involved in your city's internal disputes," he told her.

"Oy, this time, you already are," Fardinza told him as her smile widened.

Tondo and Idop rode into the Te Femma Brigade camp, followed by a dozen or so staff and aides. They were greeted by one of the queen's arbons. "Ameer Tondo, Sutrum Megatus

Idop, please follow me. The queen awaits," she told them. The two men dismounted and followed the arbon. The staff officers and aides dismounted, but they were requested to remain where they were. The arbon led the two men to a secluded setting in a wooded area nearby. The ground had been cleared of brush, rocks, and other hazards, and a large Stontza Circle had been marked in the dirt with small, light-colored stones. The queen sat on a chair with Rana Fardinza standing behind her. An empty chair was placed next to the queen. A pair of empty chairs had been placed one-third of the way around the circle to the queen's left, and another pair of empty chairs were placed one-third of the way around the ring to the queen's right.

"Ameer Tondo, welcome," the queen began, "it is unfortunate that we must meet under such trying circumstances. Please be seated." Tondo sat, and Idop remained standing, moving behind the ameer.

"What is this all about, and why has Maaryah made this challenge? It's not something I would have expected her to do," Tondo said.

"I wish you had trusted me enough to have let me know the ameera was alive," the queen replied.

"It wasn't a matter of trust, Your Highness. I felt the fewer who knew, the less chance the secret would be revealed. Not only was I protecting her, but I was also protecting the other estate residents from another attack."

"Be that as it may, I was hurt when I learned of your ruse, but I am very pleased to see that the ameera is alive. In answer to your question, Megatus Deveena ordered her to make the challenge. I was unaware of the animosity between the two. Did you know?" she asked.

"No, Maaryah and I don't speak to each other outside of official meetings. And the sisters keep to themselves. I was probably more surprised by this than anyone."

Zuni and Dori entered the clearing, with Maaryah following. Tondo almost gasped when he saw her. Maaryah's hair was cropped even shorter than the last time he'd seen her; so short was it that a person wouldn't be able to grab it. She wore a tight-fitting sleeveless tunic made from strong Te Femma cloth of mid-thigh length, revealing her muscled and well-defined shoulders, arms, and legs. Her feet were bare, and her fists unwrapped. When she noticed Tondo, a look of surprise crossed her face. Obviously, she wasn't expecting him here. He put her at ease with a smile and a wink. The queen and rana were stunned by her appearance and attire, and Idop stood staring, his good eye wide open in disbelief of her muscled form.

Hertora and Mindetta soon entered the clearing, followed by Deveena. She wore a typical green military tunic of mid-thigh length and short sleeves. She wore sandals, and her fists were wrapped in leather straps. The six women faced the queen and dropped to one knee except for Maaryah, who bowed.

"Please, stand. Witnesses, assume your places," the queen ordered. Hertora and Mindetta went to the chairs on the queen's left, while Zuni and Dori moved to the chairs on the queen's right. All four sat in unison, and the two antagonists stepped into the circle and faced each other, about ten feet separating them. "Sisters, is there no other way to settle your differences?" the queen asked.

"With respect, Your Highness, this worthless slave is a sub, not a sister. She deserves what she is about to receive," Deveena angrily growled, slamming her leather-wrapped fists together. Tondo could feel the animus she held toward his bondmate, and its hate-filled power surprised him.

"Your Highness, Deveena is not worthy to lead your brigade. I will end her short command today and spare you another embarrassment," Maaryah growled. The two rivals raised their fists in defensive stances and waited, glaring at each other.

"So be it," the queen huffed angrily. "Begin!" she shouted.

In a flash, Deveena charged forward and began pummeling Maaryah with right and left punches. Maaryah fended off Deveena's attacks with her fists and forearms, frustrating her opponent. Deveena stepped closer to Maaryah and attempted to wrap her arms around her. Maaryah moved into her advance, lowered her head, and bent at the knees. In a quick jerk, she straightened her legs, the top of her head catching Deveena squarely under the chin with a powerful head-butt, stunning the brigade commander and causing her to stagger backward, falling into a sitting position on the ground.

Maaryah stood over her and yelled, "You're not getting out of this that easy. Get up and fight!" Deveena shook away her grogginess and slowly regained her feet.

The queen leaned over to Tondo and quietly said, "That was a lucky stroke. I doubt Deveena will let that happen again; she's quite skilled."

"Maaryah could have finished her right then if she chose to. A quick kick to the head would have done it. I can see she is infuriated and wants to punish Deveena."

"As much as I like your greevayr, she will not prevail. An outsider cannot defeat a skilled sister," the queen blustered.

"Nedenna was defeated by an outsider," Tondo reminded her.

"You are exceptional, and the Messenger sent by deity," the queen replied.

"Maaryah is exceptional, too," he told her.

"I doubt your outsider is that remarkable," the queen huffed.

"Your Highness, you are about to be taught a lesson on the skill and resolve of this outsider," Tondo said with a chuckle.

"Would you care to place a wager on your arrogance?" the queen challenged.

"Certainly, Your Highness. I'm willing to bet on a sure thing. What do you have in mind?"

"While at your estate, I tasted your fine wine. I'd like ten barrels. What do you think would be a fair offering on my part?"

Tondo thought for a moment, and with a roguish smile, he replied, "If Deveena wins, you will get ten barrels of estate wine. If Maaryah wins, you will rescind the four women's banishment, including their families. Agreed?"

A flash of anger filled the queen's emerald-green eyes, then it quickly faded, "Agreed," she said with a forced smile. The queen's and Tondo's attention shifted back to the two fighters.

They were circling one another, Deveena banging her leather-wrapped fists together. Suddenly, Maaryah sprang forward and attempted to grab Deveena around the head. Deveena quickly stepped back and responded with a quick right jab that nailed Maaryah on the left corner of her mouth, cutting the skin and causing her to bleed. Maaryah wiped the wound with the back of her left hand, quickly examining the blood, her expression turning angrier. Deveena smiled and moved forward, making another attack. As Deveena advanced, Maaryah turned her left foot and leg out and swung her right leg in a roundhouse kick that Deveena partially blocked, but Maaryah's shin glanced off her opponent's shoulder and landed with enough force to the side of Deveena's head to stagger her. Maaryah followed through with a charge, putting her opponent in a headlock with her right arm and forcing her to the ground. Maaryah then began pounding her left fist into Deveena's face, over and over.

Tondo was sitting on the edge of his seat, growling his satisfaction, his fists swinging in the air. He noticed the queen and rana staring at him, so he relaxed, lowered his arms, and sat back in his chair, giving the two a sheepish grin.

Deveena tried to grab Maaryah by the hair, but it was too short. Maaryah's grip on Deveena's head tightened as she landed punch after punch on Deveena's face. It wasn't long before the Te Femman's nose and mouth began bleeding. With great strength, Deveena stood, lifting Maaryah as she did. She then dropped forward, slamming Maaryah's body onto the ground hard enough to break Maaryah's grip. Both women rolled away from each other, scrambling to their feet and circling one another as they moved around the Stontza Circle.

Maaryah quickly advanced, continually jabbing with her left fist as Deveena fended off the blows while retreating backward. Maaryah lunged for Deveena's legs, grabbing her opponent's left leg and lifting it, attempting to upend Deveena. The Te Femman interlocked the fingers of both hands and crashed them onto the back of Maaryah's neck, causing her to yelp in pain, but she continued driving forward, ramming Deveena onto the ground. Maaryah rode Deveena into the dirt, putting her left arm around Deveena's nose and mouth, suffocating her as she pounded the back and side of Deveena's head with her right fist. Deveena clawed at Maaryah's left arm, and she soon was able to get it to slide off her sweaty and bloody face. Maaryah quickly slid her left arm onto Deveena's neck and started squeezing, blocking the blood flow to Deveena's brain. In a desperate move, just before she was about to lose consciousness, Deveena slammed her right elbow into Maaryah's side as she twisted her body just enough to break the chokehold. Maaryah's right fist crashed into the side of Deveena's head, then she spun away and regained her feet.

Unexpectedly, Deveena was up and ready to make her assault, smashing a right fist into the left side of Maaryah's jaw, stunning her for an instant. Deveena quickly charged, grabbed Maaryah around the torso, and slipped around her back. Deveena began tightening her grip, squeezing Maaryah's diaphragm so tightly she couldn't breathe. Maaryah struggled to escape Deveena's devastating hold, clawing at Deveena's arms, trying to break her grip, but to no avail. Zuni and Dori shook their heads in worry as Hertora and Mindetta smiled with glee.

"It's only a matter of time now," the queen said to Tondo with delight. "Deveena has her in a death-grip, and she'll have to surrender or pass out for lack of breath." Tondo simply responded with a sagacious smile.

Maaryah leaned forward and bent her knees. She then snapped her head back, slamming the back of her head into Deveena's face. Again, she tried to break Deveena's grip but couldn't, so she straightened her legs, flipped forward, and twisted. Deveena stayed with her, not releasing her hold, but when they hit the ground, Maaryah was on top, the weight of her body smashing into Deveena, causing Deveena's grip to loosen just enough for Maaryah to break free. She grabbed Deveena's right arm as she threw her legs over her opponent's body, her right leg over Deveena's chest, and her left leg over her neck. She crossed her ankles and pulled Deveena's right arm between her legs with Deveena's elbow on Maaryah's hip. Maaryah arched her back and raised her hips, putting extraordinary pressure on Deveena's elbow in a classic arm bar. Deveena screamed in pain.

"It's over, Your Highness. Deveena must surrender, or she'll be seriously injured," Tondo explained. The queen didn't respond but only grimaced as Deveena continued howling in agony.

"Surrender!" Maaryah ordered, "Surrender to this worthless sub!" she demanded.

"Never!" Deveena yelled, her voice strained. She began pounding Maaryah's legs and hips with her free arm, but the weak and flailing blows were only an annoyance.

Maaryah raised her hips higher and pulled on Deveena's arm, increasing the leverage and multiplying Deveena's agony. Tondo wanted to intervene and end the match, but he knew it had to play out to its ultimate conclusion, so he watched as a frown covered his face.

"You're right; I am slave-stock. Now, surrender to me! If you don't, I'll break your arm!" Maaryah demanded. She raised her hips slightly higher, and Deveena shrieked louder than before. "The next move I make will break your arm!" Maaryah yelled. "Now, give up!" She pulled harder on Deveena's arm and heard a muffled pop.

Deveena bellowed in agony. "I surrender! I surrender!" she shouted. Maaryah released her, rolled away, and bounced to her feet. She stood near Deveena, assuming a defensive stance, waiting to see what her opponent would do next. Deveena rose to her knees and cradled her right arm with her left. She began moaning, rocking back and forth as pain wracked her arm.

The queen turned to Tondo and asked, "How did you know she would escape Deveena's death-grip?"

"That was one of the first moves she was taught, and she knew it well. Excuse me, Your Highness, I must check Deveena; I think she's seriously injured." Tondo walked over to Deveena, smiling at Maaryah as he did and giving her a wink. He kneeled and gently examined Deveena's arm. "The bone doesn't appear to be broken, but I think you have a damaged sinew. It will heal, but injuries like this take time," he told her. She moaned in pain and began rocking back and forth again. He rubbed his hands together to warm them and relieve her pain, but an angry look from Maaryah stopped him cold. He stood and returned to his seat.

"Rana, see that documents are drawn up rescinding the four slaves and their families' banishment and separation. Welcome them back into the realm with my blessing," the queen ordered. The rana nodded. The queen stood and announced, "Ameera, you are promoted to megatus, and you are to assume command of the Te Femma Brigade immediately. Congratulations, and may the great mother bless your efforts."

Maaryah bowed and said, "Thank you, Your Highness. It is my honor to serve you and the queendom." The queen and rana quickly left the clearing.

Hertora and Mindetta went to Maaryah and gave her a kingdom salute. "Megatus, we are prepared and fully willing to follow your commands," Hertora stated nervously.

Maaryah returned their salutes and answered, "Good. Now, help Deveena to a physician." They did as she ordered, and the three women moved out of the clearing.

Idop went to Maaryah and examined her from head to foot. Blood was on her face, and the cut at the corner of her mouth was still bleeding. Her left eye was swollen, and her left cheek was red and showing a bruise. Her arms were red and scratched, as were her legs. Undoubtedly, more bruises would soon appear.

"You look awful," he said.

"I love you, too," she replied.

Idop smiled and patted Tondo on the shoulder. "I'll leave the two of you to yourselves. Now, remember your orders: no fraternizing with members of the Te Femma Brigade," he said with a chuckle. He then exited the clearing.

"Zuni, Dori, you can go, too. I want to speak with the ameer, alone," she told them. They smiled and quickly departed, leaving the two bondmates alone for the first time in nearly three spans.

Maaryah fell into Tondo's arms and wrapped hers around his chest and back. "Hold me, just hold me, don't let me go," she cried. He held her tightly, worried he might aggravate her injuries, but she didn't object as she squeezed him with her arms.

"I've dreamed of holding you like this ever since you left the estate," he said. She looked up into his eyes, and he kissed her. She quickly recoiled in pain and laughed, still holding him tightly. They attempted to snug, but that also caused her pain.

"Just hold me, just hold me," she said, so he did.

After a short time, Tondo released her and placed a hand on her head. "I'll relieve your pain."

She gently lifted his hand away and said, "No, don't. I will live with the pain Deveena gave me just as I expect her to live with what she deservedly earned.

"Okay, have it your way." He stepped back, pulled something from his belt, and showed it to her. It was the rank badge of a megatus—two zanth diamonds encircled by the split zanth wreath denoting royalty. He pinned it onto the front of her tunic. "I'm proud of you, and I couldn't have hoped for a better commander of the army's reserve."

She smiled and said, "Lead us to victory so we can find Maari and get on with our lives." She embraced him again, and the two bondmates held each other, rejoicing in the comfort, security, and the loving warmth of each other's arms.

Tondo escorted Maaryah to her quarters. As they approached it, they saw the entire Te Femma Brigade had been assembled, and as they neared, Zuni called the sister warriors to Attention. Maaryah left Tondo and went to Zuni, stopping in front of her.

Zuni looked into Maaryah's bruised and bloodied face, then she glanced at her new rank badge and smiled. "Nedenna once said you seemed aristocratic, and I now see the proof. Congratulations on your victory and promotion. The brigade wishes to honor our new commander." She did an about-face and, in a loud voice, said, "Brigade; Ready; Salute!" All of the warriors in the brigade raised their right arms in a sharp United Kingdom salute; all but Zuni, who quickly stepped to her side of the formation, did another about-face and then raised her arm in salute. Maaryah smiled and returned the brigade's hail of respect.

After Maaryah dropped her arm, Zuni called in a loud voice, "Brigade; Ready; Two!" then, all the sisters dropped their arms in one quick motion.

"Brigade, At Ease!" Maaryah ordered in a loud voice, then she continued, "Sisters of the Te Femma Brigade, as your new commander, I expect you to train and fight harder. We must make up for some lost ground, and that we will do. Ameer Tondo assures me that he has faith in your abilities and desires that the brigade remains in the honored station as the army's reserve. You have worked hard to earn that honor, and we will prove ourselves worthy of it come the next battle," she shouted, causing the sisters to respond with cheers. "Neva Megatus Zuni, front and center," Maaryah ordered. Zuni quickly marched to her commander.

"Yes, zerr," she said after she arrived.

"You may dismiss the brigade." Zuni saluted, and Maaryah returned it. Maaryah then moved to Tondo's side.

Zuni did an About-Face and shouted, "Brigade; Attention!" The sisters snapped to the order; then, she exclaimed, "Dismissed!" The formation broke up as the sisters went their separate ways.

* * *

Idop was sitting at Tondo's desk in the ameer's HQ when Tondo entered. Surprised, Idop quickly rose and stepped around the small desk. "I wasn't expecting you back until the morning. I didn't think the fraternizing rules applied to bondmates," he said with a grin. Tondo looked askance at his friend as he moved to his chair and slumped into it. Idop gave him a quizzical smile.

"There won't be any fraternizing tonight or in the near future," Tondo said. "She has so many aches and pains she wouldn't even let me rub her shoulders. She took a hot bath and then fell asleep. She didn't even touch her meal."

"I see," Idop said, "but there will be other nights, right?"

Tondo looked annoyed. "No, there won't. The traditions of the city get in the way. She doesn't want to lose her command if she is with child, and I don't want to lose a Te Femma Brigade commander I can fully trust." Tondo leaned back in his chair as a dejected and annoyed expression covered his face. Idop didn't respond and sheepishly exited.

* * *

"Your Highness," Rana Fardinza began, "what's to be done with Deveena? She has been your loyal servant for many spans."

"Yes, indeed. She has shown her loyalty to me, and I cannot, in good conscience, abandon her. Have her summoned tomorrow after she's rested," the queen commanded.

"I'll see to it," the rana replied. "Also, there is that other matter we discussed, Your Highness," the rana reminded her.

"Of course. I will deal with that issue tomorrow, as well. See that the ameera is summoned."

Shortly after midday, Maaryah arrived at the queen's temporary residence accompanied by Zuni and the brigade's new subcommander, Neva Megatus Dori. When they arrived, they found Deveena waiting alone. Maaryah stopped several paces away, not wanting to invade Deveena's privacy nor become engaged in another unpleasant verbal exchange.

"Megatus, do you mind if I speak with Deveena?" Zuni asked.

"Of course not," Maaryah told her. Zuni went to Deveena and examined her from head to foot. Her right arm was in a sling, and both eyes were darkened with bruises, as were her cheeks. Her upper lip was swollen, and there were several minor cuts on her arms and legs.

"You've looked better," Zuni mused. "How's the arm?"

"The physician says I'll fully recover, but it will take time, just as the Feral said," she told Zuni, her words a bit slurred because of the swollen lip she was nursing.

"I'm glad to learn that. I wish you a speedy recovery," Zuni offered.

"Thank you, Zuni. I appreciate it," Deveena said humbly.

"Have you been summoned by the queen?" Zuni asked.

"Yes. I'm hoping she will at least allow me to return to the Stontza," Deveena said in a sad tone. Just then, an arbon exited and ushered Deveena into her meeting with the queen.

Deveena came out after her meeting a half-segment later with a huge smile on her swollen and bruised face. Zuni went to her. "It appears the queen gave you some good news. Will you be returning to the Stontza?" Zuni asked.

"No, she's made me governor of the mines," Deveena told her joyfully.

"That is good news. Congratulations!" Zuni exclaimed. Deveena thanked her, and then she was gone. Zuni returned to Maaryah and Dori.

"If you don't mind me asking, what did she say?" Maaryah wondered.

"The queen has made her governor of the salt mines," Zuni said excitedly. Dori whistled in amazement.

"By your responses, I'm assuming that's a good thing," Maaryah said.

"A very good thing for Deveena. The governor of the mines receives a portion of all profits from the sale of salt. She'll become quite wealthy," Zuni told her.

"Her service to the queen has been well rewarded," Maaryah observed with disdain.

"I wonder why you've been summoned?" Dori questioned.

"We'll soon find out," Maaryah told her. An arbon approached and led her and her two subcommanders into the queen's presence.

Queen Ezora was sitting on her platform, watching the three military commanders approach. A short distance from the platform stairs, Maaryah stopped and bowed. Zuni and Dori dropped to a knee.

"You may stand," the queen said. "Megatus, or should We refer to you as ameera?" the queen asked.

"Megatus will do, Your Highness," Maaryah replied.

"Ha," the queen said. "How are you feeling? We never imagined an Honor Challenge could be so brutal, and that was a particularly savage one yesterday." Maaryah's left eye was blackened, and she had a large bruise on her left cheek. Her forehead was deeply scratched where Deveena's fingernails had dug into her flesh as she tried to grab Maaryah's hair. Her arms and legs had many other scrapes, lacerations, and contusions.

"I'm okay, Your Highness; I have the ability to heal quickly," Maaryah responded.

"We're glad to hear that. Now, for the business at hand. Rana Fardinza reminded Us that all kingdom subjects must swear an oath of allegiance to King Teg-ar-mos. Is that correct?"

"Yes, tradition requires the head of each family in the gentry to offer his oath in person, before the king, Your Highness," Maaryah explained.

"So, Ameer Tondo gave his oath of allegiance to the king, and it is binding upon you as well?" the queen asked.

"Ameer Tondo and I are a special situation. The king required us to give oaths of allegiance to him separately."

"We see. So, you have sworn an oath to the king, yet you are now in command of Our brigade. Do you not see a potential conflict of interest here, megatus?" the queen asked sternly.

"Te Femma is now part of the United Kingdom, and the goal of Your Highness and the king is to defeat the Showton. I see no conflict," Maaryah replied.

"True enough for now, but what if the king and We have a dispute, particularly concerning the traditions of the city?

Where will your loyalties lie then, Megatus Maaryah?"

"Your Highness, there is no need to look for trouble where none exists. My desire is to defeat the Showton and end his threat. My loyalty is to both you and the king," Maaryah vouched.

"There will come a day of disputation; it always does. Who will you support on that day?" the queen asked in an almost threatening tone. Zuni and Dori were becoming worried witnesses to the exchange.

"Your Highness, on that day, I will join with my bondmate, the ameer."

"And what if he chooses the king over Us?" the queen challenged as her emerald-green eyes flashed.

"I will always support my bondmate. If I must, I will resign from my position. If, at any time, I do not have your full confidence, you may replace me. I serve at your pleasure," Maaryah reminded the queen.

Queen Ezora paused in thought before responding. Finally, she said, "We needed to learn what is in the heart of Our brigade commander and that We have now ascertained. You are to remain in command of the brigade. You may go." The three commanders gave the queen a Te Femma salute and departed.

After the brigade's senior leadership had exited, the rana went to the queen, "Your Highness, she would not affirm her loyalty to you above all others. What are we to do?"

"She affirmed her loyalty to the Messenger. How can I object to that? I've witnessed the Feral's loyalties, which are of a higher order than queen or king. Remember how he confronted his king about death-matches? Things will remain as they are. She is right; why look for trouble where none exists?"

# CHAPTER 14

# QWAKG-LORQ

Haptane Grunzen and Haptane T´eftoren were on a knee before the Sutro Showton. Fear embraced each army commander as they waited for their master to address them. The Showton's cold, Munnevo-red eyes glared at the two men, and although their heads were bowed low, they could feel his angry gaze fixed upon them and his burning indignation.

"Your orders were to join your armies with the other two. Why did you engage the enemy?" the Showton demanded, his lower face veiled and his angry stare burning into the two haptanes.

"The army of the United Kingdom forced us into combat, my master. We had no choice," Grunzen pleaded.

"Yes, master, we had to engage. Even though the enemy commander had chosen his ground well, he was unable to stop us, and he was forced to retreat," T´eftoren implored.

"It is a good thing he did, or else you two would now be suffering for your incompetence," the Showton growled. "I've been told you have something taken from the enemy you wish to show me. Stand! What is it?" The two haptanes quickly stood and signaled the guards at the door. The doors were opened, and two men entered, their hands bound and their feet tethered. Four guards followed, two guarding the prisoners, one carrying a bow and the other a quiver of arrows. When the group reached the center of the room, the guards pushed their prisoners to the floor and held them there with a sandaled foot on the back of each man's neck.

When the Showton saw the bows, his red eyes widened. "What's this?" he roared.

"Master, these men were captured during the battle. They call themselves archers, and they use weapons to launch shafts of wood great distances. The shafts have gravetro tips that penetrate armor and flesh, resulting in horrible wounds. These weapons caused many casualties," Haptane Grunzen told the Showton, a hint of nervousness in his voice.

The Showton stepped forward and held his hand in front of the guard holding the bow. The man handed it to him, his eyes downcast in submission, and then he stepped back. The Showton examined the gravetum weapon closely. He looked at the other guard, and the man stepped forward, nervously holding the quiver in front of himself. The Showton slowly pulled one arrow out, and its shaft made a menacing sound as it slid free. The Showton nocked the arrow in the bow, raised it, took aim at a wall, and let the arrow fly. It hit with a loud thud and sank deep into the wood.

"I know of these weapons," he said. "In my homeland, they are called qwakg-lorq." It was a guttural sound that had to be the weapon's name, but a word that no others had ever heard before, nor could they repeat. "I did not expect to find them here." He looked down at the prisoners. "Stand him up," the Showton ordered as he pointed to one of the bound men. His guard quickly jerked the man to his feet, and the Showton stood before him. He was more than a head taller than the captured archer. "How did you come by these weapons?" he growled. The prisoner looked up into the Showton's Munnevo-red eyes and shuddered. "Speak!" the Showton ordered. It was evident the man was scared out of his wits, fear binding his tongue. The Showton dropped the bow and grabbed the man tightly by the shoulders. His aura ignited, and the prisoner screamed in pain. The guards stepped away, and the prone archer crawled out of the purple pain until a guard stopped him, pinning him to the floor with a foot in the center of his back.

The man in the Showton's clutches continued screaming in agony as his tunic started to smolder. Soon, his hair began to smoke, and then it ignited in purple flames. The skin of his face started to burn and bubble; the man's screams of pain became more horrid and desperate. It wasn't long before his entire body erupted in purple flames from head to foot, and the Showton released his grip, allowing the burning body to drop to the floor. The screaming soon ended, and only a charred mass of smoldering flesh and fabric remained, a sickening odor of burnt flesh wafting through the room.

The Showton slowly walked toward the other prisoner as his aura disappeared. He signaled the guard to stand the prisoner up. After he did, the Showton grabbed the man by the chin and forced him to look at the remains of his comrade.

"Tell me what I want to know, or your days will end just like his," the Showton threatened. The prisoner nodded in submission. "Good," the Showton said, his red eyes sparkling with satisfaction. "Now, tell me, how did you come by these weapons?"

"I've been told the ameer made them," the man answered, fear straining his voice and the Showton's grip slurring his words. The Showton released him and stepped back.

"Would this ameer go by the name of Tondo?" The prisoner nodded. "How did he learn to make these weapons?"

"I am but a simple soldier. I don't know, zerr."

"Zerr? What's this zerr? What does it mean?" the Showton growled indignantly.

"It's what we're taught to say to our leaders, the army officers."

"So, it's a sign of respect, is it?" The prisoner nodded. "You may refer to me as master." The man frowned, for he carried the mark of a slave on his forehead. "Where did this Tondo come from?" the Showton asked.

"He's an outlander; he came out of the Wilderness. That's all I know . . . master," the kingdom archer shakily answered.

"Ha! Remove the prisoner and keep him alive. He may still be of use to me," the Showton ordered the guards.

After the prisoner was taken out, Haptane T´eftoren spoke, "Master, you knew the proper way to use the weapon. Tell us how you know that."

"Qwakg-lorq is an ancient weapon from my fatherland, a rather simple device. I never expected to find it here; no other people know of it. Maybe I have underestimated this Tondo. He may be more than just a simple-minded Worlder like all the rest of you."

"Certainly, he is no match for you, my master," Grunzen wormed.

The Showton's eyes brightened. "Of course not. He is already wounded, and his end will be like all the others." He turned to an attendant, "I want weapons like these crafted for our warriors," he ordered.

"Master, how many shall I have made?" the attendant asked.

The Showton looked toward the two haptanes, "How many enemy warriors were there with weapons like these?"

"A whole formation, Master, several hundred, maybe more than a thousand," T´eftoren told him.

"The mounted warriors also carried them," Grenzen added. "Another four or five thousand, Master."

"Order the smiths to make twenty-thousand of these," he said, pointing to the bow lying on the floor.

"The prisoners call them bows and the shafts they call arrows, my master," T´eftoren said.

"All right, twenty-thousand bows and two-hundred arrows per bow. Have the prisoner show our leaders how to use them. If he balks, remind him of how his friend died," the Showton ordered.

"Master, will we use these weapons in our next battle?" Grenzen asked.

"It will take time to make these weapons and for the men to learn how to use them. I won't wait that long. The women of Te Femma have resisted my control and must suffer for their folly before others hear of it. They are to be crushed! All of the residents in that troublesome city will be taken as slaves. The entire city is to be razed so that one stone does not rest upon another. After that, their precious salt is to be plowed into their fields. Te Femma will be laid waste and desolate, an example for all others to ponder. It will be an example to anyone who would resist me. This Tondo must be swept aside as quickly as possible. I still want his blue eyes in a box, and I want his eyeless head to be displayed on a pike," the Showton swore. "Now, summon Sassin and the Invincibles."

"Master, his army is unlike any other we have faced. It is well-trained and well-led, and he retook the women's city. It's not understood how he did it, but our scouts say there's a huge hole in the wall where the main gates once stood. It's as if he used magic to break the city's wall," Haptane Grunzen warned.

The Showton stared at the army commander as his purple aura ignited again, snapping and crackling its warning, causing a shuddering Grunzen to go silent. "You want to see magic, do you? Watch what I do to his army when we face him again," the Showton threatened.

# CHAPTER 15

# DISASTERS

Tondo scanned the enemy formation with his farseer from the howdah atop Myron's raster. He ended his scan and waited. He had chosen his ground well; the battlefield was only wide enough to accommodate his army, with thick woods protecting his flanks, forcing the Showton's superior numbers to stack up behind the front line units. Tondo noticed a large group of men assembled on a hillock to the rear of the Showton's army. He brought his farseer to his eye and closely examined the men mounted on tanters. It was apparent to him that these were leaders, and the veiled man in the dark flowing robes in front of the others had to be his nemesis, the Sutro Showton. Hatred mingled with excitement filled his bosom as he considered how today's victory would forever end the Showton's evil threat.

Maaryah sat in the saddle of her war-samaran, her farseer to her eye. She had it trained on the group of men who had just crested the small hill at the rear of the Showton's army. She knew immediately who the man in the dark robes was. Vengeance welled in her soul, and she forced the farseer from her eye. Her excitement waxed as her confidence in Tondo's ultimate victory grew. After the Showton's defeat, the Inquisitors would force him to reveal the location of her beloved

Maari. Maaryah's golden-amber eyes flashed with hatred as she glared at the men on the hill.

"Master, we cannot maneuver. The enemy commander has chosen his ground well. What are your orders?" an aide asked his commander, the Sutro Showton.

"Advance the line and watch," the Showton ordered. The aide signaled a hornman, who quickly sounded. Orders were given and repeated down the line, and then the entire formation stepped forward, ominous drumbeats sounding the pace. The Showton closed his red eyes and lowered his head. After a few moments, a faint purple cloud began to form above the far-left third of the United Kingdom's army. As the cloud formed, the kingdom's warriors noticed it, and their eyes turned from the advancing enemy to the glowing purple clouds roiling above their heads. Tondo also watched, wondering what the manifestation was, feeling dread growing at the center of his tzaah. He brought his farseer to his eye and trained it on his nemesis on the hillock.

Slowly, the purple clouds began to descend as they flashed with hidden energy. Tondo's warriors were soon engulfed in a roiling purple fog, and without a sound, the men started toppling, their bodies stacking atop each other. The purple haze started dissipating, and the impending disaster was fully realized. Tondo's entire left flank had been destroyed; every warrior, to the man, was down. The enemy line was nearly upon his prone men.

"Megato Zeffany, personally give Megatus Maaryah my order to have her brigade replace the left flank. Tell her the fate of the army is in her hands!" he yelled down to his mounted aide. The staff officer saluted and galloped off toward the Te Femma Brigade. "Neva Megato Hendetz, order the archers to fire on the enemy advancing on our left!" Tondo ordered another aide. The man saluted and galloped off. "Myron, move us to the left flank as quickly as possible. I must delay the enemy's advance."

Myron turned and looked at the outlander in disbelief, then he swallowed hard and yelled, "May the great god remember this: Today, I die with the Messenger!"

The raster quickly trotted toward the advancing enemy, Tondo and the hornman gripping the flagpole tightly. The kingdom archers let their arrows fly, and the sky darkened. The enemy warriors' mid and rear ranks held their pikes at an angle, covering the leading rows from the falling missiles. Most of the lethal hail was noisily deflected, and only a few deadly arrows damaged the advancing formation. Tondo's Brothers moved with their leader and formed a thin line in front of him.

The Showton opened his eyes and examined the results of his efforts. The entire left third of the enemy line was down. The lead elements of his right flank moved into the front line of the prone men and slowed as his warriors gave the unconscious enemy soldiers a merciless coup de grace. He leaned back in the saddle as an unseen smile lightened his veiled face. As he watched in amazement, the enemy commander moved his raster to the breach and stopped. Suddenly, the Showton's gleeful red eyes filled with wonder as bolts of chain lightning tore into his advancing men. Fingers of electric power flashed from the man atop the raster, passing over the heads of his thin line of defenders, tearing into the advancing formation, and ravaging nearly every assailant. In an instant, most of the attacking warriors on the Showton's right front were down, quivering in spasms of death. Only the soldiers in the trailing ranks of the formation were spared. When they saw what had happened to the men at their front, they broke and ran, throwing down their weapons and shields.

"Master, our men are down or running away. What are we to do?" a worried aide shouted in near panic.

"Release the Invincibles! Bring me his head!" the Showton ordered in a tired voice.

Tondo watched as a block formation of thousands of black-clad warriors advanced toward him.

"Zerr, here comes more. Do it again! Do it again!" Tondo's hornman yelled.

"I can't; I'm spent. Hand me my bow," he ordered. He took the bow and threw the quiver across his back. Tondo nocked arrow after arrow and began taking down every mounted target in the black-clad formation.

"Megatus Maaryah!" Tondo's staff officer shouted, "You are ordered to move your brigade to the left flank. All the men are down, and the ameer says the fate of the army is in your hands! The ameer is facing the enemy with his Brothers!" he explained as he saluted, and she returned his salute. Maaryah had seen the purple cloud forming over the army's left flank, and she knew it was going to lead to trouble, but she couldn't see its effects. The aide's panicked tone said all she needed to know; a disaster was in the making. She turned her mount and dashed to Zuni and Dori.

"Dori, take your command and support the ameer. Zuni, have your command follow me at the run. We must act quickly," Maaryah ordered. She led Zuni and her warriors on a sweep across the army's rear, breaking into its constituent three-warrior teams as they entered the trees. The main Showton line soon engaged the male units at the front, which were under Idop's command. Dori's sub-brigade moved directly to the threatened left flank.

The Invincibles continued their relentless advance toward the command raster. Myron had unsheathed his short sword for the first time in anger and was waving it in the air as he shouted oaths and curses at the deadly crush moving toward him. The hornman launched arrows from his bow, dropping one black-clad foe at a time. It was a futile effort against the seemingly numberless host before them, but the ameer had not ordered Myron to withdraw the raster. Tondo's Brothers fought valiantly, but the Invincibles' superior numbers were overwhelming. The hornman knew they were doomed, yet he would remain steadfast with his commander; his ameer; deity's Messenger.

Dori halted her mount near the command raster and started barking orders to her sisters. They quickly formed up and advanced into the oncoming black horde, the sisters whirling like buzz-saws in their three-warrior teams. Dori expected the enemy to fall back in disorder as they had at the wall of Te Femma, but it didn't take her long to realize these black-clad ferals were not so easily turned.

Tondo had been nocking arrow after arrow, taking careful aim at one mounted enemy after another. He let another arrow fly, and it found its mark. Sutro Defetane Dartez dropped from his tanter, an arrow through his heart. Tondo loosed another deadly missile. Haptane Sassin was hit on the helm, but the arrow ricocheted off the hard gravetum. Sassin screamed in pain and struggled to remain mounted. His tanter spooked and charged forward, knocking Invincible warriors out of its way with its solid spiral horns. When it was several strides away from the leading rank of Te Femma warriors, they dropped the butts of their polearms to the ground and aimed their halberds' top spikes toward the onrushing tanter. When the beast caught sight of the wall of sharp points, it planted its legs and abruptly halted, launching Sassin over its head. He flew above and past the sisters' halberds. He landed in front of Neva Megatus Dori. The Invincibles commander staggered to his feet and stood swaying to and fro in front of her.

"You're blocking my view!" she bellowed, and then she punched him hard in the face. Her fist slammed into his helm-protected forehead, causing him to go down again. Dori began shaking her injured right fist, growling in pain. An aide raised her halberd high and crashed it into Sassin's chest, sundering armor and flesh.

Several black-garbed warriors broke through Dori's line and slammed into the legs of Tondo's command raster. Tondo and the hornman fired arrows, dispatching all but one. Myron dug his heel into the raster's neck, and one of its middle legs kicked, hitting the remaining enemy warrior squarely in the chest and sending him flying over the heads of the defending sisters with an agonizing scream. Tondo and the hornman looked into each other's faces, both covered in huge smiles.

Tondo's deadly bow had disrupted the enemy's chain of command; however, the Invincibles continued their relentless advance. They needed no orders to maintain their momentum because they had been trained to plod forward until ordered to do otherwise.

Tondo's line of Brothers was nearly annihilated, and Dori's sisters were being pushed back as their losses mounted. It was only a matter of time before the enemy's superior numbers overwhelmed the Te Femmans as they had the Brothers. From atop the howdah, Tondo contemplated the inevitable and despaired. As his dread increased, he saw the mounted Maaryah come out of the trees well to the left front of his position. He smiled and watched as she formed her line and advanced it into the flank and rear of the Invincibles. Without leadership, the black horde could not react. The whirling advance of Zuni's command sliced into the back of the enemy formation. It quickly became a slaughter as Dori's sisters blocked them at the front, and Zuni's sisters tore into their unguarded rear.

"Master, do something! The Invincibles are being slaughtered. It's turning into a disaster," the aide cried.

"Order the haptanes to withdraw their commands slowly," he ordered. The aide dug his heels into his tanter and rode off. In a subdued voice, speaking only to himself, the Showton grumbled, "This Tondo is more powerful than I imagined. He can't be a Worlder. Who is he? What is he? Where did he come from?"

# CHAPTER 16

# FROM THE TREES

It was late afternoon, and it was clear that the Showton's force had abandoned the field, thereby accepting defeat. Tondo was mounted on his samaran as he toured the battlefield, accompanied by what remained of Yaddet's troop of Tondo Brothers. As Tondo passed, his men cheered his presence; another battle won; however, this one had been a desperate affair, and the realization that the Showton possessed extraordinary powers was unnerving. Tondo had grown accustomed to his relatively easy victories, but now, he was facing someone as dangerous as himself. This fact added an entirely new dimension to future battles.

As he guided his mount through the bodies of the dead, Idop joined him. "That was an amazing thing you did. You saved the army," Idop said, obviously in wonder at what he had witnessed.

"It was a desperate action by a desperate man. This Showton is unexpectedly powerful. What about the men his . . . his power touched; are they dead?

"They're alive, but it's as if they're asleep. Some are beginning to move, and I hope they'll be all right. We'll see," Idop told him. The two men guided their mounts into the midst of the fallen enemy warriors, the ones Tondo had electrocuted with his bolts of chain lightning. Not one moved. Tondo dismounted and waded into the ranks of the fallen.

"Careful, ameer, it may not be safe. Let my men examine them first," a blood-splattered Megato Yaddet offered.

Tondo examined a few of the enemy near him and searched each for a pulse. They were all dead. "No need, megato," he told those present.

"This will give the Showton sleep-terrors. He'll think twice before he faces you again," Idop said gleefully. Tondo did not share in his lieutenant's elation because he was staring at a Te Femma slave mark on the hand of one of his victims.

Several days had passed since the battle. The Showton's combined force had withdrawn, relinquishing the field to the United Kingdom army and, by so doing, admitting defeat; however, the Showton's army still outnumbered Tondo's, even after sustaining significant losses in the latest round. Tondo and Idop had many discussions concerning what the total number of enemy warriors might be. The Showton had lost two armies at Te Femma and an additional ten-thousand warriors in the last battle for a total of around forty-thousand men, some of whom had taken up arms against their old master.

The Showton's purple fog had put Tondo's men into a coma that lasted about a day. All had recovered, all but the unfortunate few who the enemy's weapons had ruthlessly dispatched before Tondo's intervention. Most of the enemy warriors struck down by Tondo's chain lightning had been killed outright, nearly three-thousand in number. A handful recovered and were taken prisoner. Even Tondo was surprised by what he had done.

Another four-thousand warriors, the so-called Invincibles, had been cut down by the sisters of Te Femma; not one had surrendered. Tondo's army had sustained about two-thousand five-hundred casualties, dead or seriously wounded, mainly from the ranks of the sisterhood and the Tondo Brothers.

Now that the Showton's force had withdrawn, Tondo called a meeting of senior officers.

"Why has the ameer summoned the three of us?" Zuni asked. One of Tondo's aides had informed Maaryah that the ameer wanted her to bring her two subcommanders to the meeting.

"I don't know, but I'm sure it's for a good reason," Maaryah told her.

Aides escorted the three women into the command tent, where the other senior commanders had previously assembled. After they entered, Tondo called in a loud voice, "Attention!" The men quickly snapped to. Then he ordered, "Ready; Salute!" All of the men saluted, including Tondo and Idop. Maaryah smiled and returned their salutes. Tondo ordered, "Ready; Two," and the men smartly dropped their arms. A low, guttural growl could be heard coming from Idop, and soon, all the other men joined in. The growl increased in volume, surprising Zuni and Dori.

"What are they doing?" Zuni asked in amazement. Dori, her right hand now bandaged, leaned toward Maaryah, straining to hear her reply over the rising din.

"They're honoring us. It's the Victor's Shout!" she told them. When the roar reached its crescendo, Tondo drew his Munnari blade, and it ignited in brilliant blue light as all the other men unsheathed their swords, holding them high, ending the roar in shouts that hurt the ears. Maaryah's smile grew wider when Zuni's and Dori's bewildered expressions turned to shock as the men raised their swords high above their heads and shouted. Maaryah bowed in thanks, and her two senior lieutenants followed her lead.

Tondo sheathed his sword and said, "Well done, sisters. Your quick action salvaged a very grave situation and, in the end, forced the enemy from the field. The rest of the army is indebted to you, and we offer you our thanks."

The meeting became a social event for the next segment or so as the sisters were praised and thanked by every feral present. The women were elated that their brigade had redeemed its reputation, and they couldn't wait to return and report this to the other sister warriors.

Idop finally called an end to the meeting, and the men exited, each offering the women a final thank you as they left. Only Tondo and the three Te Femma commanders remained. Maaryah went to him and extended her arms, and he took them, leaned forward, and kissed her on the lips.

"I never thought I'd ever kiss one of my brigade commanders," he said.

"I'm glad you waited until it was me. The others may not react as warmly," she told him, and they both laughed.

"You did well, very well. I didn't expect you to split your brigade, but it was the right thing to do. How did you think of it?" he wondered.

"I remembered your lectures, and the battle of Zhan-zorhs-varh came to mind. Even though you've always warned that splitting your force is dangerous, the situation called for it," she said.

"Chancellorsville," Tondo corrected. He turned his attention to Zuni and Dori, "You carried out your commander's plan flawlessly. I thought we were finished when the black horde advanced; however, they didn't stand a chance when you engaged. Zuni was the hammer, and Dori the anvil. Well done, sisters!" Zuni and Dori proudly smiled as they offered their thanks for the compliment.

An aide entered the tent and announced Sutro Megatus Fayeetez's arrival and his request to meet with Tondo and Idop immediately. Fayeetez's cavalry had not been present for the main battle. Instead, Tondo had his cavalry patrolling around the perimeter of the battlefield.

"Fetch Idop and have Fayeetez enter," Tondo said. The aide exited, and a short time later, both commanders entered together.

Fayeetez saluted the ameer and then turned to Maaryah, "I hear you saved the army the other day. I wouldn't expect anything less from the ameera," he told her. She thanked him and waited for Tondo to dismiss her and the other two women; he didn't.

"Tell me, Fayeetez, how did it go against the tanters?" Idop asked.

Fayeetez smiled, "We let the Showton's mounted units chase us all over the place, and when they tired, we struck. Just as Harmon advised, we strafed 'em," he said, using the godspeak term he'd learned from his senior commander. "My boys charged in, firing their arrows while standing in their stirrups. The enemy couldn't react and was cut down. Then we rode off and came around again and again. They lost over three-thousand five-hundred men. We captured more than two-thousand tanters and nearly a hundred wagons full of supplies," he told them proudly.

"Excellent!" Idop cheered.

"This has been a painful encounter for the Showton. I'm sure he'll regroup and come up with a new plan. He still has us outnumbered," Tondo warned.

"My long-range patrol has seen large animals, unlike any seen before, moving to join his army. I've been told they might be some kind of war-beast. Ameer, do you know what they might be?" Fayeetez asked.

"I can only guess. I was afraid the Showton might have creatures like that. Are they larger than thrice?" Tondo asked.

"The scouts report they are much bigger. What can we do?" Fayeetez wondered. Tondo scribbled a note and told an aide to deliver it as fast as possible. "Let's hope it takes the Showton a while to prepare for the next battle. If he does, we'll be ready for him. If he moves quickly, he'll have the advantage. I'll need you to keep us apprised of the situation and his movements," Tondo directed.

"That, I will do," Fayeetez promised. "There is another matter I need to bring to your attention."

"What is it?" Tondo asked.

Fayeetez signaled an aide at the tent door, who exited and returned with a young man being watched by two of Fayeetez's troopers. He was thin and of average height, and he was wearing the clothes of a man of gentry. His bearing was of annoyance, mingled with fear. "We captured this man in the woods, and it appears he and his party have been living there for some time," Fayeetez told him.

"Why did you bring him here? I'm sure many people live in the wild now that the Showton has invaded their lands," Idop said.

"Not many with one of these," Fayeetez replied as one of the guards handed him a grain sack. Fayeetez reached in and pulled out a crown. Every eyebrow in the tent raised at the sight.

Tondo took the crown and examined it. "Who are you?" he asked the man.

"I am Prince P′on-dre-vitz, son of King P′on-dre-vitz, the ruler of Anderez. Do what you will with me, but spare the woman and the children. They can do you no harm," he said, his head held high, but his eyes revealing his dread.

"Besides him, we captured a woman and two young boys. Four guards attempted to stop us, and they attacked, so we put 'em down pretty fast with arrows. My physician fixed 'em up. I think they'll recover, but we'll have to wait and see," Fayeetez told them.

"Okay, prince, why were you living in the trees?" Tondo asked.

"When your master's army invaded our lands, my father, the king, ordered me to leave. He knew we couldn't defeat you, and he didn't want his line of succession broken. I fear he has been killed," the prince explained.

"Probably so," Idop mumbled.

"This is not a Showton army. You are among friends here, Prince P′on-dre-vitz," Tondo said as he handed him the crown.

"Thank you. I am in your debt. You're not Showton warriors? Where are you from?" the prince asked as he took the crown, obviously relieved.

"We come from the United Kingdom of Teg-ar-mos," Idop answered.

"Ameer Tondo," Maaryah began, "maybe the prince would be interested in allying with us?"

"Yes, I would like us to enter into a treaty of mutual assistance." He turned to the prince. "Does that interest you?" Tondo asked. The prince smiled, and soon he and Tondo began negotiating the treaty's terms, closely resembling those of the treaty with Te Femma.

While the men were conferring, Maaryah asked to be dismissed, and her request was granted. As the women returned to their brigade, Zuni initiated a conversation with her commander.

"Dori and I have been wondering something that struck us as . . . as different. We'd never seen anything like it before."

"What are you referring to?" Maaryah asked.

"After the other brigade commanders left and you went to the ameer . . . " Zuni stopped as she tried to think of the right words to use in asking her question.

"Go ahead, Zuni, what do you want to know?" Maaryah encouraged.

"What Zuni is trying to say," Dori began, "is it a common sign of affection for couples in the kingdom to bite each other in the face?" Maaryah started laughing uncontrollably while the other two watched in puzzlement.

# CHAPTER 17

# A TIME TO EVERY PURPOSE

Tondo and the other commanders observed and waited for the next several days. It soon became apparent that the Showton's forces were withdrawing; whether to lick their wounds and reform or for a more sinister purpose was unknown. Tondo breathed a sigh of relief, for he had been granted time to complete his plan to counter the war-beasts he'd been advised were approaching. The description of the creatures his scouts had related was foreboding. They told him the animals were at least twice the size of thrice, with bodies covered by a hard shell bristling with horn-like spikes. They had long, heavy tails that ended with large spiked, nobs that reminded the scouts of a club head. He was told that the monsters waved these clubs in a threatening manner when annoyed.

To make matters worse, the war-beasts had a pair of horns on their heads, each one as long as a man's arm. He was told platforms had been attached to the backs of the beasts, similar to the howdah on Tondo's command raster. Men with spears were seen standing on these platforms. To the man, the scouts shared their dread of facing these monsters either mounted or on foot.

"Tondo," Idop began, "what are these creatures? How are we to deal with them?"

"They are but dumb beasts, and as long as we keep our wits about us, they will be overcome," Tondo told him with all the confidence he could muster.

Idop returned a forced smile and said, "You haven't been wrong yet. The army will follow your orders." Tondo returned Idop's smile with a nod, and Idop could detect a hint of depression weighing him down, the same bleakness that had been with him since the last battle. "Ameer, I met with the sisters this morning. Megatus Maaryah asked me to give you this," Idop said as he handed Tondo a folded piece of paper. Tondo opened it and read. A genuine smile filled his face, and Idop could see his countenance lifting. "From your expression, I'd say it's good news."

Tondo chuckled, "Yes, she's invited me to take last-meal with her this evening in her billet."

Last-meal was not the private affair Tondo had been looking forward to all day; Zuni and Dori had also been invited. He hid his disappointment, at least from the two subcommanders, and made the best of their company. Maaryah and Tondo shared what life was like at the estate during the peaceful spans, and the two Te Femmans told the bondmates about life in the City of Women before the Showton brought war to the peace-loving sisterhood. The four raised their cups in a toast to peace, then Zuni and Dori abruptly dismissed themselves. Tondo was surprised by their hasty withdrawal. Maaryah reached across the small table and took his hands. "I explained to them earlier today that I needed to speak with you in private after we ate," she said with a loving smile.

"I've been looking forward to being alone with you all day," he told her as he gently squeezed her hands.

"Tell me, my love, are we nearing the end of the war? Will our next victory be the end of it?" she asked.

"I wish I could say yes, my dear, but I fear this is not the beginning of the end." He noticed her disappointed expression, so he added, "However, I think it's the end of the beginning." She returned a weak smile, and he continued, "The Showton hasn't made it this far by being fainthearted. I know he is forming new and evil plots to expand his control. He is much more powerful than I imagined because he has developed his tzaah, and he's using it for his wicked purposes, much like the vile Gangorno, who seized control of the Cavers; however, the Showton is much more dangerous. Undoubtedly, his recent setbacks will only result in a doubling of his efforts."

"Surely, his losses must give him pause?" Maaryah wondered.

"Men like the Showton care little about losses. They only want to expand their power and their control over others. He couldn't care less how many lives it takes to accomplish his goals," Tondo warned.

"Is it possible for someone to be that cruel, that devoid of feeling? I can't fathom such a man. Even the most loathsome foreman had some concern for the slaves who served him, if only to get the work done," Maaryah told her bondmate, her golden-amber eyes filling with sadness.

"The people of this age have never faced such a vile threat. The history of my world is full of men who, for the love of power, killed tens of thousands, hundreds of thousands, even millions, and thought nothing of it. They nurtured the evil seed within their souls until it starved, choked, and suffocated every bit of good within themselves, leaving only a dark, cold, lifeless cinder of a spirit that felt no one's suffering, no one's pain. No, my precious, one more victory will not be enough. You must prepare yourself for many more battles and many more deaths." He lowered his head and fell silent in thought.

"Millions of deaths?" she gasped. Tondo raised his head and nodded. "Oy, how dreadful." She watched as Tondo lowered his gaze. Her inner-power searched his feelings. She sensed anguish and regret, a pain intense and almost overwhelming. She took a deep breath and bolstered herself. "What's the matter, my love? Something is hurting you deep within your spirit. What is it?"

"Does it show that clearly?" he wondered.

"Idop mentioned you hadn't been yourself since the last battle. He suggested I talk with you, and now that I have, I can feel it, too."

Tondo really didn't want to talk about this, and he was about to resist her intrusion into his innermost feelings, but her loving squeeze of his hands and the hurt in her golden-amber eyes convinced him to share what was causing the pain in his heart.

"I killed nearly every one of them. I only reacted to the threat. I didn't realize the power I now wield had become so devastating," he told her.

"Had you not done what you did, the army would have been crushed. You did what had to be done," she reasoned.

"Do you know we captured several men from Te Femma? They were forced conscripts."

"Yes, I did. Idop turned them over to the sisters, and they've been returned to their homes, now to live in freedom."

"Did they tell you there were others from Te Femma in the ranks . . . in the ranks of those I killed?"

"No, they only expressed their happiness that their waking sleep-terror was over."

"When they're safely in their homes, they will remember that battle and what I did to their friends and fellow sufferers. I've introduced the horror of the guns into this world, and now, by my own inner-power, I have slaughtered thousands, undoubtedly many who were no more guilty of evil than the men from Te Femma. How many more innocents must I annihilate to gain victory? I desperately want to see all the people of this land free and able to pursue their own happiness, yet I am becoming a tyrant of death. Those who survive will remember what I've done, and they will hate me as much as they hate the Showton. I despise what I'm becoming," he lamented.

"Tondo, you must stop this self-loathing! It will do you no good; it will do us no good. Those deaths are on the Showton's head, as well as all the future deaths his actions cause. His evil must be stopped, and it is now clearer to me more than ever before that you are the Messenger and the Liberator of all enslaved people, whether that enslavement is by mark or forced servitude in an evil army. As for me, I'd rather cross-over than be anyone's slave ever again. It is your duty to end it all with whatever force is required," she explained, her voice strong and convincing. She watched as his eyes filled with tears, but none fell. "What was the counsel from the sacred text of your homeland? The one your father had you repeat at the meal table. I love it. Please say it for me," she asked.

"My mother and father made my brother and me repeat it from memory all the time. It was their way of telling us to be patient in our youth," he told her.

"Please, let me hear it again," she said.

Tondo thought for a moment and then began reciting, "To everything there is a season, and a time to every purpose under the heaven: a time to be born, and a time to die; a time to plant, and a time to pluck up that which is planted; a time to kill, and a time to heal; a time to break down, and a time to build up; a time to weep, and a time to laugh; a time to mourn, and a time to dance; a time to cast away stones, and a time to gather stones together; a time to embrace, and a time to refrain from embracing; a time to get, and a time to lose; a time to keep, and a time to cast away; a time to rend, and a time to sew; a time to keep silence, and a time to speak; a time to love, and a time to hate; a time of war, and a time of peace," he repeated from memory, all the time his blue eyes were fixed on her golden-amber eyes.

"Tondo, what time is it now?" she asked, her eyes searching his.

"It's time for us to end the Showton's threat and get on with our lives," he stated emphatically, his self-doubt having melted away. He stood, and so did she. A broad smile filled his face, "The Sutro Seer is right; you are my strength. Thank you, my love." He leaned across the table, and so did she. They met with a kiss.

# CHAPTER 18

# A PLEASURE TO SERVE

The Showton sat on his tanter, wearing a dark hooded cloak and a veil across the lower half of his face, his Munnevo-red eyes burning with anger. The formation of men standing before him were the ones who had fled from the bolts of chain lightning streaming from the man atop the enemy raster. Now, their ruler, the Sutro Showton, was about to levy his punishment for their cowardice. The men were lined up in ranks of twelve, one rank behind the other.

The Showton nodded and an attendant shouted, "Haptane Grunzen, conduct the discipline!" The commander and his second-in-command moved down the front rank, the haptane holding a clay pot above his head. The man standing in front of him reached into the pot and pulled out a round, white stone. The man's worried expression released, and he smiled. The haptane moved to the next man in the rank. The second in command also carried a clay pot, and the previously drawn stone was dropped into it. Man after man drew his lot until a black stone was pulled from the haptane's pot, the unfortunate recipient of the black stone being marked for execution. The quaking condemned man was brought to the center-front of the rank, surrounded by his fellow rank members, and upon an order from the haptane, the man was beaten to death by the others with fists, kicks, and stones. The rank's survivors were then moved aside to witness the remaining punishments, and the next rank drew lots, and another brutal execution was performed. And so it went until all the ranks had drawn lots and each hapless victim executed. More than one-hundred men lay dead by midday.

"Haptane Grunzen," the Showton called. The army commander rushed to the Showton and dropped to one knee.

"Yes, master?" the haptane asked with fear in his voice.

"You and the remainder of your men are placed on half-rations for the next two wernts. This is the second time you have disappointed me. If you and your men ever fail me again, I will have your head on a pike, and your cowardly warriors will be tormented; every one of them. Have I made myself clear?" the Showton growled.

"Yes, my master. I swear, never again!" the haptane promised.

"Go, now, and train these cowards hard. If any man performs poorly, encourage him with the heavy tamer. Make him an example as the others watch." The Showton turned his mount and trotted away, leaving the haptane in his dust.

That evening, as the Showton slumped in his chair, an untouched meal plate resting on a small table at his side, he pondered. He'd been brooding all afternoon, ever since the final execution for cowardice in the face of the enemy was performed. He had a serious problem; this Ameer Tondo was more than he had expected. He was not the recreant the Showton had thought him to be; he was recklessly brave. But what concerned the Sutro Showton the most was his command of the inner-power. Could this Tondo be even more powerful than himself? Was he a Worlder? That seemed unlikely. This worrisome thought set the Showton to moping.

"Master," an attendant quietly uttered as he stepped into the tent, receiving a disdainful glare from the Showton.

"I told you I didn't want to be bothered. Leave me alone!" the Showton grumbled.

"Master, the Dark One is here. He wishes to speak with you. He says it is an urgent matter that you will find worthy of his intrusion," the attendant meekly conveyed.

"Oy, alright, have him enter," the Showton groused.

The Dark One entered and dropped to one knee. "My Master, as always, I am at your service," he said.

The Showton stood so as not to be looked down upon after giving his next command. "You may stand. What is this urgent matter?"

"I have a plan to eliminate the enemy commander, Tondo," the Dark One offered.

"You do? Go on; tell me what you have in mind," the Showton said, his red eyes searching the Dark One's veiled face for a clue to his confidence in the scheme he was about to present.

"I've learned some things about this man since I killed his woman. He is not the coward we thought he was, and he has shown himself to possess the inner-power in abundance. We must eliminate his threat before the conquered cities hear of him and gain hope," the Dark One counseled.

"Yes, yes, Nevesant, I've come to the same conclusion. So, what do you have in mind?"

"I've learned that he inspects the battlefield after a battle, and I watched him and the one-eyed beast do it after the last engagement. I can place some of my men amongst the dead next time with orders to slay him as he passes," the Dark One offered.

"It appears you have little faith in our ability to win the next battle. Let me remind you, the zondars have arrived, and they will carry the day, just as they've done before," the Showton growled, his red eyes revealing his indignation.

"Of course, my master, the huge beasts are powerful and should set his men to flight as they have others who chose to resist you; however, have you not said, 'It is wise to plan for all contingencies?'" the Dark One reminded him.

"Yes, it is," the Showton reluctantly conceded.

"Then, I will make the preparations," the Dark One said. He bowed and turned to make his exit.

"Wait!" the Showton ordered.

The Dark One stopped and bowed, "I'm at your service, master."

The Showton stared at Tondo's Champion's Dagger the Dark One had tucked into his belt. "That you took from his dwelling, didn't you?" the Showton asked, pointing at the dagger."

"Yes, Excellency, it is a trophy and a keepsake."

"And a reminder of your failure," the Showton shot back. The Dark One did not respond, but his angry eyes revealed the sting of his master's insult. "Are there not others with similar trophies?"

“Yes, two others, T′uft and Gherd,” the Dark One responded, his tone cold and subdued.

The Showton turned away and took a few steps, deep in thought. After a few moments, he faced the Dark One again. “I don’t want this Tondo killed; I want him taken alive.”

“That may not be possible, my master. One or two men lying in wait might gain a quick kill, sacrificing themselves in your service. However, he always has many guards nearby, making capture unlikely,” the Dark One explained.

“True enough,” the Showton agreed, “unless we lure him to us.”

The Dark One’s eyes lit up. “The child!” he exclaimed.

“Yes, the child,”

“But he is powerful. Are you sure you can subdue him?” the Dark One wondered.

“Our combined powers can, I’m certain,” the Showton said confidently.

“Why take the risk? Just kill him and be done with it,” the Dark One suggested.

“I want his formidable inner-power. Once captured, he’ll be . . . be encouraged to surrender it to me,” the Showton said as his red eyes expressed his glee.

“What if he refuses?” the Dark One asked.

“He may be willing to endure his own suffering, but I wonder how much pain he can watch his young daughter endure?”

The Dark One’s eyes brightened, as well. “After he surrenders his power to you, what will you do with him?” the Dark One asked.

"I'll give him to you so you can finish your assignment. I still want you to bring me his blue eyes in a box."

"And the girl, if she survives?"

"If she isn't too damaged, I may decide to keep her and train her as I did you." The Showton watched as the Dark One's eyes expressed surprise and worry. "I will not forsake you, Nevesant. As a matter of fact, it's time I add to your training. I have another assignment for you, one only you can accomplish."

The Dark One bowed again, "It is a pleasure to serve you, my master."

"We will see," the Showton said, and then he chuckled. "Let's keep this plan between ourselves for now; tell no one else."

"As you wish."

"You may go but remain near. I will send for you in a day or two." The Dark One bowed and exited the tent.

An attendant quickly entered and asked, "How may I be of service?"

"Fetch a blacksmith," the Showton ordered.

---

Two days passed, and the Dark One was just responding to the Showton's summons. He entered the tent and dropped to one knee before his standing commander.

"Yes, my master."

"You may stand. It's now time to formalize our plan. I'm sure the zondars will put the Tondo's men to flight. I'll take him captive when I win, but he is resourceful, and your counsel is well-taken. Should we not prevail, I want your two men with the trophies to lie in wait and kill the one-eyed commander. They are not to kill this Tondo, is that understood?" the Showton ordered.

"As you wish, master."

"T´uft and Gherd know where the girl is, right?" the Showton asked.

"Yes, Fortress Showtonia. If they're captured alive, they won't reveal that information. They've been trained to resist."

"Ha, I think they will if this Tondo is as powerful as I believe he is. Just make sure they carry their trophies. Those are the linchpins to this entire plan," the Showton advised.

"Once he's captured, how will he be contained? You and I cannot watch him every segment," the Dark One explained. The Showton walked over to a camp table and picked up a small hoop made from shiny gravetum. He carried it to the Dark One and held it out for him to take. The big ring was constructed in two halves, each half three fingers wide and a finger width thick. Each half had flanges bent at right angles on both ends, with a hole in their centers. The two halves were held together with a wire run through the holes and twisted.

"When he's subdued, this will be placed around his neck and secured with flared bolts," the Showton explained.

"How will this stop him from using his power?" the Dark One wondered as he examined the collar, turning it in his hands.

"It will hold energy infused into it that will neutralize his inner-power," the Showton explained.

"I don't detect anything special about this collar. Where does its power come from?" the Dark One asked.

"It has none yet. That's why I've summoned you. You have told me it is your pleasure to serve me. I want you to take this collar to the gods of the mist and entreat them to fill it with their energy," the Showton ordered, his red eyes watching the Dark One's every move. He thought he saw his puppet shudder. "What's the matter? Don't you think you're ready to converse with the gods of this world?"

"Master, I'm not worthy of such an honor. They may deem me undeserving, and you know what that means. You have faced them before. They know you," the Dark One said with terror in his voice.

"I must remain here to counter the Tondo in our next battle or until the armies retire for the cold and wet season. I am relying on you to complete this task. Take as many guards and sacrifices with you as you think you'll need," the Showton ordered, brushing aside his toady's fear.

"Master, please reconsider for both our sakes," the Dark One pleaded.

"I have made my decision, Nevesant. Not only will you do this for my pleasure, but you will also do it for yourself. If you prove worthy, the gods will likely empower you. Once you have experienced their true wonder, your conviction in our cause will be strengthened. It is the crowning piece of your training. If you are successful, you will become my trusted Second. Now, what say you?" The Showton's stare grew more intense. Reluctantly, the Dark One bowed and nodded but said nothing. "Good. Now, finish planning with your men and then select those to be sacrificed in payment for the Shadows' help. I want this done quickly, so take the boat. I will meet you in my city after my victory, or the weather causes the end of the campaign season. Hopefully, when you return, you'll find us victorious. But, as you reminded me, it is best to plan for all contingencies."

# CHAPTER 19

# BLACK FLAMES

The Dark One stood next to the boatmaster holding the ship's tiller, and both were silently staring through the mist at the massive and threatening rock formation looming ahead, jutting out of the surrounding water.

"After we pass that rock, we'll be in the realm of the gods of the mist. There is a cove on the other side, and that's where you debark," the boatmaster said.

"How will we get to land; the terrors?" the Dark One asked shakily, attempting and failing to repress his worry and fear.

"Look around," the boatmaster said, "this is the realm of Death. Nothing living remains here, at least not for long. I will put you and your party in the small boats and have you taken to shore. After my boaters return, I will wait for you beyond the rocks. It's not wise for the living to tarry long in these waters, nor on land for that matter."

"Is that the voice of experience?" the Dark One asked worriedly.

"Those are the words of our master. I bring him here every span so he may converse with them. I do not envy you your assignment." The Dark One did not answer; his cold brown eyes fixed on the dead landscape of shore, slowly coming into view through the mist.

The two longboats had just delivered the Dark One, his guards, and a herd of terrified young men and women to the rocky beach. As soon as the boats were emptied, their two-man crews shoved off and quickly rowed back to the ship. The Dark One examined the area where they had been deposited. The scene was devoid of color, every feature a shade of gray. No green tree, verdant bush, or colorful flower greeted his party; neither were the sounds of creatures heard. The mist hung tightly over them, subduing and scattering the feeble rays of the p´atezas above and smothering the sounds his party made.

"Follow me," the Dark One commanded. He and his group headed for what appeared to be a trail cut into the jagged cliffs ahead.

As they moved along the roughly hewn path, the mist seemed to form ghostly images of arms or tendrils reaching toward the living creatures as they passed. The fog grew thicker the further inland the party moved, turning the already dank day into a dusk-like shadowy world. The Dark One noticed that the rocky world surrounding him was not the least bit damp.

How could that be? he wondered in silence.

The party crested the cliff trail and moved inland until they approached the edge of a deep cavity cut into the landscape. The Dark One peered over its edge, but he could not see its floor.

"This way," he said as the others followed him along the pathway that led into the cavity's depths of mist and darkness. A segment later, they reached the floor, and the stone-strewn track ended. Only the slightest bit of light penetrated the abyss, and the heavy air was chilling. A foreboding of doom clutched at the hearts of every member of the party.

The Dark One stepped forward, signaling the others to

remain where they were. He slowly disappeared into the mist and darkness. The others waited nervously, shivering in the cold, their warm breaths visible in the chilly air. The Dark One cautiously moved forward, his right hand gripping his sheathed sword, its feel offering him scant comfort. After a few steps, he thought he heard something, possibly a call. He stopped and listened intently, but his ears detected nothing, yet the sound increased, becoming a raspy whisper, unintelligible.

"What? I don't understand?" the Dark One cautiously uttered in a hushed tone.

"Who are you, and why are you here?" the raspy voice growled. The sound was not in the Dark One's ears; instead, it echoed in his mind.

"I am Nevesant, sent by the Sutro Showton. Who or what are you?" the Dark One asked, his voice strong and loud, only the slightest quaver revealing his dread.

"I am Hubris and ruler of the other four. Our hunger is great, and we desire your life's essence. Tell me, Worlder, why you are here before our hunger overcomes our curiosity," the voice in his head warned.

"Show yourself," the Dark One demanded. The mist in front of him began to swirl, slowly forming a whirlwind of shadow. The vortex grew until it towered over him, transforming, no longer a whirlwind of mist but a column of black flames, with dark purple prominences erupting from its core, reaching out toward him with menace. He stepped back and clutched the grip of his sword tighter, yet daring not to draw it forth.

Unexpectedly, dark tongues of flame reached out of the column, quickly encircling him. A cry of pain escaped his clenched teeth. He felt something tugging at him, not at his temporal body, but something inside him, his very spirit. He attempted to move but couldn't; it was as though he were paralyzed and unable to move a muscle or even take breath. The dark flame caressed him, passed through his body, and then returned to the column of shadow. His paralysis quickly ended, and he was released. He took a deep breath and staggered.

"I now know why you are here," the voice rumbled aloud. Not only could he now hear it with his ears, but he could also feel it. "Reveal the collar," the voice commanded. He released his sword's grip and reached into his robe, removing the shiny gravetum hoop. He held it in front of himself with both hands as tongues of dark purple flames erupted from the entity's core. The collar appeared to absorb the flames, and its color transformed from its shiny, zanth-like luster into a dull black. "Take it to your master. It will now serve his purpose. But, before you go, there is something else we give you, follower of Munnevo," the voice rumbled. Four more columns of black fire formed, and tongues of multi-colored flames lashed out from each one, swirling over, around, and through the Dark One. He groaned in pain and was driven to his knees. Swirling tendrils and tongues of dark fire caressed his burning flesh and flowed through his shaking body. His pain increased until he could bear it no longer, causing him to bellow in agony.

"Enough!" Hubris commanded. The black tendrils retreated, and Nevesant's torment quickly ended. He wobbled to his feet, weakened by the ordeal. "Now," the voice began, "ten pure ones are not enough. We hunger for more Worlders. We will take all the others, as well. Do you object?"

"No," Nevesant mumbled in a feeble gasp.

"Good," the voice told him. "Tell your master we hunger greatly. He will feed us more often. Now, return to him with that message. Begone!" The five towers of black flame disappeared into the dark mist. An instant later, he heard screams coming from the other party members, guard and prisoner alike. He stuffed the darkened collar into his robe, staggered back to the trailhead, and scrambled up the wall, not daring to look back. Less than two segments later, he was on the rocky beach, waving both arms frantically in the air and shouting as loudly as he could.

"Boatmaster, someone's on the beach!" the boatman shouted from the ship's bow.

"Raise sail! Let's retrieve our lost souls," the boatmaster ordered. The Dark One watched as a sail was raised on the ship. He dropped to his knees, exhausted and spent. As he contemplated his recent experience, he thought he felt a more potent power at his center. Could it be that his encounter with the gods of the mist added to what he already possessed? He also noticed a fit of burning anger raging within himself, much more powerful than before.

# CHAPTER 20

# A REAL NASTY SURPRISE

Several wernts had passed since the last battle. The two enemy armies maneuvered as they vied for the upper hand. The Showton had found the ground he favored and assembled his force to it. Tondo chose to accept the Showton's invitation to battle, and at dusk, he began moving his army into position. By morning, the kingdom's army was arrayed in its standard formation: male foot soldiers at the front, cavalry brigades on both flanks, archers positioned behind the front line, and the Te Femma Brigade in reserve at the rear of the army.

The Showton had been caught unready to meet Tondo's army; however, by midday, all was in place. From his perch atop the raster, Tondo scanned the battlefield. Even though he had surprised his nemesis by accepting battle on the Showton's terms, his opponent had not taken advantage of the situation. Tondo's army remained in their starting positions, many of his men napping in their formations, seemingly daring the Showton to come to them.

As Tondo's men watched the enemy form their ranks, they got their first glimpse of the Showton's rumored war-beasts—the zondars. Terror gripped his men's hearts as ten massive behemoths roared and trumpeted their arrival on the battlefield. The very presence of these monsters may have caused a lesser disciplined army to flee, but not Tondo's warriors. Their confidence in the ameer—the Messenger—stiffened their resolve, and they waited, fully expecting another victory.

As the p´atezas reached its zenith, a horn sounded on the Showton's side of the battlefield, and drums set a beat. The enemy line advanced at a slow but relentless pace. Quickly and steadily, the zondars pushed ahead of the formations of foot soldiers at their flanks and rear. Tondo smiled as he watched. He brought his farseer to his eye and searched for the location of his nemesis. He was found well to the rear of his army. This time, there was no high ground from which he could manage the battle. That was a significant oversight on the Showton's part, Tondo realized. He had the advantage, and he knew his surprise would be complete.

Tondo continued to wait and watch as the war-beasts drew closer. When they were three arrow flights away, he said, "It's now time to give the Showton some shock and awe." He ordered his hornman to sound, and the call echoed across the battlefield. Tondo's central brigade, the one commanded by Nestess, split in two, half moving to the left and the other half moving to the right. As Nestess's warriors moved aside, they revealed to the advancing behemoths of war the deadly maws of Tondo's two great guns. When the war-beasts reached a line of white poles placed on the field by Tondo's men during the night, the guns erupted; one quickly following the other. Two-inch stone balls blasted from their muzzles, a few skipping across the ground like rocks across a pond. They slammed into the advancing beasts, tearing them and their riders to pieces. Beastmaster B´estra took a stone ball to the center of his chest, killing him instantly. All but two of the creatures were hit by the guns' blasts. However, one war-beast on the extreme left and another on the extreme right went unscathed. A terribly wounded beast near the center of the formation trumpeted its pain and terror, turned around, and bolted into the ranks of the Showton's men following it. Enemy warriors were knocked asunder as the monster tore through their lines. The unwounded monster on Tondo's right turned and also dashed away from the guns' roar and lingering smoke. Unlike the wounded behemoth, this war-beast's crew survived. Its mahout attempted to get the terrified beast under control but to no avail. As the zondar charged into the front rank of the men following it, the mahout grabbed a hammer tucked into his belt and drove a thick gravetum spike into the beast's head and brain, collapsing it before it could do more damage.

Haptane Grunzen watched in horror as stone balls tore into the zondars at his front. Other deadly spheres slammed into the leading ranks of his formations, ripping the men to shreds. He watched as some of his warriors wavered, a few breaking and running for the rear. "Kill those cowards!" the haptane ordered. He was not about to face his master's ire a third time. Neither were his remaining, undaunted warriors willing to experience the Showton's wrath a second time and their decimation or worse. The fleeing cowards were cut down by their stalwart comrades.

Tondo gave another order, and his hornman sounded. Nestess's men quickly returned to their starting positions, covering the guns. The gun crews worked furiously to cool, recharge, and reload their great weapons. The remaining war-beast surged forward and soon engaged Tondo's men. It advanced through several ranks, and then it collapsed, spears protruding from its mouth and eyes, the front and rear of its knees slashed and bleeding profusely.

The Showton's main line crashed into Tondo's warriors, and the battle was truly formed. A hail of arrows soon began falling into the rear ranks of the Showton's formations, and Tondo's cavalry nipped at their flanks, firing arrows into the mass of men who were unable to respond, shaking their resolve.

The Showton's tanter formations charged Tondo's foot soldiers on his left flank. As they approached, his men quickly formed hollow squares fronted by menacing metrenas, offering the tanters an unexpected briar patch of pain and death in their path. The creatures simply turned aside and dared not enter, taking their riders with them. Tondo's samaran troopers then began harassing the enemy's mounted formations, picking off both rider and mount with arrows.

After two segments, the Showton had endured enough. A Showton army horn sounded, and his formations began to make an orderly withdrawal. As they did, a purple cloud began to form over the center of the battlefield. Tondo ordered his men to break contact and pull back. The purple cloud roiled and brewed, but it did not descend.

The guns were ready to fire again by this time, so the order was given. Nestess's brigade split a second time, half moving to the left and the other half moving to the right. The guns fired once more. The retreating enemy was nearly out of range, but nevertheless, scores of Showton warriors fell as the almost spent stones hammered into their retreating ranks.

"Master, what's to be done? The enemy has prevailed," a Showton's attendant lamented.

"Silence!" the Showton shouted. "There are other means to a victory. This Tondo will not prevail. Do you understand?" the Showton indignantly yelled.

"Yes, master, of course," the attendant bleated, fearing a more painful riposte. His master turned and rode in the direction of the army's camp, his robes billowing like dark smoke in the breeze.

The two assassins, T´uft and Gherd, moved quickly and silently in the waning light of dusk, stealthily scrambling over the dead bodies. They soon settled into their hiding places, waiting and hoping for a quick strike against the kingdom's one-eyed leader a couple of stone throws distant.

Sutrum Megatus Idop sat on his mount and surveyed the scene as the Showton's formations withdrew. Things had gone just as Tondo had planned. The ameer's primary goal was to destroy the enemy's war-beasts, which had been accomplished. The United Kingdom's losses had been light, so he decided to leave the examination of the battlefield to the brigade commanders. Idop moved to Tondo's command raster and arrived as the ameer descended from the howdah and mounted his war-samaran.

"Well done, zerr; mission accomplished!" Idop said with a salute.

Tondo returned his salute and leaned back in the saddle. "I want to take a close look at a war-beast." The two commanders, followed by their staffs and Brothers, moved to where the nearest beast had been slain. They dismounted and examined the unfortunate creature.

T´uft and Gherd watched from a frustrating distance as the two men circled the fallen monster on foot. The one-eyed commander, their quarry, was much too far away to launch an assault, the zondar having been slain well into the enemy's ranks. There was no way they could get any closer without revealing themselves. They remained in their hiding places, silently waiting and watching, hoping their target would draw near.

As the two kingdom commanders examined the enemy's slaughtered beast, Megatus Maaryah arrived with her staff. She dismounted and joined the men. She stood, staring at the huge carcass. "This one escaped the gunz unharmed? Amazing, just amazing that your men brought the monster down on their own." she cheered.

Idop responded, "The guidance Tondo provided and the training the men were given filled them with the confidence they needed to deal with the beast. I'm grateful only one made it to our lines. I wonder if there are more?"

"We'll have to be vigilant. Now that the Showton has seen the guns, he will adjust his plans again; however, it's time we drive home this victory. I want the brigade commanders assembled in the morning for a council of war. We will liberate as many cities and towns as possible from the Showton's clutches before the weather turns bad. We're only three marches from Anderez. Let's meet with Prince

P′on-dre-vitz and determine the best way to free his city." The three commanders then mounted and headed toward the army's camp.

T′uft and Gherd remained in their hiding places until the midnight segment, then they stealthily withdrew to their own camp, both fearful of what might befall them upon their arrival for failing to strike down their prey.

It was early morning, and the two assassins were on their bellies before their supreme master, the Sutro Showton. "I've been told you failed in your assignment. Is that true?" the Showton grumbled, his red eyes fixed on the two men.

"Master, it wasn't our fault," Gherd pleaded.

"Excellency, we never got the chance to strike," T′uft groveled.

"Tell me what happened," their master ordered. The two men explained how the one-eyed commander didn't move into the area of dead warriors; both he and the Tondo returned to their camp without inspecting the battlefield. After listening to their explanation and their pleas, the Showton leaned back in his chair. "Very well. You will have other opportunities. You may go," he said. The two men quickly scurried away, grateful they hadn't been punished for their failure. The Showton, for his part, still needed their services.

The Tondo and his one-eyed subordinate were not as predictable as he and the Dark One supposed. This would be a long campaign, and there would be other opportunities to implement his plan. In the meantime, he had to find a way to deal with the Tondo's massive thunder-makers—his guns. Their unexpected appearance had been stunning, a real nasty surprise.

# CHAPTER 21

# WINTER QUARTERS

The isolated city of Anderez had been built on the bend of a great river, the river protecting its walls on three sides. The Showton had ordered his force holding it to withdraw. He knew it could not be saved, especially after learning that the Army of the United Kingdom had massive weapons never before encountered, thunder-makers, his men called them—Tondo's guns. The wall of a city was no longer a protection for its defenders. The Showton had already lost an army and his zondars to their malice. For now, he would withdraw reluctantly. He had taken a tremendous swath of land and could afford to surrender a little, at least temporarily. The wet season was approaching, and the weather was changing. Both armies would soon retire from combat until the warm season returned. To continue military operations during the season of inclement weather would incur unnecessary losses due to illness, disease, and exhaustion, numbers that he would have to replace, equip, and train, at least minimally. He'd already lost too many warriors, including his prized Invincibles and his well-trained war-beasts—no need to add to the toll. During the cold season, he would see the conquered cities and their provinces culled for additional conscripts. His nearly fifty-thousand in losses would quickly be replaced.

He wondered if more zondars could be readied by the next campaign season. He knew some were already being trained. He sent an order to have the beasts available for combat by the time the weather turned fair.

The thunder-makers were a major problem, though. How did the Tondo get these weapons? Although the Showton was not unfamiliar with them, he hadn't expected to find them here, in this place, and at this time. He wondered how his adversary had developed such unusual weapons, unusual for this world. Nevertheless, after some thought, he realized they were of limited worth. The thunder-makers were useful in a fixed-piece battle, such as a siege or even their latest encounter. He would have to alter his plans and introduce more maneuver into his planning, thereby negating the thunder-makers' usefulness. This would require him to remain and lead the armies facing his most threatening foe. He would also make it a point to speak with the Dark One and determine if a raid by his men might destroy or disable the Tondo's awful weapons.

The Showton smiled as he thought of his student, Nevesant, and his meeting with the Five Shadows. Indeed, it must be over by now. He wondered if his pupil survived the encounter and what lasting effects it would have on him if he had. He, himself, had been tutored by the Shadows shortly after his arrival and made more powerful than he ever imagined. It hadn't happened instantly, but over time, and his power was still growing. He had yet to fulfill his obligation to his mentors, and sometimes it made him shudder, a fact he kept to himself. With Nevesant's return, he would be able to share his concerns with another who truly understood the deadly threat they were all facing.

Fayeetez watched from atop a bluff overlooking Anderez. The Showton's force was evacuating the city without a fight. Fires had broken out, and many buildings were aflame. It was apparent the Showton's men had ended their hold on Anderez with a final round of plundering and destruction. The cavalry commander smiled, for he knew the enemy's wagons, full of supplies and booty, could never escape; he would capture most, if not all, and turn them over to the ameer. He might even be fortunate enough to trap the foot soldiers, depending on how things developed and the skill of his counterpart. He would soon see.

"Men, follow me!" he shouted. Five-thousand mounted troopers charged down the bluff and onto the valley floor, quickly engaging the hapless enemy column strung out before them, cutting down many unfortunate wretches with saber and metren lance.

Tondo, Idop, and Prince P´on-dre-vitz were at the front of the army as it wended its way toward Anderez. They watched as a lone trooper galloped toward them.

When he arrived, he saluted. The two commanders quickly returned his salute. "Ameer, Sutrum Megatus, Your Highness," the trooper began a bit winded, "Sutro Megatus Fayeetez is pleased to inform you that the enemy has abandoned the city. He is engaging them and expects to capture their wagons," the trooper announced.

"How long did it take you to reach us?" Tondo asked.

"One day, zerr."

"Thank you, neva megato. Now, rest and get some food. Remain nearby; we may need you to answer questions about the terrain ahead," Idop told him.

"Yes, zerr, as you wish," the trooper said as he saluted. The commanders returned his salute, and he turned his mount and moved away.

"Good news, Your Highness. Your city is liberated without a fight," Tondo said.

"My gratitude cannot be measured, Ameer Tondo. I must go there as soon as possible," the prince told him.

"Sutrum Megatus, proceed to the city with your Brothers troop and take the prince with you. You are fully responsible for his welfare," Tondo told him.

"Yes, zerr!" Idop said as he saluted.

"Thank you, ameer," the prince said. Idop signaled his troopers as he and the prince galloped forward with the Idop Brothers following.

The next afternoon, shortly after midday, Idop and the prince arrived at Anderez. They were greeted by Fayeetez well outside the city gates.

"What's the status? Is it safe for the prince to enter?" Idop asked.

"The city is secure, and the fires have been put out. The citizens are eager to welcome the prince," Fayeetez told them.

"Good. Your Highness, when shall we enter?" Idop asked.

"Immediately," was the prince's quick response. "Sutro Megatus Fayeetez, can you tell me the fate of my father, the king?" the prince asked.

Fayeetez took a deep breath and paused. His expression told Idop the cavalry commander was attempting to conjure up the proper words to share with the royal. "I'm sorry to report, the king has crossed-over, Your Highness. I've been told, he was . . . " Fayeetez paused to re-craft his words, " . . . the Showton had him killed sometime after the city fell. You are now the ruler of Anderez."

The prince bowed his head. It was a foregone conclusion that his father had crossed-over, but the words still brought pain. "And the queen?" the prince asked, his head still bowed.

"No one in the royal family survives, save Your Highness, " Fayeetez stated. Idop and Fayeetez sat silently on their mounts, waiting patiently for the prince to respond. They could tell he was trying to regain his composure.

After a few moments, he inhaled deeply, straightening his back and lifting his head. "I am ready to proceed." The three men advanced through the city gates, the prince leading the way with Idop and Fayeetez following behind. Idop's Brothers troop behind them, moving four abreast.

Prince P′on-dre-vitz's spirits were quickly lifted as his subjects became aware of his arrival. They greeted him with cheers and thanks. They assumed he was responsible for their liberation, and their joy reflected their gratitude. The prince slowly made his way to the palace. All along the route, his subjects had gathered, cheering his return. When he arrived at the royal residence, he dismounted and climbed the short stairway leading to the palace doors.

After reaching the top of the stairs, he turned and addressed the gathered throng. "Citizens of Anderez, it is good to be with you again. Our friends from the United Kingdom of Teg-ar-mos have made this reunion possible. Please welcome them as you have me," the prince signaled for Idop and Fayeetez to join him. The crowd cheered louder as the two commanders flanked the prince. "We will first honor our dead and restore our city, and then we will join forces with the United Kingdom and punish the Showton and his horde of criminals," the prince shouted. The crowd went wild, and they cheered all the louder. The prince turned and entered the palace. Idop and Fayeetez paused a few moments and then followed him.

As they proceeded, Idop commented, "I noticed you carefully crafted your words when the prince asked about his father. What happened?"

"The Showton commander had the king, queen, and princess put in a gravetum cage and burned to death in front of the palace. The cage and bodies were still there after more than three spans. I didn't want the prince to see that grisly sight, so I had the cage and bodies removed this morning."

"Good. I saw the remnants of the Showton's cruelty in Te Femma, and once is enough. That monster must be destroyed," Idop's voice was getting louder.

"What's the ameer's plan? Are we to wait out the cold and wet season here in Anderez?" Fayeetez asked.

"He wants to push to the coast and take Rendoto before we retire for the season," Idop told him.

Fayeetez smiled. "Then what am I doing here? I need to get my scouts forward. Please express my regrets to the prince, but I must return to my command," Fayeetez said as he saluted and then departed.

"Master, Rendoto reports enemy scouts have been spotted around the city's outskirts," the Showton's attendant reported.

"What? The Tondo couldn't have moved his army that far so quickly!" the Showton exclaimed. It was only the other day he'd received a report that the Anderez garrison had been attacked as they withdrew from the city. Several thousand warriors had been killed or captured, and the enemy had taken all their wagons, which were full of supplies and plundered loot. The Showton was expecting to hold Rendoto through the cold season, but the appearance of enemy scouts so near the city did not bode well for that plan. He couldn't be sure what this Tondo was up to; he had no reliable reports about where the bulk of the enemy army was located. The United Kingdom's detestable mounted troops were not only scouting ahead, but they were also screening the kingdom army's movements. The Showton worried that if he delayed, he might lose several thousand more warriors and even more supplies. What was he to do? His attendants had never seen their master so nervous, and it worried them. This Tondo's constant pressure was beginning to undermine the Showton's followers' confidence in their master's infallibility.

It was a miserable day; the wind was gusting strongly from the southwest. A powerful *Zerio* storm was upon the Army of the United Kingdom. From time to time, rain-drenched them and then ceased as quickly as it started. The army was at least a ten-day march from Rendoto, probably more under these conditions. The massive and heavy guns would take even longer if they could make it at all. Tondo began to regret his decision to press on to the coastal city. He had done all he could; he hadn't delayed in Anderez. Idop remained behind to receive the honors from the recently installed King P′on-dre-vitz, the Liberator.

As Tondo pressed forward, Idop and his Brothers were charged with preparing and training the promised Anderez Brigade. Anderez was not as populated as the other great cities, but Tondo was assured of at least two-thousand five-hundred recruits. He wanted these new warriors ready for battle by the end of the wet season.

In the evening, Tondo sat in his command tent, contemplating his options as gusts of wind pushed at his tent, causing the lamps' flames to jump and dance. The roar of rain on the tent skins began and stopped as he agonized about the future. A warrior covered in a foul weather cloak suddenly scampered into his tent. At first, he thought it was one of his aides, but when the covering was removed, his heart leapt; it was Maaryah. He quickly went to her, and they embraced.

"I'm glad you're here. I need to talk to someone. Someone I can share my concerns and my worries with," he said as he held her tightly against his body.

"You're worried about the weather, aren't you?" she asked.

"We need several days of clear weather if we're to make it to Rendoto. Even if we get there, I'm not sure we can take the city. The guns are getting mired in the mud, and I worry the thrice will become exhausted, unable to carry on," he warned.

"Why the rush to Rendoto?" she wondered. He watched as she paused in thought for a moment. Her eyes lit up, and she asked, "Do you think Maari is being held there?"

"I don't know. It's a city with a dock. Hermanez used to stop there. We can only hope a citizen will report she's been seen in the city. Fayeetez has promised me that finding her is at the top of his priorities."

Maaryah was torn between her love for her daughter and the welfare of the army. Her emotions prevailed. "Let me take my brigade and quickly move to Rendoto. I can seal the city before anyone escapes," she offered.

"We can't let our personal tragedy cloud our judgment. We have no assurance our daughter is there, and I won't divide the army based on hope," Tondo said firmly.

"Of course, you're right. I worry about her welfare every day," Maaryah bemoaned.

"Me, too. I promise you, we will find her no matter how long it takes."

"I know we will; I can feel it," she said and squeezed him tightly. They snugged and then separated. He offered her a chair, and she sat.

He moved his chair across from her, sat, and took her by the hands. "I don't like being this far from the ocean. Hermanez is our link to the kingdom, and I want to restore that link as soon as possible."

"We'll be all right, I'm sure of it. The Showton must be reeling from his recent defeats," she said with a smile.

Tondo chuckled and said, "Fayeetez is amazing! He took Anderez and all the Showton's warriors retreating from it. And to think, he was a simple slave laborer not that long ago."

"You had faith in him. You had faith in us all, even when we had none of our own," she told him as she leaned forward, gazing into his Munnari-blue eyes. His only response was a shy smile. They sat, silently peering into each other's eyes and holding hands. After a few moments, he leaned forward and kissed her tenderly on the lips.

"I love you," he said, and then he chuckled.

"What's so funny?" she asked.

"For some reason, First Sergeant Ames came to mind. I wonder what he would think of my current situation. The kingdom's ameer, master strategist for the king's army . . . "

Maaryah interrupted, "Don't forget, the Messenger, too."

" . . . and the Messenger. Sitting here with my lovely bondmate, a brigade commander no less, holding her hands and kissing her lips, preparing for another great battle. If I told him all that, he would say I was crazy, out of my mind; certifiably insane. But it's all true!"

"You love Fust Zergeant A-mez, don't you?" Maaryah observed more as a statement than a question.

"Yes, I guess you could say so. Although he once claimed, I was too dumb to grab my arse with both hands." Tondo laughed, and Maaryah chuckled.

"You love him like you do Idop, Fayeetez, and Ayascho," she said.

He nodded and replied, "But not like I love you." He kissed her again.

"Ameer Tondo!" an aide called from outside the tent. Tondo and Maaryah leaned back and released their hands.

"You may enter," Tondo called. The aide dashed in, followed by another man.

"Zerr, a messenger from Sutro Megatus Fayeetez," the aide reported. Tondo and Maaryah stood and faced him.

"Yes, neva megato, what's his message?" Tondo asked eagerly.

The young officer saluted, and Tondo returned it. "Zerr, good news! The enemy has abandoned Rendoto!" Tondo looked at Maaryah as huge smiles covered their faces.

"Excellent! Fabulous! Incredible!" was all Tondo could say as his worry drifted away on the wind, for Fayeetez's aggressive move had attained the army's winter quarters without a fight.

# CHAPTER 22

# THE DOCUMENT OF GOVERNANCE

The army of the United Kingdom had hunkered down in Rendoto for the cold and wet season. When Tondo and his army arrived in the city, there was no cheering or welcoming committee to greet them. The Showton's men had evacuated in the dead of night, and Fayeetez's troopers entered the following morning. As expected, the city's citizens had been traumatized by the spans under the Showton's heel. At first, the residents were suspicious that this new occupation would simply resume where the other one had ended. Fayeetez attempted to assure the people that he brought liberation, not more suffering. When Tondo arrived, he found the citizens terrified and distrusting of him and the huge army he brought into their city. Over the succeeding wernts, the people slowly warmed to their liberators' presence.

Tondo found that the Showton's occupiers had purged the entire city leadership. His first duty was to reestablish the city's self-government. This turned out to be more difficult than expected. All of the city's royals had been hunted down and killed, male and female, leaving no one with a legitimate claim to the throne. Tondo directed that a delegation of city gentry be formed to resolve the leadership issue. He then stepped back and watched as the council bickered and fought for wernts.

After much frustration, the delegation sought Tondo's intervention. He had no desire to become their kingmaker, so he proposed an entirely new form of city leadership, at least to these people, something he called Representative Government. His simple solution: let the people decide. At first, he was met with blank stares, but some delegates embraced the idea as he explained the concept.

The delegation returned to their deliberations, and a couple of wernts later, they had forged what became known as the Document of Governance. It was presented to Tondo for his approval.

The Document of Governance called for the men in each of the fifteen provinces of Rendoto to choose a single representative. The fifteen representatives would then meet and select one of their number to become the Augusta of the city for a term of five spans. After five spans, another vote would be held in the provinces, new representatives elected, and a new Augusta would be chosen from among them. Tondo said he would not approve the Document of Governance until it stipulated that both adult men and adult women be allowed to participate in the process. As an incentive, he warned the delegation that he and his people responsible for current city governance were growing comfortable in their positions of authority.

Within two days, the delegation returned with an updated version of the Document of Governance granting women suffrage. Although the document did not state that women could hold positions as province representatives or the Augusta, it did not deny them that ability. Tondo chose to let the citizens of Rendotto work out those details on their own. He approved the document, and it became the city's governing authority.

Soon after the approval, the province voting was held, and the Augusta was chosen and installed shortly after that.

While the Rendoto delegation quibbled over how the city would be ruled, Tondo sought new recruits for the army. He wouldn't form a Rendoto Brigade until one was approved by the ruler or rulers of the city. After all, city resources would be required to maintain it; however, he did agree to induct Rendoto volunteers into the army's standing formations for training. Several thousand Rendoto men had responded to the call, seeking vengeance for the Showton's numberless atrocities.

During the cold season respite, Tondo and Maaryah were often seen together strolling the streets of Rendoto. They regularly took last-meal together and occasionally first-meal. It became apparent to their lieutenants that the time their senior officers were spending together was an attempt to comfort one another concerning their growing worry for the fate and welfare of their abducted daughter, Maari.

# CHAPTER 23

# A COLD ROOM

Maari sat on her bed, a blanket wrapped around her shoulders. Another cold season had arrived, and she had a choice: leave the single open-air window unshuttered and allow light into the room or close the shutters that blocked the cold wind and the p´atezas' uplifting light. Today, the wind was coming directly through the window, chilling her cold room even more. She missed the gartz windows at her estate home more now than ever. Maari climbed out of bed, the blanket still wrapped around herself, and moved one of the two chairs in her room to the window, stepped onto it, and looked out. She was in one of the four towers of the castle. The other three towers looked alike, and she guessed her tower appeared the same. She looked down toward the wall walk below and then to the courtyard even lower, and she watched a couple of servants scurrying across it as they performed their duties. Reaching out, she pulled the shutters closed. The room went dark, only a tiny bit of light peeking through cracks around the window's wooden frame.

"There," she said aloud, "no p´atezas today; it's too cold." She returned the chair to its place and then went back to her bed and climbed onto it. It would be another dark and dreary day. *When will Parr come and save me?* she wondered in silence. It was a question Maari had asked herself repeatedly, and she'd lost count of the days. She hung her head in despair and thought about how happy she had been at the estate with Mama, Parr, Tenny, and all the others. She wondered what she could have done to avoid being taken.

When the school was attacked, she dashed out the side door along with all the other children. She ran to the manor house and entered through the kitchen door. She heard men's voices in the living room, so she hid in a low kitchen cupboard. If only she hadn't made that noise while hiding, she wouldn't be here.

She thought back to that terrible day. A wicked man, the Dark One they call him, had his mean servant, T´uft, carry her away. She winced as she remembered how the other nasty servant, Gherd, hit Tenny in the head with something. She screamed and kicked and tried to escape T´uft's clutches, but he was too strong, and his strong hands squeezed tighter, and it hurt. When they got to the big boat, he put her down, and she bit his arm. He chased her around the deck as the craft cast off and sailed away. The boaters and all of the other nasty men in black laughed as T´uft chased her around and around the boat. He finally caught her and gave her a good slap in the face. She bit and kicked him, so he grabbed her by her braid and kicked her into the cargo hold. She landed with a thud, and it hurt, it hurt a lot, causing her to wail in pain. T´uft rambled down the steps, snatched her up, and held her face in front of his.

"If ya run from me again, I'll break yer leg!" he shouted. "If ya bite me, I'll knock yer teeth out!" All she could do was howl her protest in pain and terror, unable to catch her breath, her face turning red. He tossed her into an empty storage locker, slammed the door, and latched it. "Ya'll stay in there until I feel like letting ya out," T´uft yelled, and then he was gone.

"I hate you!" Maari screamed. T´uft only laughed as he climbed the steps. She cried herself to sleep.

She was forced to remain in the storage locker, and nobody gave her anything to eat. It was cold, and the wooden deck was hard. When she asked to go to the privy, one of the boaters opened the locker just long enough to toss in a bucket. T´uft finally gave her a very hard piece of bread, so hard it was, she could hardly chew it. But Maari felt she was starving, and after she finished, she asked for another, but T´uft only laughed.

"Maybe an empty belly will take the fight out of ya, oy, my little creeper?" he growled. He pushed her back into the locker, slammed the door closed, and latched it again. Then he was gone.

In her dark prison, she listened to the boat's noises and the men scurrying around on the deck above. Soon, the bad men began bragging about their murdering escapades at the estate. She listened in stunned disbelief as they described their kills. She had seen what they did to Tenny, and she heard their descriptions of the attack on the schoolhouse and the deaths of her beloved school teacher and his bondmate. So appalling were the men's boasts that she covered her ears with her hands. She began worrying about her mother and baby brother. She cried herself to sleep once more.

Maari didn't know how long she was in the locker before she was freed from that dark box, but finally, T´uft let her out, and she was permitted to go above decks. The p´atezas rays were bright and hurt her eyes, so she shaded them with her arm as she looked around. The ship was surrounded by water; no land could be seen in any direction.

"Don't try nothin' stupid, ya little creeper, or I'll toss ya over the side and let the terrors eat ya. Now, get over there, out of the way, and sit," T´uft snarled.

Maari did as she was told, but she couldn't hold her tongue, "My parr's gonna get you! You'll be sorry!" she shouted.

"Ya ain't gonna see no parr no more. Now, sit there with yer mouth shut, or I'll stuff ya in the locker again," he threatened. When he turned away, she stuck out her tongue at him.

When T´uft finally made her go below decks, he took her to a cargo hold and pushed her into a corner near a bulkhead filled with dirty and smelly rags.

"Ya'll sleep there, but before I go, I'm gonna tie yer leg to a tie-down ring," and then he did. "There. I've given ya some slack so ya can move around a little. See, 'ol T´uft can be nice, but if ya cause me any trouble, I'll throw ya in the locker again. Understand?" She simply nodded. "Good," he said, and then he left.

T´uft fetched her early in the morning and let her wander above decks for the next several days as long as the weather was fair. She was fed three times a day, but the food was awful; however, it chased away the hunger pangs, and everyone else was eating the same thing and complaining, as well.

The boat eventually reached its destination, Te Femma. Maari was taken by the Dark One, the really, really bad man, to the palace where she was shown to a man who scared her even more than the Dark One did, the one everybody called master.

"Come here, little girl," the master ordered. She hesitated, so the Dark One gave her a shove, forcing her to take a few steps forward, her head held low. The master came down from his platform and dropped to one knee in front of her. "So, you're the daughter of the Tondo?" he asked.

She lifted her head and looked into his Munnevo eyes. At first, his red eyes and veiled face startled her and made her shiver. She took a deep breath, "Parr's gonna find me and punish you, you bad man!"

The Showton chuckled, stood, and looked at the Dark One, "What's a parr?" he asked.

"That's what she calls her father, my master."

"What's her name?"

"Maari."

He looked down at the girl, "Hoy, Maari, when you see your parr again, he'll be in bindings." The Showton faced the Dark One, "This little one impresses me. I can feel her mettle. I might be able to do something with her. Attendant!" he called.

An attendant came to him and kneeled, "Yes, master?"

"What's the name of the old woman I've seen cleaning the rooms?"

"Sorry, master, I don't know."

"Fetch her."

"I will, this instant, Your Excellency." The attendant stood and quickly exited the room.

"Oy, you weren't able to kill the Tondo?" the Showton asked.

"No, master, he wasn't there. He'd gone to the city long before we arrived."

"How do you know that?"

"His woman told me just before I killed her and her screaming brat. Stuck 'em both to the floor with a metren," the Dark One gleefully revealed.

His words hit Maari like stones. After overhearing the other assassins' boasts on the boat, she'd fretted about what had happened to her mama and baby brother but was too afraid of what she might learn if she asked. Now, the Dark One had declared them dead. She wailed in torment and charged him, her little fists pounding his torso. He grabbed her by the neck and held her at arm's length, squeezing until she started making gurgling sounds and clawing at his grip.

"Behave yourself, or I'll squeeze until you turn blue," he threatened. He released his hold, and she dropped to her knees. She clutched her neck, gasping for air. He placed his foot in the middle of her back and pushed her chest to the floor, pinning her to the stone, her arms flailing.

She screamed in anger and anguish, her little heart breaking. "Parr's gonna get you! He's gonna kill you!" she bellowed. He put more weight on the foot holding her down, forcing the breath out of her, and silencing her threats.

"Shut up, you little creeper, or I'll cut out your tongue!" he warned. She went silent but continued to struggle under his foot. The Showton laughed as he watched the spectacle of this little girl challenging his lead manslayer.

The Showton's attendant returned, shoving before him a terrified old woman. He brought her into the room and pushed her to the floor at the Showton's feet.

"Master, this is the woman you ordered me to fetch. Her name is Purda," the attendant told him. She lay prostrate on the floor, whimpering in fear.

"Old lady, have you ever cared for children?" the Showton asked.

"Yes, master, I had two of my own 'til the Black Scourge took 'em," she puled, obviously in fear for her life.

"Stand up," the Showton ordered, and she did as he commanded, struggling to lift her aged body off the floor, her eyes downcast, not looking into the Showton's veiled face. "Do you think you can handle this one? She's quite spirited. She just attacked the Dark One, armed only with her tiny fists."

Purda cast her eyes upon the struggling child under the Dark One's foot. "I'll teach her proper respect, master," Purda replied, feeling much more at ease, realizing she wouldn't be punished for some unknown transgression.

"Good; see that you do. I'm putting this tyke under your care. You are responsible for her welfare, and if anything unfortunate should happen to her, I will be most displeased," the Showton warned.

Purda glanced into his red eyes and quickly looked down. "I will care for the child most carefully, master, as you wish."

"Take her now and leave us," the Showton ordered.

Purda dipped to one knee in genuflection. She then went to Maari. "Stop your struggling, child, and take my hand," she said. The Dark One lifted his foot, and Maari jumped to her feet and was about to bolt away; however, Purda was much too quick and grabbed her by the upper arm. "Stop that!" Purda ordered.

"You're hurting me!" Maari yelled.

"Stop resisting if you want it to stop hurting," Purda growled. Maari calmed down, and Purda relaxed her grip a bit. The old woman then marched out of the room with Maari in tow.

Purda's and Maari's relationship began with the two as antagonists. Maari was belligerent, and Purda was unyielding. Purda's method of getting Maari to comply was simply withholding the child's meals until she did what she'd been told. Maari quickly began obeying because she had already learned, while on the boat passage, that she couldn't win when defying those who provided her with food. At first, she hated the old woman as much as all the others, but as she became more compliant with Purda's wishes, she warmed to the old woman, and Purda warmed to her.

Although Purda was no surrogate for her loving family, over time, she became more of a friend than a foe. Their relationship improved considerably on the long overland journey they took from Te Femma to the Showton's newly built city, all the time under the watchful eyes of their Showton guards. After their arrival, Maari was taken to her new abode, a room located near the top of one of the castle's four stone towers. It was a dismal place, hot in the warm season and freezing in the cold. It was dark and dank, the only illumination coming from a sizable open-air window.

Life for Maari was one boring day after another. Purda was reluctant to let her charge out of the room because the old woman's life was literally on the line, especially if the child ran away. They spent many segments in Maari's room talking. Purda shared her love for her two children, a little boy, Fento, and a little girl, P′atta, who were taken by the Black Scourge a long time ago. Maari could see the tears welling in Purda's eyes, and she took her hand. Maari would tell Purda about her mama and parr and Tenny and her life on the estate. Purda was amazed to learn of her parent's kindness, although she never revealed it to the child. Purda even made a simple rag doll for Maari and smiled as she watched her charge nestle and love her simple gift as P′atta had done so long ago.

After many wernts had passed, Maari managed to convince her custodian to take her into the nearby fields and woods a few times so they could enjoy the fresh air and beauty of nature. However, each time they went out, Purda would tie a cord around Maari's waist, leading her along like a creature on a leash. Even at her tender age, Maari felt it degrading, but it was something she was willing to endure to get out of her dismal cell.

On one of the excursions to the woods, while Purda was napping with one end of the cord tied around the elderly woman's wrist, Maari noticed a woodland creature in the tree they were sitting under, watching them from a not-too-distant branch. Maari reached into the leather purse-like pouch she always carried with her on these trips, her outing bag as she called it, and pulled out a sandwich. Maari tore off a piece and placed it on the ground in front of herself. She watched as the furry creature sniffed the air and then scampered down the tree trunk, darting from place to place, pausing to search for danger quickly. When it reached the ground, it slowly approached Maari's offering, its nose continually sniffing the air.

Maari got her first clear view of the creature. It was small and could easily fit in her cupped hands. It had a tiny pointed face, huge brown eyes, and big ears that continually seemed to be turning in different directions. The little creature had fluffy, tan-colored hair all over its body and on its long tail.

As it slowly crept closer to Maari's offered treat, she could see its feet. Both front and back feet were like tiny hands with long, slender fingers and thumbs. When it got to the morsel of food lying in the grass, it reached out with its two front hand-like feet, grabbed it, lifted the tidbit to its mouth, and began munching away. Maari couldn't restrain herself and giggled. The little creature sprang off its long hind legs and grabbed the bark of the tree trunk. Then it scampered into the branches.

Maari's giggle not only startled the little creature but also caused Purda to awake. The old woman looked around and blinked her eyes until she could get her bearings. "Oy," she began, "I must have fallen asleep. Quickly now, my girl, finish your sandweetz. It's time to go back to the castle." Maari gave a disappointed groan but did as she was told, then the two headed back to the castle.

Since the warm season was upon them, Maari convinced Purda to take her out of the castle more often. Each time they went out, Maari would go to the same tree where she had seen the little creature. Purda would fall asleep, and the furry critter would come down and snatch an offering from Maari. Eventually, she was able to hand-feed the little ball of fur.

Sometime after that, the little creature jumped onto Maari's shoulder and sat there for a while, its nose sniffing the air and its big ears constantly moving in all directions, its bulging eyes fixed on Maari's face. In time, the creature allowed her to touch and then pet it. Maari soon found a particularly favored spot to scratch, and one of the little creature's hind legs began involuntarily thumping the ground as Maari scratched its chest and belly.

"I will call you Tumper," she whispered, not wanting to awaken the quietly snoring Purda. The name she chose came from a wondrous bedtime story her parr had often shared with her; it was a favorite. She reminisced about those happy times and a favorite story she begged her father to repeat night after night. It was a fantastic tale of woodland creatures who could talk to one another and about a baby creature whose mother was slain by wicked men. Suddenly, sadness overcame her, and she began to weep silently. Tumper looked at her face, sprang to her shoulder, and began licking the tears running down her cheek.

"That tickles," she quietly uttered as she wiped away the moisture from her other cheek. Purda snorted, causing Tumper to spring from Maari's shoulder and dash into the tree's branches. A short time later, Purda was awake, and their excursion ended.

That night, after last-meal and Purda's final visit for the day, Maari lay on her bed, gazing out of the unshuttered window. Her eyelids grew heavy, and she was about to fall asleep when she noticed something sitting on the window ledge. It was Tumper. She threw off her blanket and dashed to the window. Little Tumper jumped onto her shoulder and hung on as Maari started to return to her bed, stroking Tumper's head and back. Before reaching her bed, she detoured to her outing bag and opened it. By this time, Tumper had learned that scrumptious treats came from that bag, so the little creature jumped from Maari's shoulder into it, cleaning out every scrap and crumb it could find. Maari carried her outing bag, with Tumper inside, to her bed, climbed in, and waited for her new pet to finish its snack.

For the next segment or so, Maari and Tumper played together until Maari fell asleep. When she awoke in the morning, as the p´atezas' warming rays reached her window, she found Tumper curled in a ball on her blanket. Maari was thrilled when she saw her tiny friend had remained the night. She began rubbing Tumper in its favorite spot, and its hind leg began thumping the blanket. Suddenly, Tumper sat upright, resting on its hind legs, its ears searching out an unheard sound. In a flash, the little creature jumped to Maari's shoulder and then to the top of Maari's wardrobe. It hid in the shadows, peering down with its huge brown eyes. The door opened, and Purda entered carrying a tray with their first-meal. She placed the tray on the table and faced Maari.

"Have you washed your face, my girl?" Purda asked.

"Not yet." She hopped to the washstand, poured some water into the basin, cupped her hands, and splashed water onto her face. She grabbed a towel and dried off. She then went to the dining table and sat.

"Aren't we forgetting something?" Purda asked in a scolding tone.

"Oy! I forgot," Maari said. She quickly went to the wardrobe, removed her sleeping gown, and pulled out a clean tunic as she glanced at the two huge eyes watching her from above. She quickly changed, then returned to their table and sat.

The two had a friendly meal together and talked about the colorful birds they had seen the previous day on their excursion. Every now and then, Maari would sneak a glance at the top of the wardrobe, where she could see Tumper's huge eyes watching them. She slyly dropped a few morsels of food onto the floor and pushed them against the wall with the side of her foot.

When they had finished eating, Purda gathered their wooden plates and the remaining food and exited. After the door was shut and latched from the outside, Maari reached down, collected the food she had pushed aside, and held it in the palm of her hand. Little Tumper sprang from the wardrobe to the bed, and then it bounded to Maari's shoulder. The tiny creature climbed along her arm and began munching on the food Maari was holding in her palm.

Tumper became Maari's steady companion, and the two played together day after day. It was such a joy for her to have a friend to play with, and it brought a bit of happiness to her gloomy confines. Tumper would hide in Maari's outing bag on excursion days and was carried into the woods. When Purda wasn't looking, Maari would open the case, and Tumper would bound out and scurry into the trees. It would always return when Maari placed a morsel from her sandwich—which often had a corner missing when she pulled it out of the bag—on the ground or in the palm of her hand. Purda was inevitably napping, and when she stirred, Tumper would dart into Maari's outing case, ready for the journey back to the room.

The weather was changing, and another cold season was approaching. As Purda and Mari were returning from their outing, they noticed the masts of the big boat as they exited the woods. Maari hated it because it represented the pain she felt for the loss of her mother and baby brother, and her abduction from a loving home. The two passed by it without uttering a word. Purda marveled at its colossal size, and Maari hated its presence.

As they approached the open city gates, Purda suddenly stopped. Maari looked up and saw her staring straight ahead in fear. Maari looked in the same direction and saw the Dark One standing in the middle of the gateway, his dark robes rustling in the gentle breeze. Purda and the Dark One remained staring at each other for a long time, neither making a move nor a sound.

Finally, the Dark One spoke. "Come here, old woman, and bring the child," he angrily ordered. Purda grabbed Maari's upper arm, and they moved to him. When they arrived, Purda dropped to her knees and pulled Maari down with her. Maari struggled until she shook free from Purda's grip, then she stood, glaring at the evil man she hated. Her anger and fear grew within her, and she wanted to yell her loathing at the monster who had killed her mama and brother; however, she had learned from past experiences that such a display would only cause her pain, so she could only stand, seething and shaking with hate.

"Why did you leave the castle with the child?" the Dark One demanded. His dark-brown eyes and his tone displayed the enmity he held toward the old woman.

"Master, I took her into the woods for some fresh air. Keeping her cooped up in a dark room isn't good for her. She might get sick," the old woman pleaded. He bent down, grabbed Purda's upper arms, and yanked her to her feet.

"Don't you ever take her outside the castle walls again!" he shouted, his nose nearly touching hers. Unexpectedly, he was surrounded by a black, shadowy aura so chilling that the old lady's breath could be seen.

She groaned in pain, "Master, it hurts!" she cried. At first, the black aura scared Maari, and she stepped away until the cord around her waist stopped her retreat. When she heard Purda's groans and pleas, anger overcame her fear, and she charged into the painful rays and kicked the evil man several times in his ankles and shins. He released the old woman, and she collapsed to the ground. He then back-handed Maari, and she, too, hit the dirt. The Dark One stepped back and lifted his arms shoulder high, reveling in his newly acquired power, laughing his glee. Soon, the aura began to fade, and he lowered his arms.

Looking down at the old woman sprawled in front of him, he growled, “I will kill you if you ever take the child out of the castle again. The Showton has plans for her. If she needs fresh air, take her to the castle courtyard or along the wall walk, nowhere else.” He turned and tramped away. Maari stopped rubbing her face, jumped to her feet, and tried lifting Purda. The old woman struggled to her feet as Maari steadied her as well as she could.

“I hate him!” Maari cried, “I hate him!”

“Now, now, child, hold your tongue. Such outbursts will do you no good. These are hard times, and we must be careful if we want to survive.” Purda’s eyes searched Maari’s face. What could the Sutro Showton want with such a precious child? she silently wondered as fear and worry for her charge clutched at her. They headed back to Maari’s room, Purda limping and holding her hip as Maari helped her along.

The cold season was now upon them again. Purda had recently brought her word that the Dark One had been summoned away by his master, the Showton, and he had departed on the great boat. Maari smiled gleefully, for that evil man brought a deathly gloom to the castle that hadn’t been there before his arrival. Purda seemed happier or at least less fearful now that he was gone.

Maari's custodian had just left, latching and securing the door from the outside as she always did. Maari shuttered the window and sat on her bed, wrapped in a blanket. Little Tumper sprang from the top of the wardrobe and landed on the bed in front of her. She scratched her pet, and its hind leg began thumping the blanket, causing her to giggle. She stopped and stared at the wall on the other side of her gloomy room. She had been in this awful place for so long that she couldn't remember how many days it had been. She wondered where Parr was and when he was coming for her. A tear trickled down her cheek and dropped onto her blanket.

# CHAPTER 24

# BETRAYED

The Dark One strode down the gangplank and onto the dock of Panemento, a large coastal city twenty marches south of Rendoto. A small delegation of Showton attendants greeted him.

"Excellency," an attendant began with a bow, "we have prepared for your journey. Follow me." The attendant led the way to a cluster of waiting tanters held by helpers.

"I was surprised to learn that Rendoto was abandoned without a fight. Why?" the Dark One asked as they walked on.

"The last battle went poorly because the Tondo unleashed a horrible weapon that slaughtered the zondars. The men call these awful monstrosities thunder-makers, for they erupt with a roar of thunder, belching fire and smoke, spewing forth huge stone balls that tear asunder all flesh they touch. The master says even city walls cannot protect the defenders anymore. He thinks that's how the City of Women was taken," the attendant explained.

"I see," the Dark One muttered. "I knew something must have gone poorly when the master wasn't waiting for me in his city. The sooner we eliminate this Tondo, the better. Let's hurry to His Eminence and learn what's to be done." The party mounted their tanters and rode off toward the east.

The Showton had established his winter quarters in the city of Nudart, located about fifteen marches south of Anderez. Depending on the weather, the journey to Nudart was expected to take twenty to thirty days. Fortunately for the Dark One and his party, the weather was cooperative, and they arrived in only eighteen. The Dark One was immediately ushered into a private meeting with his master, the Sutro Showton. He entered and dipped to one knee.

"You may stand, Nevesant. Show me the collar," the Showton demanded.

The Dark One retrieved the dull black gravetum collar from his robes. "It will now serve your purpose, master," he said as he handed it to the Showton.

"You have done well. We are now ready to implement our plan. I have learned that the one-eyed commander is in Anderez, and the Tondo is in Rendoto. Take your men to Anderez and kill the commander there. Be certain at least one of your men survives the attack and is captured alive. When that is done, return to me."

"Master, I have heard that this Tondo has weapons the men call thunder-makers, and by their reactions, something fearful and devastating. Would it not be wiser to kill the Tondo outright and end his threat forever?"

"Nevesant, need I remind you we have discussed this before? There is more to gain by his capture than you can imagine. He is more like me than he is like you or the others of this world; I'm sure of it. When I take his inner-power, mine will double, at least. Then, nothing will be able to stop me. And you will be at my side. Tell me, did the gods of the mist impress you?" the Showton asked with a wry smile.

"They terrified me and devoured all the others. Do you really plan to free them from their prison?" the Dark One wondered.

"That is their hope, not mine. I will use them, but only when I must. As you have seen, the cost of their assistance is high, and they cannot be trusted. If they are ever allowed to escape the mist, I fear we will all be doomed."

"They demand to be fed more often," Nevesant informed his master.

"Yes, yes, they always hunger for the essence of the living. If they have their way, they will devour all living things. We must be cautious in dealing with them, giving them only what they need, not what they want," the Showton explained. The Dark One nodded his understanding. "Good. Now, take your men, kill the one-eyed commander, but make certain one or both of them are captured. I've sent Zedo ahead to gather as much information as he can. He will meet you at the South Ford Tavern outside of Anderez. Be sure no one can follow your trail in or out of the city. We will go to my fortress and prepare for the Tondo's arrival when you return."

"Do you think he's that foolish?" the Dark One wondered.

"With his woman and infant dead, the girl is all that is left of his family; he'll come. He's shown us he's no coward. Now, take your leave and make haste," the Showton commanded.

"As you wish, master," the Dark One replied, and then he exited the room.

The Dark One found Gherd and T´uft lodging in a building not far from where he met with the Showton. He entered and looked around, and T´uft noticed him first, "Master, you've returned. You've been gone for a long time. Where did you go?"

"The Showton sent me on an errand to the perpetual mist," the Dark One proudly stated. Gherd and T´uft stared at him in disbelief, for they knew what lurked there.

Gherd was the first to overcome his shock and surprise. "Master, did you see 'em? What do they look like?"

"Like nothing you have ever seen with your natural eyes. They took everyone but me," the Dark One admitted.

"What did they do?" T´uft wondered.

"They engulfed the others with shadow and devoured them. That's all I can tell you," he declared. His two lackeys could only gawk, and after a few moments, he asked, "Do the two of you still have the things I gave you from the Tondo raid?"

"Yes, master," Gherd answered. T´uft nodded.

"Where are they?" the Dark One asked.

"I keep mine here," Gherd said, patting his chest.

"Me, too," T´uft said. "I keep it with me all the time. Don't want no sneak thief to get it. The Shadows know, there's enough of 'em 'round here."

"Let me see them," the Dark One ordered. Both men hesitated. "Don't worry; I'm not going to take them from you. I didn't get a good look at them before."

The two men pulled at the straps around their necks and let

their trophies hang in front of their chests; T´uft had Maaryah's medal, and Gherd had the Victor's Laurel. The Dark One stepped to each man and examined his item. "Nice craftsmanship," he said. "You can put them away." He waited for the men to tuck their prizes under their jerkins. "The master has an assignment for us. We set forth for Anderez. Fetch mounts and provisions; we leave immediately."

Bento had been the proprietor of the South Ford Tavern for over twenty spans. He assumed its daily management long before, when his father became too frail to continue in that role. Bento became the owner when his father crossed-over. Now, he and his woman, Parji, ran the establishment, helped by their twelve-span old daughter, Henna, who served the patrons and as a maid for cleaning and preparing the four rooms on the second floor. It was a good life and provided the family with a modest living; however, as of late, business had been terrible even though the tavern was located on the main trail from Anderez going south toward Nudart. It was located just south of the only ford across the great river for many marches in either direction. Bento expected business to improve after the P´on-dre-vitz family again ruled Anderez; unfortunately, it hadn't. No one from Anderez came this way, and no one came from the south because the Showton's army lurked somewhere in that direction, near or in Nudart. Anyone in their right mind wouldn't even head south from the city; however, as of late, the tavern had a guest; a quiet man who kept to himself and didn't want to be bothered. He sat at the table closest to the fireplace, smoking his pipe and drinking his brew. Bento tried to strike up a friendly conversation with the man on the day he arrived, but it was immediately apparent that this visitor wanted to be left alone. Bento had learned by experience that it was best to leave this kind of traveler, a loner, to himself and not ask any questions. So long as he kept paying, he wouldn't be bothered. The man had been there for three days, only leaving the tavern to check on the care of his mount.

The rain was coming down in sheets on this day as the wind howled through the trees and over the rocks. It was a good day to be indoors, enjoying the comforts of a dry room and a warm fire. Surprisingly, three men quietly entered the tavern.

A dangerous-looking man with a veiled face strode up to Bento, "Are you the keeper?" he asked.

"Yes, my liege. I am Bento. How may I serve you?"

"We want warm meals, large brews, and dry beds. See that our mounts are cared for," the Dark One ordered. He pulled two shiny zin coins from his robe and handed them to Bento. The tavern keeper hadn't seen zin for so long that he almost jumped for joy.

"Thank you, my liege, thank you! You will be served immediately," Bento said with a broad smile. He yelled over his shoulder, "Henna, the best brew for our visitors! Parji, serve them warm food and bread, all they can eat! My liege, please excuse me. I will shelter and feed your mounts." He quickly left, but before he went through the door, he noticed the other two patrons had joined the loner at his table near the fireplace. Young Henna quickly appeared, prepared three brew flagons, and delivered them to the table just as the three newcomers sat.

"Girl, fetch me another," the loner snarled.

"Yes, my liege," Henna replied as she scampered away. She returned in a flash with another flagon. Parji rushed in from the kitchen, holding a heavy, black gravetro kettle by its handle. She placed it in the center of the table, dipped a large ladle into it, and began scooping its contents into wooden bowls she had also brought. After all four men had a bowl of steaming food sitting in front of them, she took four flat, spoon-like wooden utensils from her apron and handed one to each patron. Henna returned with four small loaves of bread and placed them on the table. The men quickly passed them around and began eating as Parji and Henna stepped back, waiting for their guests' next request.

The Dark One pulled the veil under his chin, looked over to the women, and in a stern voice, said, "Leave us. If we need anything, we'll call you."

"As you wish, my lord," Parji said as she grabbed the kettle's handle and was about to carry it back to the kitchen.

"Leave it here," the Dark One demanded. Parji released it, bowed, and returned to the kitchen with Henna closely following. The Dark One addressed the loner in a quiet voice, almost in a whisper, "Zedo, what do you have for us?"

"Master, I've been inside Anderez. The guards are very vigilant. Just getting through the gates was trouble. Fortunately, I was in Anderez before it was retaken, and I knew a few names. I told the guards I was visiting family now that a P´on-dre-vitz again rules the city, and they believed me. I can come and go as I please; they've grown accustomed to my face. It may not be so easy for the three of you."

"What else have you learned?" the Dark One asked.

"The one-eyed beast's name is Idop. He is in Anderez to build and train a large fighting force for his army. There's more than two-thousand warriors training already," Zedo explained.

"When and where is the best place to kill him?" Gherd asked.

"He always has guards and attendants around him; they're with him everywhere he goes; he's never alone," the spy replied.

"He's got to sleep. What about night?" the Dark One asked.

"I think that's the best time to do it. You'll have to get into the palace. That's where he sleeps." Zedo quickly looked around the room, checking to see if anyone was watching. He pulled a folded sheet of paper from his jerkin, unfolded it, and handed it to his master. "I paid one of the palace maids a pretty price for this. It's the innards of the palace. That black dot is where Idop sleeps, always alone and with no warriors other than the usual palace guards; two here and two there," he said, pointing on the map where the guards' duty stations were located, denoted by black Xs.

"How do we get in?" T´uft wondered.

Zedo pointed to another area of the map, "Here. After you enter the city, toss a grapnel up there and climb the inside wall; it'll be easy. That puts you close to Idop's room. You'll only need to deal with these two guards. After you've killed him, drop a rope over the outside of the wall, here, where I'll be waiting with tanters."

The Dark One sat silently examining the map for a few moments, then said, "Good work, Zedo. We'll do it tomorrow night."

"But master, how will the three of us get into the city?"

T′uft asked. The Dark One didn't answer and sat in thought.

The tavern door opened, and Bento scurried in. "My liege, your mounts are well fed and in a nice dry place," he announced.

"Come here," the Dark One ordered.

Bento scurried to the table. "Yes, my liege?" he asked when he arrived.

"This brew is excellent. Where did you get it?" the Dark One wondered.

"The regular house brew I make myself, but my best customers get the brew I haul in from Anderez."

"By wagon?" the Dark One wondered.

"Yes, my liege. I gotta get supplies from time to time," Bento explained.

The Dark One smiled, reached into his pouch, and pulled out another zin coin. He tossed it to Bento, "More brew and bread," he ordered.

"I'll be back in an instant, my liege," Bento stated gleefully and quickly darted away.

"That's how we're getting into the city," the Dark One quietly announced as he refilled his wooden bowl from the kettle.

The four guests had arisen in the morning to the savory aroma of cooking victuals wafting up the stairs. The men ate a full meal and were preparing to depart after completing some early morning business. The Dark One finished wiping blood from his black sword and stepped over the lifeless body of Bento. T′uft came out of the kitchen.

"You done?" the Dark One asked.

"Yes, master; the woman and girl are dead," T´uft declared. The two men exited the tavern and moved to the small barn nearby. Gherd had finished hitching two draft samarans to the small covered wagon. Zedo was mounted, leading the party's three tanters by ropes.

"We should arrive in the city just before dusk. You go to the meeting place on the outside of the wall after dark and wait for us there. Don't let anyone see you," the Dark One ordered Zedo.

"Yes, master," he replied, then he was off. The other three men climbed aboard the wagon and headed out. They forded the stream and continued along the rutted northbound trail.

Rain pelted the wagon off and on throughout their journey to Anderez. They arrived just before the gates were to close for the night. In the growing darkness, the trio in the wagon was met by a lone guard.

"State your business," he sternly ordered.

"We're picking up supplies for the South Ford Tavern," the Dark One declared, his veil tucked under his chin.

"How's 'ol Bento? I haven't seen him in spans, not since that evil Showton got here with his wicked army. I'd a never expected Bento to hire anyone to do work he could easily do himself. He's too tight with his coin," the guard said.

"Bento is slowing down now that he's getting up in spans. He's still tight with his coin, though. All he's giving us is a dry place to rest our heads and meals, at least until the wet season ends. Then, we'll be moving on," the Dark One explained.

"That sounds like Bento. All right, you can proceed. Hurry along; we're about to close the gates," the guard told him. The Dark One waved his thanks, and the wagon rolled forward.

The trio found an alley off a quiet city road and waited until the midnight segment. They emerged from the wagon wearing their black garb, and the three manslayers stealthily moved along the base of the wall before the palace complex. It was easy to scale the wall from the inside, as Zedo had indicated on the map.

After all three were on the wall walk, they dispatched a sentry, placed a grapnel at the corner of a merlon and embrasure, tossed the free end of the attached rope over the outside of the wall, and quietly moved into the palace itself. The Dark One had memorized the map, and the other two simply followed him. It wasn't long before they reached the guards' post. The Dark One indicated with hand signals for the other two to take them out. Their leader created a distraction using his inner-power to knock over a table on the opposite side of the guards. The sentries immediately reacted, turning towards the sound and raising their weapons. The two assassins quickly approached them from the rear and, in a flash, attacked. The two guards went down without making a sound.

The Dark One signaled for Gherd to look around the hallway corner nearby. Gherd quietly moved to it and peeked around the corner. He signaled the all-clear, and the other two silently moved to him. The Dark One looked around the corner, then stepped into the short hallway. A few strides ahead of him was a heavy wooden door. He tapped Gherd on the shoulder and indicated their target, Idop, was through that portal. Gherd quietly crept forward. When he was halfway to the door, he unexpectedly stopped for an instant, dashed into a shadowy alcove, and hid. Suddenly, a low rumble filled the three assassins' ears as if coming from a distance. The Dark One looked in all directions trying to figure out what was happening. The stone floor began vibrating, and the small tables and stands in the hallway and alcoves bounced along the floor, a few toppling over, sending pots and small statues crashing to the stone floor.

"Groundshake!" T´uft grumbled.

After a few moments, the rumbling subsided, and the shaking ended. The door to Idop's room burst open, and the assassins' target stood in the doorway with a sword in hand and wearing only his night-wrap.

"That's Idop! Gherd, kill him!" the Dark One ordered. Gherd, still unsettled by the groundshake, delayed for an instant, giving Idop time to defend himself. The manslayer quickly advanced, and the two men engaged, Idop parrying Gherd's initial strike. Suddenly, Idop was surrounded by a white aura, which chilled the air and caused frost to form on the nearby door and wall. Gherd wailed in pain and jumped back, leaving himself wide open for a killing thrust. Idop quickly took advantage of his vulnerability, and the assassin dropped to the floor, face down, and didn't move.

A detachment of guards turned the corner of the main hallway and spotted the startled intruders. The Dark One pulled a throwing-star from his robe and threw it at his prey. Idop instinctively swept the air with his left arm. The star's trajectory suddenly curved, sending the deadly missile off target just enough to only nick Idop's left ear, sinking deep into the doorjamb rather than embedding in his skull. The Dark One uttered a curse under his breath, and without hesitation, he betrayed his loyal follower, T´uft, striking him with a hard blow to the back of the man's head with the pommel of his sword, causing his comrade to collapse unconscious to the floor. The Dark One turned and dashed down the hallway in the opposite direction of the advancing guards. Idop charged after him and nearly crashed into the guards as they met at the intersection of his short hallway.

"Sutrum megatus, my apologies," one of the guards uttered. "Are you all right?"

"Yes! You, hold this man. You, secure the one over there. The rest of you, follow me!" he ordered as he pointed.

They chased the Dark One as he rambled down the halls and out to the wall. He quickly stepped over an embrasure and slid down the rope. When Idop got there, his sword slammed down on the thick strand, cutting it in twain. The Dark One free-fell the last ten radi or so of his descent, toppling over when he hit the ground. He scrambled to his feet and dashed to the waiting Zedo, who was holding the tanters. The Dark One jumped atop the nearest mount, and the two men were off in a flash, disappearing into the darkness.

Idop could only watch as the interlopers galloped away, escaping into the night. He turned and marched back into the palace, where the other two intruders were being held. One of the would-be assassins was on his feet, and the other was still lying face down where he fell. A pool of blood had formed around his torso. Idop strode up to the standing assassin, his good eye staring into the man's face.

"Who are you?" Idop demanded. T´uft said nothing and simply stared back at him in silence. "Why are you here?" Idop growled. Still, T´uft said nothing.

"Zerr, I found this hanging from his neck," the guard said as he handed Idop Maaryah's medal. He recognized it immediately, and in an instant, he reacted by punching the assassin as hard as he could with his right fist while still holding his sword. T´uft dropped to the floor, momentarily stunned, rubbing the side of his face, trying to relieve the pain. He spat out blood and a tooth.

"Search the other one," Idop ordered. Gherd's body was searched, and the blood-drenched Victor's Laurel was found. It was also handed to Idop. He looked down at T´uft and growled, "I pity you when you're brought before Ameer Tondo."

The Dark One and Zedo followed the great river, heading downstream for half a march. Nevesant continually glanced over his shoulder, hoping upon hope he wouldn't catch sight of a horde of mounted palace guards bearing down on him. Every quick glance revealed only an angry blue Munnari glaring down on him threateningly, sending a chill through his body. He pushed his tired mount even harder, but he could never escape the blue munna's intimidating presence.

At dawn, the assassins found an area with a slow-moving current and had their mounts swim to the south side. Several days later, the Dark One made his report to the Sutro Showton.

"Tell me what I want to hear, Nevesant, the one-eyed commander is dead," the Showton said, looking down at his kneeling Second.

"Unfortunately, I cannot, master. He lives."

"Another failure? I'm beginning to lose confidence in your abilities. Tell me what happened," the Showton demanded, his ire rising.

"We were ready to strike, my master, but a groundshake struck first, and it awoke the entire palace. The guards were upon us in an instant. Idop killed Gherd, but I made sure T´uft would be captured. I barely escaped, allowing you to hear this report," the Dark One offered in meekness.

"A groundshake, you say?" The Dark One nodded. "More misfortune; curse the blue moon!" The Showton stopped and thought for a moment. "You say T´uft was captured alive?" he asked.

"Yes, master, alive, I'm sure. The trophy was hanging from his neck," the Dark One told him, attempting to temper his failure.

"Very well. You may stand. The main purpose of your mission has been accomplished. Reluctantly, I'm satisfied," the Showton admitted as his anger eased slightly.

The Dark One stood and said, "Master, I have a troubling discovery to report."

"More bad news, Nevesant?" the Showton wondered.

"The one-eyed commander possesses the inner-power. I saw him use it against Gherd, and he deflected my throwing-star in mid-flight with a sweep of his arm," the Dark One explained as he looked into his master's worried red eyes.

"Before, you told me there was nothing special about this

man. Don't you think such a revelation is special?' the Showton grumbled.

"Master, I was quite thorough in my questioning. No one ever mentioned it. He must have hidden his power from the others." the Dark One whined.

The Showton pondered his servant's words for some time. He took a deep breath and said, "This army of the United Kingdom is becoming more than troublesome. How many more of their accursed leaders possess the inner-power?" The Showton turned his back to the Dark One and took a few steps as he silently pondered. Soon, he returned and stood before his Second. "We will proceed with our plan to capture the Tondo. Let us go to my city and prepare for his arrival."

# CHAPTER 25

# HEAVY LADEN WITH WORRY

Two wernts had passed since the attempted assassination, and now Idop was standing before his commander and close friend, Ameer Tondo.

"It's good to see you, Idop. Have you come to personally report that the Anderez Brigade is formed and ready for battle?" Tondo asked.

"It will be ready to join the army when the weather turns fair," Idop promised, "but that's not why I've come to Rendoto." By Idop's demeanor, Tondo could tell that something dire had brought him here. Tondo's smile dropped from his face as he waited for Idop to continue. "A couple of wernts ago, three Showton assassins made their way into the Anderez palace at night, most likely planning to kill me. Their plot was foiled at the last instant by a groundshake. It awoke everyone in the palace, and the guards assembled. I killed one of the assassins, another was captured, but the third escaped."

"The timing of that groundshake must be more than good luck. The gods are protecting you, my fortunate friend," Tondo said as his smile returned. "Is that what you came to tell me?" Tondo asked, a bit mystified by his subordinate's need to make his report in person. Idop signaled an aide, and T´uft was brought into the room, held in bindings, and placed before Tondo. T´uft looked up into Tondo's blue eyes and shuddered. "Is this the assassin you captured? Why bring him to me?" Tondo wondered.

"He was carrying this," Idop told him as he pulled Maaryah's medal from his jerkin and handed it to Tondo. He watched as his commander's eyes examined it, and then Tondo's glare locked onto the assassin standing before him. Tondo's aura ignited, and the room turned red. He dropped the medal, and his eyes went wild. He lunged at the bound man in front of him, pushing T´uft to the floor, and then he began slamming his right fist into the man's face over and over. Idop and the guards stepped back, escaping the heat of Tondo's burning vengeance as he continued pummeling his victim.

"Tondo, stop; you'll kill him!" Idop yelled. Tondo continued his assault, undaunted. "Tondo, he may know where Maari is!" Idop yelled. Tondo's fist stopped in mid-swing, and he stood. He took a deep breath and forced his aura down. The enraged Tondo stood staring at the unconscious T´uft, whose face had been turned into a bloody mess, the prisoner's clothes smoldering from the heat of Tondo's vengeful aura.

After he had calmed, Tondo moved in front of Idop. "Has he said anything about Maari?"

"He hasn't said a word since we captured him. When we begin to question the brigand, it's like he goes into a trance and becomes oblivious to everything around him. Even pain doesn't bring him out of it, and he stays like that for segments. The dead assassin had this," Idop told him as he handed Tondo the Victor's Laurel. Tondo examined it and handed it back to Idop.

"I'll make him talk," Tondo declared. "Fetch me a large bucket full of water," he ordered an aide. The aide dashed out and soon returned, carrying a heavy wooden bucket with water slopping over its brim. The aide quickly handed it to his commander. Tondo walked over to the unconscious T´uft and set the bucket down next to him. Tondo grabbed him by the scruff of the neck, pushed his head into the bucket, and held it there. It wasn't long before T´uft regained consciousness and began struggling. Tondo continued shoving the brigand's head under the bloody water, keeping it submerged for a long time as the other men in the room started to squirm at the sight. Finally, Tondo released his prisoner, and T´uft rolled away from the bucket, coughing and sputtering as he took in huge gulps of air.

After T´uft stopped coughing, Tondo knelt beside him and pulled him up until their noses nearly touched. "You're going to tell me everything I want to know," Tondo snarled. T´uft weakly smiled, rolled his eyes back, and fell into a stupor. "Okay, so you want to do this the hard way. Good, just what I want!" Tondo growled. He lifted T´uft's limp body, stuffed his head into the bucket again, and held it there until his prisoner began struggling once more. After a long delay, Tondo pulled the manslayer's head above the water level. "I can keep this up all day," Tondo declared, and then he stuffed his prisoner's head back into the bucket and held it there as the man's legs kicked and his body contorted. After another lengthy delay, Tondo pulled his suffering victim up and let him catch his breath, but only for an instant. He then stuffed T´uft's head back into the bucket.

"Tondo!" Idop cried, "You're going to kill him this way. Stop! This isn't you."

"Ha, it's me, all right!" Tondo lifted T´uft's head above the water. "If this vestang doesn't talk, he may as well be drowned," Tondo growled. He then pushed the brigand's head into the bucket again.

T´uft was growing weaker, and Tondo could feel his victim's strength failing. He pulled T´uft up and tossed him aside like a rag doll. "Fill the bucket again," he ordered. Another bucket was brought in, and it filled the other. Tondo hovered over T´uft like a raptor preparing to swoop down on its prey. The assassin attempted to crawl away, but Tondo grabbed him by the foot and dragged him back to the bucket. He held his prisoner's face just above the water level. "Are you ready to tell me what I want to know?" he growled in an angry voice.

"Never!" T´uft screamed.

Tondo pushed the assassin's head under the bloody water and held it there until T´uft stopped struggling, and then he pulled him up. T´uft didn't move, and the others thought he'd been killed.

"Wake him up. I'm not done with him, not by a long-shot," Tondo barked using a godspeak term. Tondo's victim was prodded, pushed, and slapped until he began moving again. When he did, Tondo grabbed him and held his face just above the water level. "Are you ready to talk, or would you like some more of this? And believe me, I'm enjoying it."

T´uft nodded, "Hoy! Ha. All right, enough," he said in a dispirited tone.

"Good," Tondo growled. He lifted his prisoner and plopped him into a chair, his arms still bound. "Everybody out!" he ordered. "Idop, you can stay." Tondo grabbed another chair and sat across from the bound man. Water and blood dripped from the brigand's face and hair. "Tell me your name," Tondo ordered.

"T′uft."

"How did you get this?" Tondo asked as he picked up Maaryah's medal and held it in front of the assassin's face.

"My master gave it to me."

"What's your master's name, and how did he come by it?"

"He's called the Dark One. He was in the Big House when I went in, and he tossed it to me," T′uft admitted.

"So, you were one of those who raided my estate. Did you attack the woman in the Big House?" Tondo thundered, his anger seething.

"No," was T′uft's curt reply.

"Then, who did?" Tondo demanded. The prisoner delayed answering, so Tondo got up, placed the bucket between their chairs, and then sat again. T′uft stared at it in horror. "Who attacked the woman?" Tondo barked.

T′uft took a deep breath, "May Munnevo forgive me. My master did," he replied.

"The Dark One?" Tondo questioned. T′uft nodded. "You took a young girl with you when you left. Is she alive?" Tondo's blue eyes were burning into his victim's soul. The discouraged man nodded again. "Where is she?"

"The Showton sent her to his city some time ago. That's all I know."

"His city?" Tondo wondered.

"Fortress Showtonia, on the coast south of Panemento," T′uft volunteered.

"How far south?"

"I guess, ten marches or so," T´uft told him.

"Where's she being held in the city?"

"I don't know. Probably the Showton's castle," the prisoner replied, his eyes fixed on the bucket at his feet.

Tondo grabbed him by the jerkin and pulled him closer, his blue eyes burning into T´uft's dark-brown eyes. Tondo's glare continued for a long time as his tzaah probed the prisoner's veracity; the assassin groaned under the big man's probing glare. Tondo finally pushed him back into the chair.

"Guards!" Tondo called. Two guards quickly entered. "Take this man and watch him closely," he ordered. The guards lifted T´uft out of his chair and literally carried him away. "Idop, have Harmon assemble the Rangers," Tondo ordered.

"Hoy? You're not planning to go to that place, this Fortress Showtonia, are you? That would be madness! Anyway, I don't trust this brigand. Something seems very wrong about all this. When the assassins were discovered, I thought I saw the one who escaped hit T´uft in the back of the head and knock him out. I didn't believe my eyes, but now that I've learned the rest, I think this is a trap," Idop warned.

Tondo pondered his lieutenant's words as he paced back and forth, rubbing his brow and flexing his bruised knuckles. After many long moments, he stopped his pacing and faced Idop. "Trap or not, I can't allow Maari to languish in some prison now that I know where she is."

"Even if she's still in the city, how will you find her? She could be anywhere," Idop warned.

"If she's there, I'll find her," Tondo answered.

"How?"

Tondo didn't reply and simply thumped his chest, the center of his tzaah. "Now, fetch Harmon and the Rangers," Tondo repeated.

Two segments had passed since his confrontation with the captured manslayer. Tondo was standing in the middle of a hollow square formed by the Rangers, twenty-five men to a side. The Ranger unit had been increased to half-troop size and consisted of one-hundred highly trained and motivated men. These were the warriors who would lead the way and engage in perilous missions. They knew the risks and reveled in them.

"Rangers, At Ease!" Tondo began, and the men relaxed. "I have assembled you here to make a personal request. I plan to conduct a dangerous mission, and I need some men willing to go with me. This is not an official army operation, and it is hazardous. Many, possibly all, of those involved may not return. I am looking for a handful of volunteers willing to risk their lives by following me into a deadly place. I cannot say more about this operation, other than we will be taking the boat after it arrives. No one will think less of you if you choose not to volunteer. If you are willing to go with me, take one step forward." Without hesitation, all one-hundred men stepped forward. A lump grew in Tondo's throat, and he blinked back the tears forming in his Munnari blue eyes. These men were indeed his best, willing to risk all by following him into danger. "Thank you, men, but I can't take all of you. Sutrum Sestardus

Harmon, I assign you the task of selecting eight men to go with me," Tondo ordered.

"Zerr, it would help if I knew the details of the mission," Harmon responded.

"Yes, of course. Dismiss the Rangers but keep them nearby. We'll meet as soon as they're released and go over what I have in mind," Tondo told him. He then ordered the formation to Attention and turned it over to Harmon. Tondo returned to his headquarters.

A quarter-segment later, a serious-looking Harmon exited Tondo's HQ and quickly marched to the waiting Rangers. Everyone was still there; no one had left the area. Harmon ordered the men into rank formation and at attention. After a short delay, as he pondered his assignment, he called seven names, "Pundi, Tindo, Gando, Mundez, Vetz, Sensi, and Brand. The men whose names I've called will meet with me. The rest of you are Dismissed." The formation broke up, and many disappointed faces could be seen. The chosen men gathered around Harmon.

"You only called seven names, sutrum sestardus. The ameer said he wanted eight," Brand noted.

"I'm the eighth man. The ameer has discovered where his daughter is being held. Maari is my second daughter, my daughter's daughter. My love for her is so great, I am willing to trade my life for hers," Harmon responded. "All right, men, sit down and hear me out. The ameer doesn't want this information released until after we've left on the boat, so if I learn that any of you have opened your big mouth, I'll have your skin, and you'll be off the mission. Understood?"

“What’s the plan, sutrum sestardus,” Gando asked.

“We’re going to free Maari. There’s no guarantee she’s still where he was told she is, but he has to try to find her and bring her home. We’ll be going into that vile Showton’s own city, just the nine of us, and rescue her. Also, there’s a possibility we’ll be walking into a trap,” Harmon explained, and he watched as the men looked at one another in surprise. He paused for a few moments to let his words sink in, then he continued, “If any man wishes to change his mind, me and the ameer will understand.” No one responded, so Harmon continued, “This is your last chance to back out. We’ll start preparing and training as soon as we’re done here, and once you’re on the boat, there’s no turning back.” Harmon paused again and waited, his eyes scanning the faces of the chosen Rangers.

Finally, Vetz spoke up, “Sutrum sestardus, you know none of us are going to back out and let the ameer down. As for me, I’d follow him into the domain of the Five Shadows,” the Ranger said with a chuckle. The other men joined in with laughs of their own, accompanied by their own comments of dedication to their commander.

“Good!” Harmon exclaimed, “Let’s get to work.”

Several days after Tondo’s meeting with the Rangers, the *Anterra* tied off at the Rendoto dock. The gangplank was put in place, and a contingent of Te Femma elite guards scurried down it. Four guards proceeded to a point position well off the dock. The remaining guards formed a double column facing each other from the lower end of the gangplank and across the landing to dry land. Several arbons scurried down to the dock and gathered together near the point-guards. The unfolding scene had stopped all work in the area as everyone wondered at the unexpected activity. Two Te Femma Brigade warriors, enjoying some off-duty time nearby, knew precisely what was happening: Queen Ezora had arrived, making an unexpected visit.

The queen soon appeared and deliberately strode down the gangplank, closely followed by Rana Fardinza. The queen and her senior adviser marched across the dock and onto solid ground; they looked around. The rana noticed the two Te Femma warriors nearby and waved them over.

The two sister warriors quickly scrambled to the queen and kneeled. "Your Highness, how may we serve you?" one asked.

"One of you announce my arrival to Megatus Maaryah. I've come to inspect the brigade. The other, take two arbons to the city's governing authority . . . rana, what's he called?" the queen asked.

"He's called the Augusta, Your Highness," the rana told her.

"Take the two arbons to the Augusta so they can announce my arrival. I'm curious to learn how this government chosen by the people functions. You may go," the queen ordered. The two warriors stood, gave the queen a Te Femma salute, and dashed off to their assignments.

Maaryah was sitting on her samaran, watching a troop of newly arrived Te Femma replacements going through their drills, when one of her aides galloped up and saluted. "Zerr," the aide breathlessly began, "Queen Ezora has arrived by boat and wishes to inspect the brigade."

Maaryah returned the aide's salute, then ordered, "Have Neva Megatus Zuni and Dori assemble the brigade."

"Zerr, Neva Megatus Zuni has already ordered the brigade assembled. She suggests you meet the queen at the dock. She is sending appropriate transportation for Her Highness," the aide told her. Maaryah smiled. Zuni was an excellent subcommander who didn't wait for orders unless necessary.

"Excellent," Maaryah replied. "You come with me. Have you ever met the queen?" Maaryah asked the aide.

"No, zerr," she responded.

"Ha, Neva Megato Donnie, this is your lucky day." The two women turned their mounts and ambled off in the direction of the city dock.

By the time Tondo learned of the queen's arrival, she had already met with Maaryah. He'd been informed that she was currently on her way to the Te Femma Brigade's assigned district in the city.

"Idop, this is it. The Rangers and I are off. You'll have to meet with the queen. Please convey my apologies for not being here," Tondo said.

"The queen's not the one I'm worried about meeting. Maaryah will be madder than a wet frizzard, and I'm afraid she'll take her anger out on me," Idop told him.

"She's never killed a one-eyed man before, and I doubt she'll start now," Tondo said over his shoulder as he exited his headquarters on his way to the nearby dock.

Tondo and Yaddet stood near the tiller of the *Anterra*, watching a red p´atezas sinking slowly below the horizon as Hermanez guided the ship out to the open sea.

"Maaryah won't be the only one madder than a wet frizzard. The queen will be, too," Hermanez warned.

"Can't be helped, boatmaster," Tondo replied.

The following morning, Rana Fardinza entered the queen's room displaying a worried expression. "Rana, why the concerned look on such a beautiful day? What is troubling you?" she asked.

"Your Highness, I've been informed that the boat has departed. It left as night was falling."

"Hoy! Boatmaster Hermanez assured me he would remain here until I was ready to return to Te Femma. I don't like being stranded. Megatus Maaryah is a friend of his. Speak with her and learn if she knows what's happening. I don't appreciate this surprise."

After her short meeting with Rana Fardinza, Maaryah and the rana rushed to Tondo's headquarters to determine why the boat had left without warning. The two women were ushered into the ameer's office and found Idop waiting there.

"Megatus Maaryah, Rana Fardinza, how may I help you?" Idop said with a smile; however, Maaryah detected a hint of worry in his unpatched eye.

"Boatmaster Hermanez promised the queen he would remain here until she was ready to return to Te Femma. Do you know why he left so abruptly and when he'll return?" Maaryah asked.

"The boat was needed for an urgent mission that couldn't wait," Idop told her.

"I wasn't informed of an urgent mission. What is it?" Maaryah asked. Idop did not immediately respond, giving Maaryah a worrisome clue. "Idop, what's going on; where's Tondo?" she asked, her tone expressing her sudden concern. Rana Fardinza watched the exchange between these two close friends and quickly surmised something very serious was in the works. Idop walked to a small table near a wall and removed a cloth covering two items. He picked them up and handed them to Maaryah. Her eyes widened as she stared at the medal and laurel.

"A few wernts ago, assassins tried to kill me in Anderez. One was killed, one escaped, and one was captured alive. They were carrying these awards. I brought the captured assassin here, and Tondo got him to reveal where Maari may be held."

"Tondo has taken the boat to fetch her!" Maaryah exclaimed, hardly able to contain her joy.

"He's going to the Showton's own city with a handful of Rangers, including Harmon. I fear for them," Idop admitted.

Maaryah's joy was quickly dashed. "What do you mean?"

"I think it's a trap, and I told him so. He wouldn't listen to reason. You know how stubborn he can be. Now, he's off, 'Into the belly of the beast,' as he put it," Idop explained. Maaryah's worry grew, and tears filled her eyes. Her son was dead, her daughter abducted, and now, her bondmate, and her father were engaged in a desperate and potentially deadly rescue mission. She couldn't bear to hear anymore, and she bolted from the room with Rana Fardinza on her heels.

Maaryah never said a word on their journey back to the Te Femma Brigade area, and she wiped away tears as they ran down her cheeks. She dashed into brigade headquarters and right past Dori. She rushed through the door that led to her quarters and quickly slammed it shut.

"What's wrong with her?" Dori wondered as she looked to the rana for an answer.

"The ameer has left on a dangerous mission to rescue their daughter. He may be going into a trap."

"Oy! I'll go to her," Dori offered.

"No, let her be for now. She needs to be left alone with her worrisome tears. I must take my leave and tell the queen what is happening," the rana said, and then she left.

"Your Highness, the boat left because Ameer Tondo has mounted a rescue mission for his daughter, and Sutrum Sestardus Harmon, Maaryah's father, went with him. It could be a trap. Maaryah is beside herself with worry," the rana told the queen.

"That poor child. She's lost a son and a daughter, and now she may lose her broesayr and father. I must go to her and offer what comfort I can," the queen told the rana.

The door to Maaryah's quarters slowly opened, and the queen quietly entered. She moved through the living room to the only other door and quietly opened it. Maaryah was lying on her bed, sobbing. Queen Ezora entered the room and silently closed the door. She moved across the room and sat on the foot of the bed. When she did, Maaryah noticed her and sat up. She quickly wiped the tears from her eyes and took a deep breath, attempting to gain control of her emotions.

"My sister, do not be ashamed of your tears. You have suffered much, and you are heavily laden with worry. Here, let me hold you," the queen offered. Maaryah fell into the queen's embrace as her tears began flowing again, her body shaking as she sobbed. "To love a man so is a blessing . . . and a curse. I envy you, and I sorrow with you. He's in the hands of deity now. May the gods bless his mission and safeguard their Messenger, granting him a speedy and safe return."

# CHAPTER 26

# MUNNARI ECLIPSED

Hermanez pulled out his charts and laid them on the table in the boatmaster's cabin. "Before all this nasty business with the Showton started, I charted most of the coastlines of the Great Gulf," he said as he searched through his charts. Tondo said nothing and only watched. "Ha, there it is. Panemento is here, and I suspect the Showton's city is somewhere along this coastline," the boatmaster said, pointing to areas on the chart.

"When will we get there?" Tondo asked.

"Two days, if the weather holds. We can't just sail up to the city's dock, if it has one, and tie off. If you're planning to make this raid at night, I'll have to find a cove near the city and let you off there," Hermanez explained. The usually mirthful boatmaster had been deadly serious and all business since they left Rendoto.

"We must remain far out to sea during the day and only approach the coast at night. Don't want no Showton eyes seeing our sails in daylight," Tondo warned. He paused in thought for a moment, then continued, "We can scan for lights at night and hopefully learn the city's location that way. When we find it, I will need to go ashore a few times at night to explore and probe the area. I also need to learn where in the city Maari is being held."

"One trip to shore is dangerous enough, and now you tell me you'll be making several. You'll be dodging Showton guards, but don't forget, terrors are out there, too. Idop is right; you're Munnoga-touched," Hermanez carped.

"It must be done. I can't conduct this mission without reliable information. Right now, I have none," Tondo explained. Hermanez simply growled, revealing his displeasure with the ameer's audacity.

A few nights later, Tondo and Hermanez, aided by their farseers, noticed a collection of lights onshore. The following night, Hermanez guided the *Anterra* to a cove south of the lights. Tondo, Harmon, and two Rangers climbed into a longboat and oared their way toward shore. The four men rowed as quietly as they could. They feared drawing the attention of someone on the beach, but they also didn't want to attract any terrors that might be lurking in the area.

They reached land safely, and Tondo and Harmon moved inland. The other two Rangers pulled the small longboat into the trees, covered its track in the sand as well as they could, and waited for the other men to return. Tondo figured he had less than four segments to collect as much information as possible before returning to the ship well before first light. Hermanez needed two to three segments to move the boat out to the open sea and beyond sight of land.

Tondo's first night of reconnoitering confirmed that they had found Fortress Showtonia. He and Harmon also learned that all of the gates to the city were closed at dusk and secured until first light on the following day. On the party's return to the ship, they sighted a terror's ominous dorsal fin. Tondo altered his plan and told Hermanez his party would remain ashore and not return to the boat for the next two days. He would then return and make final plans for the rescue attempt. During the two days ashore, he and Harmon found a secluded area of the city wall they felt was scalable and not too distant from the castle's wall. Tondo also received a distinct impression that Maari was held in the southeast tower. After two days and nights ashore, he and his party returned to the ship and made their final plans.

A mild *Zerio* squall blew in from the southwest, delaying the rescue attempt for another day, but Tondo and his Rangers were ready to go after it passed. It was an overcast night, dark and cold, faint skyglow from the moons' light, diffused by the clouds, provided just enough light for the men to see a short distance. They rowed the longboat as quietly as possible, hoping to make it to shore without notice. Unfortunately, Tondo's luck had run out, and a giant dorsal fin was seen circling their small craft.

"Tondo, we've got an unwelcome visitor," Harmon whispered as he pointed toward the fin taller than a man moving toward them. The men pulled their oars harder, and the longboat's speed increased, but all knew that if the beast chose to strike, they could not escape its hideous jaws. The fin circled the boat two times as every man's eyes nervously followed it. During its third circuit, the monstrous terror turned and headed straight for the craft.

"Here it comes!" one of the Rangers shouted in horror.

"Quiet!" Tondo ordered in a whisper. He raised his right arm, and a bolt of lightning streamed from his fist, striking the water in front of the rapidly advancing fin. The terror rolled onto its side and then went belly up, its momentum causing it to gently nudge the craft's stern, shoving it sideways and spinning it around. The men rowed furiously, pulling away from the monster as Tondo pushed the tiller over, correcting their course. After a few moments, the beast wiggled its body, rolled over, and disappeared into the depths. Tondo looked into the blackened, smiling faces of all eight comrades from his position at the tiller, their wide, bright eyes and white teeth reflecting the dim light streaming down from the moons' and stars' scattered light.

It wasn't long after their encounter with the terror, the boat landed on the sandy beach. The men quickly scrambled out and carried it into the trees. Two Rangers swept away the party's footprints in the sand using bush branches as brooms. These two men were to remain with the boat and guard it. Tondo and the other six Rangers headed toward the city, carefully avoiding two sentries patrolling the beach not far from where they had landed. Tondo moved his party into the woods and approached the city from the landward side. During his reconnaissance, it had become clear to Tondo that the city was well guarded both outside and inside. This fact led him to conclude that Idop was probably right. They were moving into a trap; however, he knew from experience that it was challenging to remain one-hundred percent vigilant one-hundred percent of the time, and he was sure it was no different for the Showton's guards.

Tondo and his Rangers soon reached the portion of the wall they intended to scale. A grapnel and rope were handed to him. He stepped back, swung the rope, and tossed the line and hook upward as far as possible but well short of the wall's parapet. Using his inner-power, he pushed and guided the grapnel until it cleared the rampart, lodging in the cracks of the stone. He could feel his inner-power declining, first by the substantial effort in warding off the immense terror and now this.

Nevertheless, Tondo had to press on, and sensing his daughter's nearness drove him onward as he climbed the rope, crossed over the parapet, and moved into the shadows. Harmon and three more Rangers also made the climb. The other two men remained at ground level, guarding the rope, the other's planned escape route.

A sentry soon appeared, making his usual rounds. Silently, Tondo signaled for one of the Rangers to take him out, which was done with deadly efficiency. The Ranger quickly changed into the sentry's armor and began patrolling the wall. The Showton sentry's body was pushed over the outside of the parapet, and the two Rangers on the ground drug it into the woods and covered it with foliage. Tondo and the remaining three men quickly and silently moved to the inner wall, scaling it next.

They were now within reach of the southeast tower, where Tondo was sure Maari was being held. One of the Rangers coiled the grappling line they had just used and threw it across his back. The four men then headed across the castle courtyard and through a doorway, Tondo leading the way. They scurried up several staircase levels, stopping at its highest point. Tondo carefully looked around a corner. He saw two guards flanking a door, a doorway he could feel that led to Maari. He ducked back to the head of the stairs and silently instructed his team on their next move. He returned to the hallway corner with his three companions closely following. He waved his arm, and a small table in an alcove on the far side of the guards fell over, and the statue resting on it shattered on the stone floor, scattering shards in all directions. The two sentries immediately turned and faced the noise, and their backs turned toward Tondo and his men. Two Rangers silently charged the guards, and the sentries were down in a flash, hardly making a sound. Tondo and Harmon rushed to the door, removed the latch pin, and moved into the room as the other two Rangers dragged the unconscious guards' in and quietly closed the door. It took the men a few moments for their eyes to adjust to the near darkness after going through the torch-lit hallway. In the faint light streaming through the window opening, Tondo saw a bed and a small, dark-haired child sleeping there. He moved to her, kneeled, and gently covered her mouth with his hand. An instant later, Maari's eyes bolted open. She gasped and attempted to roll away, but Tondo held her in place. He leaned over her and moved his face just above hers, "It's Parr, my girl. You must be quiet," he whispered. Maari's eyes became even wider as she wrapped her little arms around her father's neck. He removed his hand from her mouth and embraced her.

"I knew you'd come. I knew you'd rescue me," she sobbed in joyous relief.

"Quiet, it's a dangerous time; we must move silently and quickly," Tondo warned as his eyes filled with tears of happiness. She nodded in understanding, rolled out of bed, and into the arms of the kneeling Harmon.

"Parr-parr!" she exclaimed.

"Shush!" he warned. She hugged him and went silent.

Unexpectedly, the door burst open, and a person rushed in. "What's going on here?" Purda demanded.

Mundez grabbed her from behind and held a knife to her throat as he kicked the door shut. "Make another sound, and it will be your last," he warned.

"No!" Maari shouted. Harmon shushed her again.

"What are you doing here, old woman?" Tondo demanded.

"She's Purda. Please, don't hurt her!" Maari cried.

"You picked a bad time to come in here," Tondo told her.

"I heard a noise in the hallway and noticed the guards were missing. Maari is my charge, and I had to make sure she was all right. Are you her parr?" Tondo nodded. "You must go. Both the Showton and the Dark One are here. They've been waiting for you."

"We're about to leave. Harmon, take Maari," Tondo ordered, and then he headed for the door.

"Don't go! It's nearly time for the guards to be changed, and you'll be seen and outnumbered," Purda warned.

"Okay, we'll go out the window," he said, causing a look of wonder to fill Purda's face. Without orders, Mundez planted the grapnel in the window's corner and dropped the rope over the outside. Tondo signaled for him to go, and he rappelled down to the castle wall walk thirty feet below. The second Ranger, Vetz, quickly rappelled down and waited at the rope in case Maari fell.

Harmon prepared Maari. "Now, climb on my back and hold tight."

"Wait!" she cried. She dashed to the table, grabbed her outing case, and threw the flap open. She held it in front of herself and waited. Little Tumper leaped from its hiding place atop the wardrobe to the bed and then to Maari's shoulder. The little creature scampered down her arm and disappeared into the purse-like bag. Tondo and Harmon watched in wonder as Maari closed the flap and put her arm through the strap, moving the bag until it was hanging down the center of her back.

"Quickly, my girl, climb aboard," Harmon urged. She did as she was told. "Hold tight now; it's a long way down." He stepped onto the table that Mundez had placed below the window and climbed through, his legs hanging over the edge. He then wrapped the rope around the D-ring attached to his harness and pushed off, sliding down the rope and landing with a quiet thud when his sandaled feet hit the stone wall walk.

After Harmon and Maari dropped from view, Tondo turned to Purda, "All right, we'll do the same. Climb on my back; you're going with us."

"No," Purda exclaimed. "I'm too old and frail to make this escape; I'll only slow you down. I will use my wits. Now, cut me here," she said, pointing to her left shoulder.

"Are you absolutely sure you want it this way?" Tondo asked, his eyes wide in surprise.

"Ha! Now, be quick about it," she demanded. Tondo didn't have time to debate the issue, so he brought his sword down on her shoulder with a partial swing, and she gave a muffled cry of pain. Then, in a labored tone, she groaned, "You must knock me unconscious; don't delay." He punched her in the forehead, and she went down. He went to the window and slid down the rope in a flash. When he reached the wall walk, he whipped the rope, loosening the grapnel, and with a bit of help from his inner-power, the hook came free and plummeted downward. It stopped in mid-air before it was about to hit the stone, and Tondo grabbed it. He then began coiling the rope. Tondo tossed it and the grapnel to Vetz, who readied them for another descent by the party. Mundez was ordered to rappel first and quickly slid down the rope. With Maari still on his back, Harmon went next, and as they climbed over the parapet, the sound of many approaching feet caught their attention.

"Go! Get Maari away from here. Don't wait for me. Remember my standing order." Tondo shouted. Harmon rappeled down and stood near Mundez. Tondo yelled to Vetz, "Hurry, I'll cover you!".

"No, zerr, you go first!" Vetz shouted back. For an instant, the two men were locked in a battle of wills, only to be broken by the appearance of two veiled and dark-robed men followed by a gaggle of guards.

"See, Nevesant, I told you he'd come!" the Showton blustered.

"He's a bigger fool than I guessed," the Dark One scoffed as he drew his black sword and pointed it at Tondo. Vetz advanced and confronted the Dark One. Tondo could feel the black-robed villain's tzaah preparing to lash out at the Ranger approaching him, and Tondo blocked it with his inner-power. The Showton watched the three men as they engaged in combat; Vetz with his sword, Tondo with his unseen power, and Nevesant with both. Suddenly, the Dark One was blasted backward, slamming into the castle tower's stone wall, propelled there by a blast of energy from Tondo that was not only felt but could be seen as a rippling wave. The Dark One lay unmoving. For an instant, the Showton was shocked by what he had seen, but he quickly recovered and engaged Tondo, assaulting him with bolts of purple energy.

Tondo's lone ally, Vetz, was set upon by several Showton guards, and he was forced backward toward the parapet. While shielding himself from the purple energy streaming toward him, Tondo pulled his tomahawk from his belt and let it fly, slaying one of the guards about to strike down his comrade from the rear. Tondo continued slapping aside the Showton's purple bolts, and they ricocheted in all directions, one deflected bolt slamming into a Showton guard, killing him outright. Another guard circled to the rear of Vetz and was about to strike a killing blow when Tondo threw his sword like a spear at the assailant, piercing his chest and propelling him over the wall. His body crashed to the courtyard, landing near Harmon's feet, causing Maari to shriek in horror.

"Don't delay!" went the call from Vetz above. Harmon quickly retrieved Tondo's sword, then he and Mundez dashed to the outer wall. The Ranger posing as the sentry had dispatched the two guards stationed at a side gate, allowing the other two Rangers waiting on the outside of the city, Sensi and Brand, to enter. Harmon's collection of Rangers heard the approach of several men, so they quickly dashed through the woods. Unexpectedly, Sensi and Brand turned and moved toward the approaching threat, preparing to take them on and allowing the others to make their escape.

The Dark One struggled to his feet and tried to regain his bearings. The first thing he saw was one of the guards falling over the edge of the wall. He watched as another guard fell to the blade of the skilled fighter the others were confronting. The Dark One took a deep breath and advanced into the fray; his black sword pointed at Vetz. Tondo could feel the Dark One's inner-power rising again, and he watched as a black aura surrounded the man in dark robes. Simultaneously, the Showton's assault grew more intense, and it was all Tondo could do to protect himself. As the Dark One advanced on the Ranger, the guards felt the chill of his aura and scattered. Nevesant swept the air with his left arm, and Vetz was blasted over the wall, and he smashed onto the hard courtyard far below, his body bloody and broken.

Tondo was left alone to face the Showton, the Dark One, and a steadily increasing cohort of guards. He dug deep within himself and called upon the reserves of his inner-power. He blasted forth his chain lightning, but the Showton blocked it. He could feel himself weakening and realized his fending off the terror and his other tzaah efforts had reduced his reserve of energy more than he realized.

The guards began to advance on him, their weapons reflecting the light of the Showton's purple energy and Tondo's red aura. Tondo reached over his shoulder, pulled his short sword from its scabbard, and waved it threateningly at the advancing guards. The Dark One focused, and his black energy pushed toward Tondo as a red shielding bubble appeared, protecting Tondo from the dark, menacing rays.

Harmon, still carrying Maari on his back, and the two remaining Rangers accompanying him made it to the hidden longboat and the two Rangers guarding it. The four Rangers quickly dragged and carried the boat to the water's edge. Harmon lifted Maari from his back and placed her in the boat.

"Sit, child, and don't move!" he ordered in a stern and worried tone. He turned and looked toward the castle, amazed by the purple and red glow lighting the castle walls and reflecting in flashes from the clouds above.

The Showton's and Dark One's combined powers continued to bear down on Tondo. His red bubble was beginning to shrink as his inner-power ebbed. A Showton palace guard cautiously moved around him and carefully approached from behind. The guard raised his pole-arm and slammed it onto Tondo's red energy shield. The weapon shattered, and the guard was thrown backward and knocked prone. Tondo was driven to his knees, and his red aura began to shrink even more.

Harmon and the remaining Rangers watched in horror as the red light streaming from the castle faded and went out. As they watched, the purple glow grew brighter, and they feared the ameer had been overcome. The shouts of angry men were heard, and the Rangers turned to see twenty or more Showton guards charging along the beach, heading directly toward them.

"Shove off and get in the boat!" Harmon ordered.

"The ameer, we can't leave him!" Pundi cried in desperation.

"We can't help him now. His orders are to return to the boat. We've got what we came for," Harmon shouted. The men shoved the boat into the surf and jumped aboard. They began rowing with all their might, pulling away from the beach as quickly as possible, ignoring all concern for the terrors.

"Parr! Where's Parr? Don't leave him!" Maari wailed. The men didn't respond, tears streaming down their blackened cheeks as they pulled at the oars with all their might.

Startlingly, a pike splashed into the water next to the boat. Several more pikes followed, one hitting the boat's transom and sticking there. Harmon, manning the tiller, reached back and dislodged it, letting it drop into the longboat's wake. He took one last look over his shoulder, and as he did, he saw the clouds over the castle parting, revealing Munnevo eclipsing Munnari. Harmon turned forward and hung his head, his heart breaking.

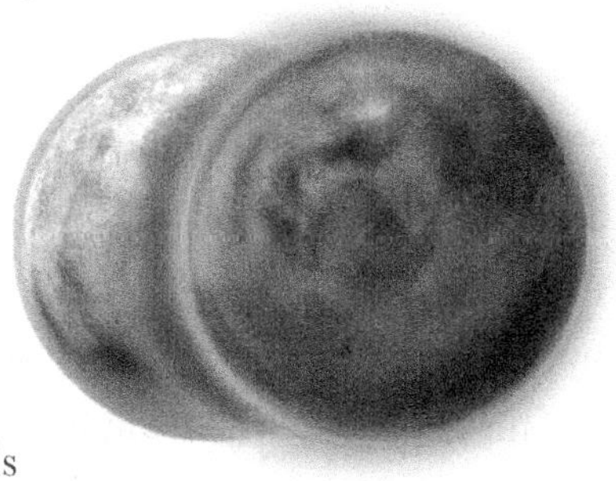

The longboat reached the *Anterra* without further incident. Maari was handed up to a pair of boaters, and the remaining Rangers climbed aboard, Harmon being the last. Boatmaster Hermanez watched in disbelief as the longboat emptied, and Tondo was nowhere to be seen.

"Harmon," he called, "where's the ameer?"

"He fell!" was Harmon's painful reply.

"What are my orders?" Hermanez asked.

"You know what his standing orders are, 'Return to Rendoto with or without him,'" Harmon reminded the boatmaster. Painfully and reluctantly, Hermanez ordered the stone anchors aweigh and the sails raised.

# CHAPTER 27

# THE DULLARDS' GUEST

Early the following day, the Sutro Showton sat in judgment of the guards who had failed to apprehend the invaders who'd retrieved the girl. His Munnevo-red eyes displayed his anger, and his tone emphasized his frustration at losing his prize, the little girl named Maari, causing his aura to ignite, surrounding him in a pale purple glow that sizzled and snapped. His attendants and guards shuddered at the display, for they feared greatly whenever their master was upset. In the past, it had always led to death, sometimes many deaths. Obviously, the twenty or so guards lying prostrate before him would receive a severe punishment for their failure. The only remaining question was, would the Showton's anger strike out at others?

"Defetane Ant´ebbo, were you the commander of the guard last night?" the Showton growled.

"Yes, master," one of the men groveling at the Showton's feet feebly answered.

"You were advised that an attempt would be made to take the girl. Why did you allow her to escape?"

"It couldn't be helped, master. The intruders were very skilled and efficient in their attack. I truly didn't expect them to come by sea," the defetane replied, his voice quavering.

"Were you not advised to watch both land and sea?"

"Yes, master, but a terror has been feeding offshore for several wernts. Only insanity would guide men coming from the sea," the defetane whimpered.

"It appears they were Munnoga-touched enough to succeed due to your lack of vigilance. Attendant Superior Neehoer, how many lashes does it take to kill a man?" the Showton grumbled.

"It's commonly believed that forty lashes from a heavy tamer will result in death, Your Excellency," the attendant replied.

"See that this man is given forty-one. Inform the flogger that if the defetane remains alive after forty-one lashes, he will receive forty-one himself," the Showton declared.

"As you wish, Your Excellency," the attendant superior fawned.

"See that the others receive thirty-nine, and those who survive, strip them of their rank and pay. They will work as slaves in the army for five spans."

"Excellency, after the five spans are over, what's to be done with them?" Neehoer asked.

"Release them from my service and see that they never return. Brand their cheeks as a sign to everyone of their unworthiness," the Showton decreed. The attendant bowed in response. "Now, remove this worthless scum. I never want to see any of them again," the Showton proclaimed.

The unfortunate wretches were pushed and prodded out of the Showton's presence, many weeping in anticipation of their forthcoming brutal punishments. The Showton leaned back as his aura faded, but it still remained visible, crackling and snapping its ominous warning.

"Bring in the old woman," he ordered.

Purda was brought into the room by two guards holding her by the upper arms, her feet hardly touching the floor. When they were a couple of steps from the Showton platform, the guards shoved her down, and she collapsed in a heap, her face barely above the floor.

"Old woman," the Showton began, "where is the young girl I assigned to your keeping?"

"Master, she was taken from me by armed men. I tried to stop them, but I am only an old woman, weak and frail. When I intervened, they mercilessly sliced me with a weapon." She pulled aside the top of her bloody gown, exposing a nasty-looking sword cut on her left shoulder. "After they slashed me, one of them hit me with something, and I don't remember anything after that." She raised her head and looked up at the Showton, giving him a clear view of the large bruise on her forehead.

The Showton glared at her for several long and foreboding moments. He leaned back on the throne, and his Munnevo-red eyes gleamed as he chuckled, "It seems you are one of the few in this castle worthy of your keep." He turned to Attendant Superior Neehoer and ordered, "She will not be punished. However, since the child has been taken, there is no longer a need for her services. I release her from my favor. See that she is escorted out of the castle," he ordered. Neehoer nodded, and the two guards grabbed her by the upper arms and carried her out.

Purda and the guards marched down the castle hallways. She was taken through the main gateway of the fortress wall and dumped. The guards turned and marched back into the castle without saying a word. Purda sat on the ground, collecting her thoughts. She had survived her encounter with the Sutro Showton, certainly fairing better than the unfortunate ones summoned into the Great One's presence before her. But now, what was she to do? Her few personal items were in her room—what was once her room—in the castle. She didn't even have a cloak or a single eez coin. She had gone through hard times before, and she was a survivor, but she was much younger then. *What am I to do now? What am I to do when night falls? Where will I find shelter from the cold? How will I get my next meal? Could I beg for alms? she wondered silently. No! The cold-hearted residents of this wretched burg wouldn't part with a coin, even if it were carved from wood. I must rely on myself, my wits, and my own personal industry. But what is that to be now?* These disturbing thoughts cascaded over her, and she despaired. She began to weep.

Purda suffered through a miserable night. She went to the tree where she and Maari had gone to enjoy their outings. She covered the hard cold ground with branches from trees and bushes. She slept under a blanket of fallen leaves. In the morning, she awoke stiff, cold, and hungry. She waited near the main gate of the castle and was fortunate enough to meet a friend who served there, a friend who fetched her personal items and her pouch of eez coins—her life savings. Purda gave her friend five coins for her help, and then she moved on to a new life. She eventually became a washerwoman, serving the many guards and warriors who came and went in the Showton's city. It was a hard life, much harder than working in the castle, but she was still alive, and the thought that the little girl, Maari, was no longer in the clutches of the evil Showton gave her solace.

Tondo awoke, his body sore and stiff. He was sitting on a cold, stone floor where filthy, moldering straw lay. A small window in the stone, high above on the opposite wall, hardly more than a slit, provided scant illumination to his dungeon, and as he looked around, that was the best description he could think of: a dungeon. He took a deep breath, and the stench of this miserable place was sickening. His back was against the hard stone blocks of a wall, and his wrists were shackled to the stone at shoulder height. His ankles were also shackled, and chains extended to rings in the stone floor nearby. He felt something around his neck, but he couldn't see what it was.

"Well, todo, you're in a fine fix now," he mumbled to himself.

He then thought of Maari and the others and wondered if they'd made their escape. If they had, it was all worth it. Maaryah will be thrilled to be reunited with their daughter. Then he thought about the pain she would suffer when she learned he didn't return with the others. His poor bondmate, she had been through so much already. Now, she had to deal with that, as well.

He heard a sound and looked in the direction it was coming from. He saw a short man with a dirty face and hands, garbed in filthy clothes, coming toward him. Must be one of the guards, Tondo guessed. The scullion grabbed a torch from a nearby sconce and kneeled in front of Tondo, examining him from head to waist. His face drew closer to Tondo's, and in the torchlight, he could see the guard's green teeth, and as the guard's face came closer to his, he could smell the man's foul breath and rancid body odor.

The guard looked into Tondo's eyes, and his face beamed. He exclaimed, "Drueg, ya gotta see this. He does have blue eyes, just as they says." Another man, looking and smelling much like the other, approached and squatted in front of Tondo.

"Ha, you're right; now, if that don't beat all. Hoy, how did you get them blue peepers?" Drueg asked.

"I got them from my mother," Tondo answered, then he added, "Step back a bit. Your foul smell is killing me."

Both guards laughed uproariously, then Drueg leaned forward and said, "I don't think our smell's gonna kill ya. The master has plans for ya, and ya ain't gonna like 'em."

The other guard, holding the torch, leaned forward and examined Tondo's face. "Hoy, Drueg, what's that on his face?" Drueg came closer, took a long look, and then rubbed his stinking fingers down the left side of Tondo's face.

"Don't know, Moeg; it's kinda prickly," Drueg said. Moeg ran his filthy fingers down the right side of Tondo's face.

"Never seen noth'n like it. Hoy, what's on your face?" Moeg asked.

"It's called a beard or whiskers," Tondo told him using the godspeak terms.

"Drueg, did ya hear what he said? Does ya know what it means?" Moeg wondered. Drueg simply shook his head. "Oy, what ya say we have a little fun with this fool before we tell the masters he's awake?" Moeg asked.

"What's ya got in mind?" Drueg wondered with glee.

"I always like hearing big men scream, and he's a big 'un, he is," Moeg said with a smile. Tondo didn't like what he heard one bit, so he concentrated and focused his tzaah on a blast that would push the two reprobates away. When he released the surge of energy, nothing happened. He tried again, and again nothing happened. Suddenly, he felt vulnerable and naked.

Moeg stood, handed the torch to Drueg, went to an open-topped wooden box, pulled out a wicked-looking device, carried it back to Tondo's location, and dropped to a knee. Moeg held it in front of Tondo's face and said, "Big men cry like babies when I screw this down on their thumbs and fingers. I wonder how loud yer gonna scream," Moeg laughed. Drueg also whooped, continuing with annoying cackling snorts. Tondo was having none of it, at least not without a fight. He reared his head back, crunched his abdominal muscles, pushed off the wall with his shackled arms, and slammed his forehead into Moeg's nose. The degenerate fell backward, stunned, and groaning in pain. He grabbed his face and withered in misery, his legs kicking and bending in spasms of agony.

"He broke my nose! He broke my nose!" Moeg yelled in a muffled and distorted voice. He rose to his knees, blood gushing from his nostrils and pouring onto his filthy chest, legs, and the moldering straw on the floor. He pinched his nostrils closed with his left hand and snatched the torch from Drueg's grip with his right. "I'm gonna burn him. I'll roast those blue eyes of yern," he threatened, his words muffled and even more distorted.

"Don't do it, Moeg! Ya heard the master's orders," Drueg warned.

"I'm gonna make him pay, anyhow. If I can't burn him, I'll mash his fingers good! Grab his hand," Moeg ordered. Tondo formed a fist as Drueg did as he was told. With great effort, Drueg extended the fingers on Tondo's right hand and grabbed Tondo's thumb with his left. Moeg dropped the torch and picked up the thumbscrew from the floor where he had dropped it. Just as he was about to position it on Tondo's fingers, it went flying through the air, crashing at the feet of a wicked-looking man wearing black robes and a veil across the lower half of his face. The menacing-looking newcomer was standing at the base of the stone stairs. Tondo watched as the two guards turned, and as soon as they recognized who it was, they slinked away and groveled in front of the new arrival.

"I told you I was to be notified when he awoke. Why the delay, and why were you planning to use this device on him without my order?" the Dark One growled. He kicked the thumbscrew lying at his feet with the side of his sandaled foot, and it scooted across the floor and hit Moeg in the forehead.

The guard gave a muffled cry of pain, then he howled, "He broke my nose with his head, master. He needed to be taught some rah-spect," Moeg pleaded, his voice still distorted as blood gushed from his nostrils.

"I told you he was dangerous, and it appears you had to learn that for yourself, the hard way. Now, put that thing away, and don't bring it out again without the Showton's orders," the Dark One demanded. Moeg picked it up, slinked away, and dropped it back into the box.

The Dark One approached Tondo and stood in front of him. He moved his outer robes aside, displaying the Champion's Dagger tucked into his belt. Tondo's stare centered on his stolen blade for a while, and then he looked up into the wicked eyes of the veiled man hovering over him. The Dark One pulled the dagger from his belt and went to one knee.

"You recognize this, don't you?" he said, displaying the gem-encrusted award in front of his prisoner's face. Tondo didn't respond, but the hate in his eyes spoke for him. "Ha, I'm the one who killed your woman and child," he declared, evil glee displaying his pride. "Had you been there, I'd a killed you, too. But, in time, when the Showton is done with you, I'll complete my task."

"How brave you must be to attack an unarmed woman and her infant; undoubtedly, one of the Showton's greatest warriors," Tondo spat, his tone dripping with sarcasm. The Dark One placed the dagger's tip under Tondo's chin and pushed up slightly, forcing Tondo to raise his head up and back due to the pain.

"Be careful with your insults, fool. You're in the Showton's domain now. He may choose to have your tongue ripped out and fed to the frizzards," the Dark One threatened. He then looked past the grimy streaks running down Tondo's cheeks, the tracks left by the two guards' filthy fingers, and he stared at the stubble of Tondo's beard. "What in the name . . . Is that hair on your face? Are you some sort of beast-man?"

"There's only one beast in this room, and it's not me," Tondo spat. The Dark One pushed the dagger's blade higher, penetrating Tondo's flesh and causing a trickle of blood to flow down its edge.

"You're as foolish as you are dense. Your new master will put an end to your conceit," the Dark One spat as he removed the dagger from under Tondo's chin and stood. He looked at the two guards and ordered, "Drueg, Moeg, clean him up and prepare him to go before the master. Now, heed my words. He's not to be underestimated or toyed with. Is that clear enough for you two dullards to understand?"

"Yes, master, we'll clean him up; no make'n sport, as ya wish, Great One," Drueg blandished. Moeg mumbled something indecipherable, which the Dark One chose to ignore.

"When the master is ready for him, I'll send down the guards," the Dark One told them. He then turned and tramped up the stairs.

Moeg and Drueg disappeared into the bowels of the dungeon, and when they returned, each one was carrying a bucket full of water. They stepped in front of Tondo and quickly doused him. Moeg took a grungy towel from around his neck and began rubbing it in Tondo's face, removing the grime deposited on his cheeks. As he scrubbed Tondo's face, he'd shove his prisoner's head into the stone wall, exacting his petty revenge. Tondo endured the abuse with silent animus.

Tondo was left to ponder his parlous situation for the next segment or two. In his previous life, he had wondered from time to time how he'd handle being a prisoner of war. Now, he was one, shackled and chained to a wall. He expected no mercy, especially from the one he had tormented: the Sutro Showton. A quick death was all he could hope for, but he was sure his nemesis had other plans. He steeled himself and worried if he would die with honor.

Tondo repeatedly tried to use his inner-power for half a segment or so. He could feel it burning within his bosom, but nothing happened when he released its energy; however, he could feel a warming sensation coming from the device around his neck. He quickly surmised the device was blocking his tzaah. Depression overtook him, and he leaned his back against the cold stone. Hunger began to gnaw at his stomach, and thirst nagged at his dry throat. He could hear the two reprobates quietly talking nearby. "Hey!" Tondo yelled, "I gotta go." The two dullards laughed and continued their chatter. "I gotta go!" Tondo yelled again. His guards didn't move and continued their quiet babbling. *No food, no water, no relief. Todo, you better get used to it,* he thought to himself.

# CHAPTER 28

## WHAT IS TRUTH?

As the light from the window slit high above grew brighter, indicating midday, Tondo heard the sound of heavy footsteps coming down the stairs. Four armed and armored guards soon appeared, marched to his place, and stopped, the guards staring down at him. Moeg and Drueg, each holding a hammer and chisel, quickly dashed over to them.

"The master is ready for him; break the fetters," a guard ordered.

"As ya wish, seshtane," Drueg replied. The bolts securing Tondo's shackles were broken, and the guards yanked him to his feet. He stretched and shook the stiffness from his aching muscles. Tondo's hands were quickly bound at the wrists with a leather cord.

"Don't make any sudden moves, or you'll suffer for it," the seshtane threatened.

Tondo didn't immediately reply as he stared at the band on the seshtane's finger; it was his bonding ring. "That's my finger band," he grumbled.

"Not anymore," the seshtane growled. "Be thankful I didn't take your finger too." Tondo glared at the seshtane, who responded by backhanding him across the face. "Lower your eyes, and never look at me in that manner again. You have no pride; you have no will; you have no life. The sooner you accept it, the easier the remainder of your miserable existence will be. Follow me, or I'll have you dragged up the stairs by your feet."

"I'll walk," Tondo said, his eyes downcast. *No need to cause myself unnecessary pain; however, I'm adding you to my blacklist,* Tondo angrily thought in chilled silence.

Tondo followed the seshtane up the stairs and through the hallways. Two guards held him firmly by the upper arms, and the third guard followed the others, his Showton pike's point held against the center of their prisoner's back, making the passage unnecessarily painful for Tondo.

It took only a short time for the group to reach the heavy wooden doors undoubtedly leading to the Showton's Great Hall and his doom, Tondo guessed. The seshtane stopped and waited. After a heart-pounding delay for Tondo, the doors slowly opened, and the seshtane advanced; Tondo followed. The Sutro Showton sat atop his regal platform, his hand holding a scepter, and most of the throne engulfed by his flowing robes. The lower half of his face was veiled in the same manner as the Dark One's, who was standing alongside the scaffold. The guard behind Tondo prodded him along with his pike, obviously attempting to impress his master. The seshtane stopped a couple of strides short of the platform's stairs and dropped to one knee. The two guards on Tondo's right and left lifted their prisoner off his feet and slammed him to the floor. The third man drove his pike into Tondo's back, breaking the skin and causing him to stifle a cry of pain through clenched teeth.

"Master, the prisoner you called for," the seshtane said, his head held low.

"You may stand. Raise the prisoner's head. I wish to examine his face," the Showton ordered. The seshtane stood, went to Tondo, dropped to a knee, and grabbed him by his long hair. He yanked Tondo's head up, giving the Showton a clear view of the prisoner's face. Tondo gritted his teeth and growled in pain as the seshtane pulled his head higher, causing the guard's pike to dig deeper into his back.

The Showton placed his scepter on the platform, rose to his feet, slowly walked down the platform's stairs, and stopped in front of the prisoner. "Raise him up. I want to look into his eyes," the Showton ordered.

The seshtane released Tondo's hair, stood up, and nodded to the guards. Tondo was jerked to his feet and held tightly by his upper arms. The third guard's pike dug deeper into his back, and Tondo growled in pain. The Showton stared into Tondo's Munnari-blue eyes as Tondo stared back into the Showton's Munnevo-red eyes. Neither man moved as they peered into one another's soul. After what seemed an interminable period, the Showton took a step back.

"You may release your hold on him," the Showton told the guards. "Seshtane, you and your men are dismissed." The Showton scanned the room and ordered, "The rest of you will leave, all but the Dark One." The guards and attendants quickly exited the room. The Showton's Second, the Dark One, promptly moved to his master's side, his hand on the grip of his sword. The Showton turned his back to Tondo and stepped away.

After the room cleared and the great doors were closed, the Showton turned around and stepped in front of Tondo again. He closely examined Tondo's whiskered cheeks, and then he smiled.

"Where are you from?" the Showton asked.

"The United Kingdom."

"Really? And before that?"

A puzzled look crossed Tondo's face, but after a short pause, he responded, "The Wilderness."

"And before the Wilderness?" the Showton asked. Tondo said nothing, his eyes searching the Showton's face. "You don't belong here. You are not like the others—these Worlders—are you?" the Showton stated. When Tondo didn't answer, the Showton continued, "And neither am I." The Showton pulled his veil below his chin, revealing a five o'clock shadow. The Showton turned around and walked away from his prisoner. "You are not from this world. Where are you really from?" the Showton asked over his shoulder.

Tondo's eyes widened as he contemplated what he had just seen and heard. "I'm from Earth. Where are you from?" Tondo asked.

The Dark One slapped Tondo hard across the face with the back of his hand. "You don't ask questions here. You're only allowed to give answers," the Dark One growled.

"What method of conveyance did you use?" the Showton asked.

"I can't remember the words, and there's nothing in world-speak that can describe it," Tondo explained, all the time under the threatening glare of the Dark One.

"Ha, indeed, if it's anything like the method that brought me here, this simple tongue will need to grow in order to explain it; however, it matters little at this point. You are a gift to me. It appears that visitors to this world receive a greater portion of inner-power than Worlders. Are you aware of that?" Tondo shook his head. "I will take your inner-power and combine it with my own and become invincible," the Showton gloated. He turned and faced Tondo, his purple aura ignited, and he closed the distance between himself and his prisoner.

The Dark One drew forth his black sword and held its tip in front of Tondo's face. "Don't move, or you'll feel the bite of my blade," he warned. Tondo could feel the sting of the Showton's aura as he drew nearer, but as he did, the purple haze began to be sucked into the band around Tondo's neck, like smoke into a vent. The Showton abruptly stopped his advance and stared with disbelieving eyes. Tondo quickly realized what was happening, and a smile slowly crept across his face. The device around his neck, meant to shunt his inner-power, was also affecting the Showton's tzaah, and the look on the Showton's face made it clear that was not part of the plan. Tondo wanted to make a snide and disparaging remark, but discretion held him in check, discretion and the tip of the Dark One's blade hovering menacingly before his eyes.

The Showton turned around and tromped up his platform stairs. He knocked his scepter aside, and it flew off the platform. He slumped to his throne. He sat in thought for a few long moments as his aura slowly faded. The Dark One continued to glare at Tondo, seemingly waiting, or hoping, for his prisoner to do or say something that would free him to strike. Tondo simply stood in silence, a smile his only act of defiance.

"Master, allow me to remove his smirk at the neck," the Dark One growled. The bound prisoner could see the Showton contemplating his Second's appeal. Tondo's muscles grew tight as he prepared to react. He would not go down like a dumb beast to slaughter.

The Showton leaned back and said, "No, I will take his power; it will only require more time than I originally planned." An evil smile rose on the Showton's face, and his mirthful glare fell upon his prisoner. "It's such a pity," he said. Tondo only responded with questioning eyes. "I was fond of the little girl. She showed great promise, and I planned to train her myself. Now, she has crossed-over, just like all the others who foolishly followed you into my snare." The Showton watched as Tondo's smile fell from his face. "Nevesant, put away your sword and come stand beside me," the Showton ordered. Reluctantly, the Dark One sheathed his black sword and moved to a position next to the platform. "Yes, she's gone," the Showton continued. "You weren't planning on my boat, the Showton, pursuing them after they deserted you. They were chased into shallow waters, and your boat was dashed to pieces against the rocks. I understand the terrors were well-fed that day. Your effort has come to naught, an utter failure. Worse than that, you've killed your own daughter, the last of your family, I'm sure."

Tondo's mind was racing. Could this be true, or was his nemesis engaging in a cruel deception? Tondo knew he had planned and prepared well. Hermanez was too good a boater to let his ship flounder upon the rocks. Yaddet was aboard as well, yet doubt nagged at him, and he began to despair.

The Showton's smile grew as he watched Tondo's expression change. He felt his gambit was working. He would weaken his adversary's will to live, and when his defenses were crumbling, he would strike. He desperately needed Tondo's extraordinary power if he was ever to cow the Five Shadows and bend them to his will. He doubted physical pain and suffering would do the trick. Also, he worried that doing so might lessen his prisoner's coveted tzaah. He would assault Tondo's emotional health, not his physical well-being, at least not more than necessary. I will demoralize him. He silently assumed that a few detzamars under the hands of the two dungeon morons would weaken anyone's resolve. He would also destroy Tondo's hope and sow seeds of self-doubt.

"Now that I have you, I will easily crush your army in the next encounter. Then, those who assisted you in revolt will be dealt with, especially the women of Te Femma. I plan to make an example of them. Their suffering will be magnified and heralded throughout my domain," the Showton blustered.

"That may prove to be more difficult than you imagine," Tondo flatly stated. The Dark One bristled at Tondo's retort, but he did nothing.

"Their fate is already sealed. That's the simple truth," the Showton replied.

"That's only your opinion. Truth will resolve itself over time," Tondo declared.

"What is truth?" the Showton asked absentmindedly. To his surprise, Tondo simply stood, his eyes blinking, searching the

Showton's expression. The Showton answered his own question, "Truth is what we make of it." He watched as Tondo's expression changed to unbelief. "You doubt my words; why?"

"Believing a thing to be true does not necessarily make it so," Tondo stated. The Showton eyed him as he contemplated his prisoner's declaration. It had been a long time, a very long time, since anyone had challenged him intellectually. He decided to confront his adversary with a battle of wits, which he knew he would easily win. "Tell me then," the Showton began, "what do you think truth is?"

Tondo thought for a moment, then answered, "That which is true is the ultimate outcome of one's research."

"The ultimate outcome, you say?" Tondo nodded. "Reaching an ultimate outcome is fleeting at best. Today's ultimate outcome is tomorrow's superstitious falsehood," the Showton fired back.

"Not always, but I see your point; however, true beliefs and true statements correspond to the actual state of affairs one is examining," Tondo explained.

"The actual state of affairs is always changing, as well. As one delves deeper into the mysteries of existence, new truths always come to light. For example, one of my world's great scholars defined the motions of all the heavenly objects. His findings became laws that others based their premises on. Unfortunately, upon closer examination—a more detailed and accurate exploration—it was found that these laws do not always hold true. A new truth was discovered that explained these motions more accurately. So really, what was truth and what was folly?" the Showton asked.

"That sounds like Newton's and Einstein's theories. Are you from Earth?" Tondo dared to ask as his eyes shifted to the Dark One.

"I know nothing of those words. Now, answer my question, if you can," the Showton barked.

"A set of logically consistent beliefs must cohere to one another in order to be justified. In your example, the former was simply clarified by the latter. True belief is to know something and believe it is true," Tondo explained.

"Ha, that may be so for the physical world, I will grant. Nevesant, hand me your sword," the Showton ordered. The Dark One unsheathed his black blade and handed it up to his master with a bow. "Nevesant, do you have any idea what we are discussing?" the Showton asked.

"Master, why waste time with this fool?" was his Second's tort reply.

"Because he has deep thought, something the rest of you lack. Now, where was I?" the Showton said, and then his eyes scanned the black sword he was holding. "Justified true belief is much simpler to attain in the physical world. What about moral truth? Is murder bad?" he asked, causing the Dark One's annoyed expression to shift to glee.

"Murder is evil, and evildoers commit murder," Tondo quickly replied.

"If that's so, you must be an evildoer, for you have slaughtered thousands," the Showton retorted.

Tondo lowered his eyes and thought in silence for a moment as a wave of guilt passed over him. Maaryah's counsel sprang from his memory. He looked up and said, "The death of souls in war rests upon the heads of those who perpetrate war. Killing combatants in battle is unfortunate, but it is not murder. Therefore, it is not evil."

"Kings and rulers have their victims executed all the time. Then, are they not evildoers?" the Showton asked as he turned the black sword in his hand, examining both of its deadly edges.

"The fate of evildoers is written in the laws of justice. A king has the right to condemn the guilty, just as the people have the right to condemn an evil king," Tondo explained.

"The people are a mob of halfwits, and if it weren't for men of our superior intellect, they would soon begin slaughtering each other as they do on my world and undoubtedly as they do on yours. I bring order and stem their chaos before it overwhelms them. I'm doing them a favor," the Showton revealed.

"Those you subjugate hate you," Tondo told him.

The Showton laughed, "Let them hate me, as long as they fear me."

"You bring suffering and death. You nurture the evil seeds and partake of their ghastly fruits," Tondo grumbled.

"Nurture the evil seeds? That statement has a familiar ring to it. Where have I heard that before?" the Showton wondered.

"Eezayhod, the priest," the Dark One said.

"Are you a priest, too?" the Showton asked.

"No. Master priests from the temple at the Ancient City taught me that within the heart of man are planted the seeds of his being, good seeds and evil seeds, placed there by the gods, allowing man to choose for himself, good or evil. The greatest decision in life is choosing which seeds to nurture," Tondo declared.

"The gods?" the Showton laughed. "You now turn to silly superstitions?" the Showton huffed. "We are the gods of this world, and you are my prisoner. That makes me the supreme authority, wouldn't you agree?" the Showton said with a smile as he waved the black sword in the air.

Tondo watched closely, wondering if the Showton would strike but unwilling to let the words of his nemesis pass without a rebuttal. After a short delay, he said, "Neither you nor I are gods. Do you really believe your spirit is more precious than anyone else's? You justify your addiction to power by claiming to make order of chaos, yet there is no chaos to . . . "

"There will be!" the Showton angrily interrupted. "It's just a matter of time before this world's far-flung cities turn against each other. I am saving them from that bedlam."

"That is only your excuse for seeking power," Tondo claimed.

"So, you're alleging that the pursuit of power is evil? You need look no further than your own reflection. I have learned that you had attained your own degree of power, until now. You must be a very evil man in your own right; is that not so?" the Showton teased.

"The pursuit of power is not necessarily evil unto itself. It is how that pursuit is carried out and what one does with the power he attains. I have always sought to uplift those around me, not slaughter them," Tondo stated.

The Showton pondered his words for a moment, then asked, "So, you've received training from the priests, have you?" Tondo nodded. "It appears we have that experience in common. You see, I have also received training; training from powers beyond your imagination," the Showton boasted.

"Undoubtedly, those powers followed the promptings of the Tempter," Tondo accused.

"The Tempter? Ha, the Tempter. The influence of the Tempter stems from the same source. Have you ever felt the Tempter's promptings?" the Showton asked. Tondo nodded again. "Of course you have. Those promptings, that influence, comes from the gods of the mist. Both me and Nevesant, here, have seen them, felt their power, and experienced their wonder."

Tondo looked perplexed. "God's of the mist? Who are they?"

"The Five Shadows," the Showton told him. Tondo's expression turned to disbelief. "You doubt my words. Why?"

"The Five Shadows are only a myth and a curse, nothing more," Tondo stated firmly.

The Showton smiled widely and rested the black blade across his thighs. "Nevesant, are the Shadows a myth?" he asked.

"No, master, they are real and fearsome! I have seen them, all five of them. Their influence nearly overwhelmed me. All who were with me were taken by them; only I survived the encounter," the Dark One declared with such forcefulness and fear in his voice that it caused Tondo to wonder if the Showton's claim could be valid.

"Maybe I should have our guest taken to them so he may experience their hunger for himself. What do you think of that?" the Showton asked, his eyes searching the Dark One's face.

"It would be a fitting end for this skeptic; however, I was looking forward to removing his head from his shoulders myself," the Dark One replied.

"You could take him there and watch. What do you think of that?" the Showton offered with a cruel smile.

"One encounter with the gods of the mist is enough for me. I'd rather you send someone else," the Dark One admitted.

Tondo didn't like the sound of any of this. If the Dark One was resisting his master's wishes, maybe there was some substance to this claim.

"That's all right; I'm not done with him yet, anyway. I will take his power in due course. After that, you can take his empty shell and do with it as you please." The Showton's menacing red eyes turned to Tondo. "How long ago did you arrive on this world?"

Tondo thought for a moment and replied, "It was fifteen, maybe twenty spans ago."

"I've been here about the same time. Quite a coincidence, wouldn't you say?" The Showton paused to ponder, and Tondo simply stood in silence, staring at his nemesis. "I wonder," the Showton mumbled absentmindedly. "Does your world believe in alternate realities?"

"Some do," Tondo replied.

"Do you believe in such a possibility?"

"I guess I do, although the evidence is still too thin to give me much confidence in the theory."

"Don't you think it quite a coincidence that you and I arrived here at nearly the same time? Did you expect to end up on this world?" Tondo shook his head. "Me neither," the Showton admitted. "I wonder," he repeated. He handed the sword back to the Dark One and stood. He stepped down the stairs and stopped in front of Tondo. The two men stood eye-to-eye, staring, and delving into each other's soul. A shiver unexpectedly ran down Tondo's spine. "Hmm, could it be?" the Showton wondered to himself.

"Hoy?" Tondo asked.

"Could we be of the same lark-quin?" the Showton remarked thoughtfully.

"I don't understand. What's lark-quin?" Tondo wondered.

"Mystics and some scholars from my world believe our lark-quin—referred to as spirit in this world—is shared across all the realities. If that is true, you and I may be of the same lark-quin, the same spirit," the Showton surmised. He smiled as a look of horror crossed Tondo's face.

"That's impossible! We don't even look alike," Tondo growled.

"Outward appearances have nothing to do with it. It is said that our lark-quin, our spirit, has an infinite capacity to occupy all the realities. In this way, our lark-quin shares infinite lives, growing by infinite experiences, and gaining a knowledge of all things," the Showton expounded.

"Ridiculous! We share nothing!" Tondo exclaimed.

"Why do you say that? You and I are more alike than you imagine," the Showton laughed.

"You are a tyrant and a murderer. I seek to free all people and give them choice. Life is precious to me," Tondo rebutted.

"Is that so? You may simply be a reflection of me. I bring order and regimen to a culture that was doomed to go down the same path our worlds have. The freedom you claim to bring to these people will only result in more deaths than you or I can imagine. You call me a murderer, yet you have brought the horrors of advanced weapons from your wicked world to an innocent land unprepared to receive them. You know full well where your thunder-makers, your gunz as you call them, will lead these people; to more deaths and sufferings than anything you could blame me for. Now, who's the tyrant; who's the murderer?" the Showton retorted.

The two men stared into each other's eyes as both seethed with anger and hatred for the other. "Guards!" the Showton finally shouted. The seshtane and his three men marched into the room. "Take this prisoner back to his keepers. Have him scourged. I don't want him killed or injured in such a way that could lead to death, but he's to suffer, thereby gaining full knowledge of my power over him," the Showton ordered.

"Yes, master," the seshtane replied as he raised his left arm in salute. Tondo was forcefully removed, a guard's pike digging into the center of his back again.

After the prisoner and his guards had exited and the great doors closed behind them, the Dark One went to the Showton and asked, "Master, have you heard from the boat? Has it returned already?"

"Hoy?" the Showton responded, seemingly a bit confused by the question.

"You said his boat had been destroyed and the child killed. You could only know that if your boat has returned," the Dark One explained.

"It was simply a ruse, a ploy, a means of weakening his will. Didn't you notice the fear in his eyes when I told him that? I'm certain my boat will soon return with the girl or a report of her death. Possibly, it will return, having captured the other boat.

Now, wouldn't that be good news?" the Showton chortled.

Tondo was led down the stairs and into the depths of the castle's bowels by his guards. The two dungeon dullards greeted them.

"What does the master want us to do with the prisoner?" Drueg asked of the seshtane.

"He's to be scourged."

An evil and wicked smile covered Moeg's face, wrinkling his swollen nose. "Now, yer gonna pay for what ya did to me," he growled.

Tondo's mind was racing. In the past, he'd been able to extricate himself from what seemed a hopeless situation; either by ingenuity or luck, he had escaped the predicament. There appeared to be no way out this time, and he found it difficult to believe his fate was sealed.

The guards took him to a heavy wooden grate attached to a wall. One of the guards removed the leather binding holding his wrists together, and then the guard with the pike digging into his back pushed him face-first against the grate. The other two guards tied him by the wrists to the grating. The seshtane took his dagger and sliced Tondo's jerkin in two up the center of the back. He then cut away the fragments and let them fall to the stone floor. Moeg and Drueg disappeared into the shadows and quickly returned, each holding a brutal-looking scourge—a whip with many leather thongs attached to a handle. Moeg walked over to Tondo and held his scourge where Tondo could see it. Each thong was braided and had several pieces of sharp bone fragments woven into its length.

"I'm going to flay the skin off your back with this heavy tamer, and I'm going to enjoy every stroke," Moeg snarled.

"Let me see that," the seshtane ordered. Moeg handed him the scourge. The seshtane examined it closely and handed it back. "The master doesn't want him killed. Use something else."

An angry look crossed Moeg's face, but it quickly changed to submission. "Yes, seshtane, we'll fetch the others," Moeg bitterly groused. The two simpletons scurried back into the shadows and quickly returned with different scourges. Tondo was watching over his shoulder as Moeg handed his to the seshtane for examination. It was similar to the previous one, except this one didn't have pieces of bone woven into its thongs. Instead, each thong was knotted in several places along its length.

"This will do," the seshtane said and handed it back to Moeg.

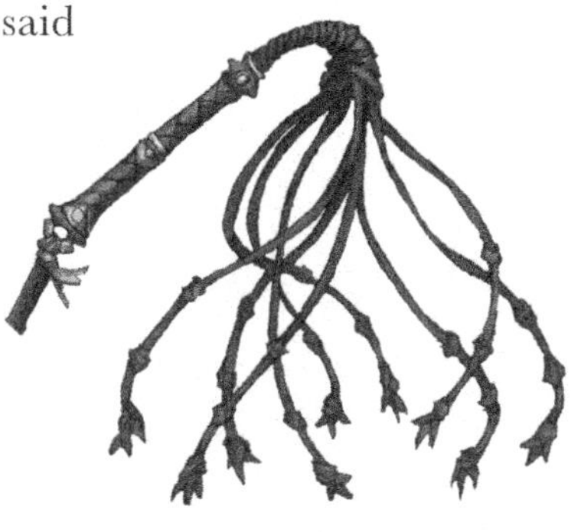

"How many?" Drueg asked.

"The master didn't say. I'll tell you when to stop," the seshtane told him.

Moeg took a position on Tondo's left, and Drueg took his place on Tondo's right. Moeg held his scourge in his right hand, and Drueg had his in his left.

"Begin!" the seshtane ordered. Moeg struck first. Although painful, it didn't seem as bad as Tondo thought it would be. Drueg struck second, and the pain increased substantially. Moeg's second strike felt like fire searing his back, and Drueg's next strike drove Tondo's pain off the chart. He remembered how he'd once burned himself picking up a hot machine-gun barrel. This was ten times worse. Moeg struck again. That was a hundred times worse.

Tondo took stroke after stroke, and he lost count at around fifteen. His only respite was when Moeg and Drueg stopped to trade places, shifting their scourges to the opposite hand. At some point during his searingly painful ordeal, Tondo heard someone screaming in agony, and he quickly realized it was himself. Not long after that, he lost consciousness.

# CHAPTER 29

# SAIL ASTERN!

Hermanez was on the tiller flanked by Harmon and Yaddet. Dawn was breaking, and no land was in sight. The boatmaster shouted to all his boaters, "Keep your eyes open for sails!" The boaters responded with a thunderous bellow, indicating they'd heard. A brilliantly red p´atezas slowly climbed above the horizon. At midmorning, one of the boaters shouted, "Sail astern!" Everyone turned in that direction, and Hermanez put his farseer to his eye and watched as another boat appeared from the mist.

"Just as I feared, the *Zerio* was in the city," he grumbled.

"Can we outrun it?" Yaddet asked.

"We'll know in a couple of segments," Hermanez replied.

Every sail the *Anterra* could raise was already set. The ship was running before the wind, making the tiller's feedback unnatural. It took all the boatmaster's skills to maintain control because the slightest mistake could cause the ship to turn wildly and stall. By midday, it became apparent that the *Zerio*, now renamed the *Showton*, was gaining on them.

"Will they catch us before dark?" Harmon worriedly asked.

"Yes," was Hermanez's curt and nervous reply. The boatmaster turned the tiller over to his second in command, Arbreno, and then focused his farseer on the *Showton*. For a long time, he watched the ship as it constantly reduced the distance between them. Finally, he lowered his farseer and turned to Harmon and Yaddet. "It appears to have a crew of at least twenty, and I also counted twelve warriors onboard. There could be more below decks. Yaddet, I want only boaters up here. I'll call you when it's time. Harmon, place a couple of Rangers at the door to my cabin, and you, along with one or two other Rangers, wait inside. I'm not about to let those vestangs take the girl after the price we've paid to rescue her. The *Zerio* should catch us by late afternoon, so stay alert," Hermanez declared. Everyone took their places and waited as the boaters scurried over the ship, coaxing all the speed out of her they could.

As the boatmaster had predicted, the *Showton* pulled even with the *Anterra* when the red p´atezas hung low in the western sky.

"Ha, my boaters!" Hermanez called, "After they start throwing over grappling lines, you throw yours. We're gonna take back the boat they stole from us!" Hermanez vowed. The boaters cheered and readied. The *Showton* drew closer, a boater on the enemy ship hurled a grappling line, but it fell short. The *Anterra's* boaters responded with laughs and insults. The enemy boaters retorted with oaths, curses, and threats. It wasn't long before another line was thrown, and this one grabbed the railing and hung there. Several more followed, and the *Anterra's* boaters also cast their lines. Their crews pulled the boats closer until their hulls touched with a loud bang that shook both ships. *Showton* assailants began swinging over to the *Anterra* on ropes.

"Yaddet, get those vestangs!" Hermanez yelled.

Yaddet and an entire brick of Tondo Brothers, twenty-five strong, spewed forth from the cargo hold and immediately attacked the *Showton* pirates. A vicious hand-to-hand melee erupted as men shouted curses at one another. The clang of sword against sword rattled up and down the deck. After a quarter-segment, the outnumbered and overmatched *Showton* attackers began fleeing back to their own ship.

"Go get 'em, boys!" Hermanez yelled. *Anterra* boaters and Tondo Brothers swung by ropes or jumped to the other ship. *Showton* boaters began cutting the grappling lines in a desperate attempt to free their ship from impending capture, but it was too late. After another quarter-segment, all *Showton* boaters and warriors were either captured, severely wounded, or killed.

"Master Hermanez!" Yaddet called from the stern of the *Showton*, "What do you want done with the *Showton* men?"

"Put 'em in bindings and lock 'em in the cargo hold. Keep your men over there and guard the prisoners closely. I'll send Arbreno and some of my boaters over to manage the *Zerio*," Hermanez shouted back.

It was dusk by the time the two ships separated and set their courses for Rendoto. Harmon had brought Maari to the stern of the *Anterra*, and they watched as the last rays of day reflected off the scattered clouds. Maari stood with little Tumper sitting on her shoulder.

"I wish Parr was here," she said wistfully. "Now, what's going to happen to me? Am I going to live with you, Parr-parr?"

"No, child," Harmon told her, a bit confused by her question. "I'll take you to your mama."

Maari looked up at Harmon, her eyes wide with excitement, a huge smile covering her face. "Mama's not dead?" she nearly shouted, hardly able to control her joy.

Harmon kneeled as Hermanez and Yaddet watched with tender hearts. "Of course, she's not dead. She's waiting for you," Harmon told her. Maari jumped into his embrace as her arms wrapped around his neck. He hugged her as little Tumper licked his nose, causing him to jerk his head back and stare in surprise. After his shock, he smiled. "Why did you think she had crossed-over?" he asked.

"The mean man they call the Dark One said he killed her and little Harmon, too," she told him.

"Your mama is alive, and she misses you very much."

"And baby Harmon?" she asked.

Her parr-parr looked into her face with sad eyes, "Little Harmon isn't with us anymore." He watched as her eyes filled with tears, and she hugged him again and wept. Harmon returned her hug but kept his eyes fixed on Tumper. The creature sat on Maari's shoulder, its huge eyes staring at Harmon and its ears constantly moving. After a few moments, Harmon leaned back and looked into her face again. "You have to be strong. You are all your mama has now," he said.

"Parr-parr, Mama has you, too," she noted.

# CHAPTER 30

# TROUBLE ALWAYS COMES IN THREES

Nearly four wernts had passed since the ship left Rendoto. Maaryah was beside herself with worry. Idop had told her the mission was expected to take two wernts, and he tried to comfort her by suggesting the delay could be caused by a change in plans or possibly a storm at sea. His efforts to calm her apprehensions weren't working. *Could it be that she sensed my own concern and worry at the delay?* If the ameer failed to return, the burden of winning the war would fall to him, the second in command; a thought that terrified him.

Idop could see her standing atop the Rendoto city wall near the rear gate, an excellent place to view the ocean and search for the boat. She carried her farseer there every morning and scanned the horizon until it became too dark to see. Inclement weather couldn't interrupt her vigil. She refused to break her watch even to eat; an aide or subordinate would bring her some food at each midday segment.

Just as she thought her faith in Tondo's return could not diminish any further, she saw the *Anterra* clear the point of land at the entrance to the bay. Her spirit soared, and she scanned the ship with her farseer. She saw a child standing next to a warrior. "That has to be Maari!" she shouted and began hopping up and down on her toes. When she lowered the farseer, she couldn't believe what she saw; a second boat cleared the point. "That must be the *Zerio*!"

Maaryah rushed to the dock and waited for the ships to arrive, hopping up and down on her toes with excitement. Slowly, ever so slowly, the *Anterra* approached. There wasn't room for two ships to dock at the same time, and she noticed the *Zerio* had dropped her anchors in the middle of the bay. The *Anterra's* gangplank was maneuvered into place. Maari scampered down it and rushed into her mother's waiting arms. Maaryah went to her knees as they embraced, hugged, and squeezed each other as they sobbed in joyous reunion, their spirits soaring.

After their long embrace, Maaryah, still on her knees, held Maari at arm's length and examined her from head to foot. "Oy, how you've grown," she noted. Over three spans away from the influence of the Blessing of the City had a marked effect on the child. She had grown much faster than she would have if she'd passed the same time at the estate. *No matter,* Maaryah thought, *As soon as I get her back to the estate, her growth will continue at the usual slow and normal pace.*

"Mama, where's your braid? It's gone! What happened?" Maari cried.

"I've become a warrior like Parr. I had to cut it off," her mother explained.

Maaryah noticed her father waiting next to her. She stood and hugged him, then said, "Papa, thank you for bringing my Maari back to me." She looked around and then to the ship.

"Where's Tondo? Is he on the other boat?" She looked at her father and noticed his downcast eyes. "Papa, where's Tondo?" she cried in near panic.

Harmon looked into her amber eyes and, in a sad voice, said, "He's not with us."

For an instant, Maaryah was paralyzed, unable to comprehend what her father had just told her, yet not wanting to come to a realization of the truth. After a long, torturous delay, she understood. "No! No! It can't be. No!" she wailed and fell into his arms. It was all Maaryah could do to avoid falling apart in front of her daughter. She scooped Maari into her arms and hugged her until Maari began to fidget. She stopped embracing her daughter but continued holding her. "What happened? Tell me everything." Harmon explained in detail how the mission unfolded and Maari's rescue. He also noted that Tondo wasn't the only loss; three Rangers hadn't returned. When Harmon finished, she asked, "Did you see him fall?"

"No, daughter, none of us did."

"Oy? You left him! How could you?" she shouted in anger.

"We had no choice but to leave; it was by his command. We were set upon by a host of Showton guards. Had we delayed even an instant, all of us would have been killed, and Maari would have been stolen again," he explained, and then he continued, "I recovered this."

Harmon slipped his arm through a rope attached to a cloth-wrapped bundle he was carrying across his back and handed it to Maaryah. She carefully set Maari down and took the bundle. She untied the ropes securing it and unwrapped the cloth. It was the Munnari Blade. She uttered a muffled cry of despair and brought her left hand to her mouth as her right hand held the sword. Harmon watched as she struggled to control her emotions, her pain-filled amber eyes staring at her father in disbelief.

After much effort, she pushed back her ravaging sorrow. "No one saw him fall?" she asked. Harmon shook his head in response. "He hasn't crossed-over! I refuse to believe otherwise. The unnamed god wouldn't allow it," she proclaimed.

Harmon simply nodded, not wanting to argue the point and add to his daughter's suffering. "I must report to Idop," he finally said.

"Yes, of course," Maaryah replied. She gave her father a snug, then scooped Maari into her arms again, "Are you hungry?" she asked.

"Yes, and so is Tumper," Maari told her.

"Tumper? Who's Tumper?"

"Tumper's my friend," Maari said as she moved her outing bag from her back to her front and opened the flap. Maaryah peered in and saw two huge brown eyes looking back at her.

"Oy, my goodness! I must see that you're both fed," Maaryah said. She tucked the Munnari blade into her belt, gave her father another snug, picked up Maari again, and started walking to her brigade headquarters, carrying her daughter and fighting an overwhelming desire to collapse to her knees in despair.

Mother and daughter were inseparable throughout the remainder of the day and into the next. Maaryah even permitted Maari to sleep in her bed that night, a real treat for the young one. Maaryah tried to hide her aching heart over the loss of her bondmate, but even at Maari's tender age, she could see and feel her mother's sorrow.

Late in the afternoon, as Maaryah reviewed a report from one of the wing commanders, Maari stopped playing with Tumper and went to her mother's armor stand. She stood staring at it, moved to the weapons stand, removed her mother's sheathed dagger, and took it to her.

Maaryah looked up and stopped what she was doing. "What is it, my darling?" Maaryah asked.

"Mama, I want to be a warrior just like you. I want to go back and find Parr," Maari told her, still holding the dagger.

"Ha, you would be the bravest of all my warriors, but you must wait until you're taller and can use something longer and heavier than a dagger," her mother explained.

"I know," Maari said in a disappointed tone, "but I want to look like a real warrior, just like you do, Mama." Maaryah smiled and took the dagger from her daughter.

"Your Highness," Rana Fardinza began, "the boat has returned. There are now two boats in the bay; the *Anterra* at the dock and the ameer's second boat. I've been told there was a battle at sea, and the ameer's boaters prevailed and captured the other one."

"A battle at sea! That's astonishing! I would never have imagined such a thing was possible," the queen exclaimed.

"Was the ameer's mission to rescue his daughter successful?"

"Yes, his daughter has been returned to her mother; however, the ameer didn't come back. The report is he was killed by the Showton and his guards," the rana sadly informed the queen.

Queen Ezora jumped to her feet, "The ameer has been killed? This is horrible! How can we defeat the Showton without him?" the queen blurted. She began pacing back and forth, worry etched on her face. After some time, she stopped and faced the rana, "Poor Maaryah. See if there is anything I can do for her and the child."

"As you wish, Your Highness. I hate to bring this up after such tragic news, but we have a new problem you must deal with, now that the child has been returned," the rana said.

"Ha. I must return to our city; I've been gone much too long. Unfortunately, we can't wait throughout Maaryah's mourning period. Let her grieve in peace for a couple of days and then summon her," the queen ordered. Rana Fardinza nodded.

Two days had passed since the ships had returned. The news about the loss of the ameer had spread like wildfire through the ranks of the army and Rendoto's residents. A pall of depression descended over the city like a dank and chilling fog; sadness and worry clutched at everyone.

Maaryah had just put Maari to bed, and she was sitting in her office behind the desk, holding her head in her hands, her elbows planted firmly on the flat surface.

Why did it always have to be this way? she wondered.

Throughout her life, it seemed that a tragedy of greater importance closely followed every instant of joy. When she and Maari were reunited, her spirit soared with the unbridled joy of their reunion. Maaryah's happiness had been immediately dashed by the shocking and painful revelation that Tondo hadn't returned. She wanted to curse the unnamed god for his cruelty or indifference. Wasn't Tondo his messenger? How could the great god abandon him? How could the great god abandon her again?

Unexpectedly, she was engulfed by an unseen comforting influence, and the words of the Sutro Seer came to her, 'Your strength and power come from the source of all good: the great god whom you are angry with.'

An impression—an epiphany—focused her thoughts. Could it be that this was the great god's plan all along? Tondo and herself and all the others the Messenger had touched were the tools by which the great god's work was unfolding. If that was indeed the case, Tondo must still be alive. Suddenly, her worry and anger eased. A feeling of confidence replaced the empty hole at her center. Her heart jumped at the hope. Maybe she simply was grasping at straws, but at least it was something to grasp.

An aide entered Maaryah's office, "Zerr, Megatus Nestess desires to speak with you," she said.

Maaryah leaned back and wiped the dampness from her cheeks. "Let him enter," she told her aide. The sister exited, and Maaryah stood. When Nestess entered, she went to him and extended her arm. Nestess started to bow, looked perplexed, and finally reached out and took her by the forearm, and they shook in greeting.

"Ameera Tondo, thank you for meeting with me," he said.

"Think nothing of it, and please refer to me as megatus. We are equal warriors in arms. Please sit," she told him. Her statement put Nestess at ease, and he sat in the chair in front of the desk. Maaryah returned to her chair and asked, "What is it, Nestess? You seem worried."

"We, the army that is, have a problem. Sutrum Megatus Idop hasn't been seen for two days. He refuses to meet with anyone and remains in his office." He leaned forward and, in a near whisper, continued, "I'm hearing rumors that he's been drinking heavily." Maaryah's eyebrows furrowed, and Nestess leaned back. "Since the ameer's crossing-over, his aides tell me he hasn't been himself."

"Tondo hasn't crossed-over!" Maaryah shot back, causing Nestess expression to change to wonderment. "No one saw him go down, and until someone can prove otherwise, he's alive."

"Yes, of course," Nestess said in a condescending tone.

"What do you want of me?" Maaryah asked.

"You're the sutrum megatus' friend. Can you talk with him? See why he's turned to drink?" Nestess wondered.

"That doesn't sound like Idop. He's never been a drunkard, not even after losing an eye. Okay, I'll meet with him," she declared.

"I'm sorry, Megatus Maaryah, but the commanding officer's orders are, he's not to be disturbed," Idop's aide told her.

"Is he in his office?" she asked.

"Yes, zerr."

"Then, I'm going in. Attempt to stop me at your peril," she threatened. The aide recalled his commanding officer's description of the Honor Challenge as he examined the powerful-looking woman towering over him. He quickly stepped aside. Maaryah entered Idop's office and closed the door. She found Idop sitting in his chair with his head and chest lying on the desk. He was quietly snoring, an overturned cup near his left hand and a Munnari short sword near his right. She looked around the office and counted four empty pitchers of wine and an empty wineskin on the floor near his chair. It was a pathetic sight, and it saddened her, but only for an instant.

She turned around and opened the door, shouting to an orderly, she commanded, "Bring me a bucket of water. Make sure it's cold water." After a short wait, she was handed a heavy wooden pail. She closed the door, walked over to Idop, and dumped the entire vessel onto his head and back. Idop roared in surprise and anger, jumping to his feet, sword in hand. He staggered backward a few steps before gaining his balance, water pouring off his hair and down his face, obscuring his vision.

"What in the names of the Five Shadows!" he yelled. "I'll kill you!" he threatened, waving his sword in front of himself as he wiped the water from his face with his left forearm.

"Idop, how dare you threaten me!" Maaryah shouted back. "Look at you! You can't even stand without wobbling. What's wrong with you?"

A couple of Idop's aides were standing near the doorway to their commander's office, their ears near the door, worried expressions on their faces.

Megatus Nestess entered the orderly room and cleared his throat, getting their attention. "What are you two doing?" he gruffly asked.

"We're trying to determine if we should enter and protect our commander," one of the aides answered worriedly.

"Is the ameera with him?" Nestess asked. The aides nodded. "Leave them be; they're old friends," he told them with a wry smile. The aides looked at each other and stepped away from the door.

"Megatus, can we help you?" one of the aides asked.

"In half a segment, tell the sutrum megatus his brigade commanders request a meeting with him. They're waiting outside," Nestess told him.

"Yes, zerr, half a segment."

"Idop, this isn't like you. What's the problem?" Maaryah wondered.

"Your bondmate has gone off and gotten himself killed. That's the problem," he grumbled.

"He's not dead! No one on the mission saw him fall. The great god wouldn't allow it," Maaryah told him. Idop wiped his face again with his forearm and threw his sword onto the desk.

"Alive or dead, he ain't here," Idop groused.

"So, that's what set you to drink? You miss your friend?" Maaryah asked.

"I miss the ameer's leadership. I may have the title of army commander, but he's the one who made the great plans. The plans that succeeded. He's the one with the inner-power that could counter the Showton's. He's the Messenger. I'm none of those things."

"Idop, straighten your back! Tondo taught you what you need to know. You, too, have the inner-power. You may not be the Messenger, but the Messenger has shown us what we must do. Undoubtedly, this is all part of the great god's plan. We now must save our own world. Pull yourself together and act like the commander this army desperately needs, especially now," Maaryah scolded.

Idop was a bit puzzled by Maaryah's statement, but his head hurt too much to think, so he didn't. "Is Tondo still alive?" he asked, his good eye searching her face in hope.

"I refuse to believe otherwise. He may have escaped; you know how resourceful he is. He may have been captured, alive," she said.

"Captured! You've seen what that vestang does to his prisoners. By the name of the great god, may that not be his fate. Why did he act so foolishly?" Idop repined as he ran his fingers through his soaking wet hair.

"You must find him. You owe him that. He didn't give up on you when you acted foolishly during the Brigand Campaign, did he? He risked his life to bring you back," Maaryah reminded him. Idop lowered his gaze, a bit ashamed of himself. "Now, sutrum megatus, what are you going to do?" Maaryah demanded in a stern voice.

"I'll do everything I can to find him and bring him back," Idop promised.

"The best way to do that is to kill that vestang, the Showton," she firmly declared.

Idop slowly walked to a nearby table and opened the lid of the tiny chest sitting on it. He lifted a large finger band. Maaryah identified it immediately because it was the ameer's signet ring. He returned to Maaryah and handed it to her. "Tondo told me to give this to you if he didn't return. Also, his Munnari armor is in his quarters. He said the mission called for stealth, so he left it here."

She stood in silence as tears welled in her eyes and soon began streaking her cheeks.

Idop signaled for Maaryah to sit, and after she did, he also sat. "Tell me about Maari. Is she all right?"

Maaryah and Idop enjoyed each other's company for a while before one of his aides interrupted, "Zerr, the brigade commanders request a meeting with you."

"What do they want?" Idop asked.

"Megatus Nestess says it's for yours and the ameera's ears only," the aide replied.

"Alright, have them enter," Idop told him as he and Maaryah stood. The brigade commanders were ushered in and pressed against the small room's walls.

"Oy, what's this all about?" Idop asked.

"Zerr, the brigade commanders have talked it over, and we think it would be wise if we stopped campaigning and returned to the kingdom, especially now that we've lost the Messenger," Nestess said.

Maaryah couldn't believe what she had just heard, and in disgust, she asked, "Nestess, did you say you want to give up and abandon the field?"

"It's not just me, Megatus Maaryah. All of the brigades want to go home. We can't win without Ameer Tondo. Also, after learning of the ameer's loss, the men are grumbling; they want to return to the Blessing of the City," he added.

"I was never consulted, and I'm a brigade commander," she noted.

"You command the women. They're not from the kingdom," Megatus Pydeez told her.

"Te Femma is part of the kingdom by treaty, or have you forgotten that fact, Pydeez?" Maaryah glared at the man. Her scowl then fell upon Nestess. "Nestess, why does the ameer call you Stonewall?" He lowered his head in shame. She continued, "Because you're steadfast and reliable. Now, where is your resolve?" She then walked around the room, and as she did, she touched each ex-slave's mark, which was every brigade commander present. "Tondo put his life on the line for each of the marked here. He could have returned to his estate and lived the good life, and the rest of you would still be shoveling stink out of your master's stalls or doing some other menial task for a master who hated you for being lower than frizzard dung. He argued with royalty and all the great ones of the kingdom to give you a chance to live up to your potential. And this is how you repay him; by giving up?" Maaryah was becoming furious.

"Ameera, the Messenger has crossed-over. We cannot win," Megatus Savas whined.

"How do you know he's dead? Did you see him fall? Did any of you see that? Sutrum Sestardus Harmon was there, and he didn't. The great god wouldn't abandon his messenger.

Have you no honor or self-respect? It's the duty of each one of you to find him," she ordered.

"I know this is a difficult time for you, ameera, but we can't go forth on only hope," Megatus Gheedan reasoned.

"Gheedan, it's always been about hope. Tondo's hope for us. His hope freed the slaves, and his hope has made the kingdom a place where the marked can prosper. If this army surrenders the field, how long do you think it will take before the Showton's forces approach the East Gap ready to turn us all, freed-men and freeborn alike, into slaves? We're here, and the Showton is reeling from his defeats. It's time to drive forward to victory and end his menace while he is weak. We must never surrender to a tyrant. As for me, the Te Femma Brigade will advance alone if necessary," Maaryah's anger could not be contained any longer, and her orange aura ignited, startling the men.

"You have the inner-power!" Nestess exclaimed as he and the others shielded their faces from the burning rays and stood in awe.

"Yes, and so does your commander, Idop," she declared.

Fayeetez burst into the room and looked around. "What's this all about?" he demanded as he stared in surprise at the lucent ameera.

"The brigades have lost their nerve and wish to crawl home," Maaryah snapped as her aura faded.

"Outrageous!" Fayeetez spewed. "The mounted warriors are going forward, not backward."

"Enough!" Idop shouted. "I decide where this army goes, not the brigade commanders. Megatus Maaryah is right. We don't know for sure the Ameer is dead. We have an obligation, a duty, to do all we can to find him. The best way to do that is to destroy the Showton. And I say, the sooner, the better. Now, return to your commands and prepare them for our upcoming campaign season. Tell your men we will return to the Blessing of the City only after the Showton is dead. We will defeat the enemy and rescue the ameer if he's still alive, and I for one will pray to the great god for his safe return . . . " Idop was interrupted as Zuni and Dori entered the crowded room. "Oy, what is it? Why have you come to this brigade commanders' meeting unannounced?" Idop grumbled in a perturbed tone.

"Our apologies, zerr, but the queen has summoned Megatus Maaryah, and she is to report immediately," Zuni told him.

Idop turned to the ameera and nodded, "You're dismissed. This meeting is over anyway." Maaryah quickly stepped out of the room with Zuni following, but Dori remained with the men. When she didn't leave with the other two women, Idop suspected something was up. "Why are you still here? What's going on?" he asked.

"Zerr, we have a problem," she looked around the room and caught each commander's eye. "The army has a big problem. Let me explain."

Night had fallen, and Maaryah marched through the dark streets with Zuni at her side. They passed a few small gangs of men gathered outside sleazy taverns. When the men saw two women approaching through the darkness, they thought they might have a little fun at the women's expense; however, when the ruffians noticed the women were armed and most likely Te Femmans, they slinked back into the shadows and let them pass unaccosted. These brutes had learned from past experience or rumor the Te Femmans were not to be confronted if one valued his well-being.

Maaryah kept an eye on the hooligans and a hand on the grip of her sword; Zuni did the same. They would have preferred to detour around this part of the city, the Dregs, as it was called, but it was the most direct route to the queen's hall and temporary residence. After the two women emerged from the ghetto, they relaxed.

"What does the queen want with me?" Maaryah finally asked.

"The arbon didn't say, but I can guess," Zuni stated.

Maaryah looked at her, "Tell me what you think this is about."

Zuni went on to explain why she thought Maaryah had been summoned. When she had finished, Maaryah was beside herself with worry.

"Trouble always comes in threes," Maaryah mumbled under her breath.

"What did you say?" Zuni asked.

"Trouble always comes in threes. It's an old kingdom adage. Too often, it's true. First, Tondo didn't return; then Idop and the brigade commanders lost their nerve; now this. It's enough to make me scream," Maaryah angrily told Zuni, her worry now replaced by a new resolve.

"Your Highness, Megatus Maaryah has arrived," the arbon said.

"Very well," the queen replied, her tone expressing the unpleasant task before her. She climbed the stairs to the temporary throne platform and sat. "Have her enter." Maaryah marched in alone, approaching the throne. A couple of strides short of the platform, she stopped and bowed.

"Your Highness, you summoned me?" she asked.

"Ha," the queen said, then she stood and went to Maaryah. She took her by the hands and said, "My child, Our deepest and most heartfelt condolences for your loss. The ameer is sorely missed. What can We do for you?"

Maaryah stifled a smile when referred to as a child, for she was probably close to twice the queen's age. But this wasn't a time for mirthful thoughts. Her amber eyes grew stern, and she said, "Ameer Tondo is not lost. His return has only been delayed."

The queen looked at her with concerned eyes. "Of course. I hope that is the case," the queen said, her voice expressing disbelief. She released Maaryah's hands, returned to her raised throne, and sat. "We were greatly pleased to learn your daughter has been returned to you. How did she fare during her ordeal?"

"She told me she was well cared for by an elderly woman the Showton assigned to her keeping," Maaryah told her.

"Praise the great mother!" the queen exclaimed. "We can only imagine the joy of your reunion."

"For a moment, my joy was full until I learned her father hadn't returned. It's now my duty to see that he does," Maaryah told her, guiding the exchange to the likely purpose of the queen's summons.

"That responsibility rests with the army, not you. Now that you and your daughter are reunited, We are sure you will be spending all of your time teaching and training her," the queen said.

"I'll be spending as much time with her as my duties permit," Maaryah explained.

"Megatus Maaryah—Ameera Tondo—it is your duty as the child's mother to raise her and pass along your knowledge and many worthy attributes. You can only do that when she is under your direct personal care and instruction. That is why the traditions of the city require a mother to forsake any occupation or daily duty that interferes with a mother and daughter relationship. The battlefield is no place for a child. Surely you agree," the queen pronounced.

"When the weather changes, and before the army begins the next campaign, I will have Boatmaster Hermanez deliver her to Lady Idop in the kingdom. She will be responsible for her until our victory is secured and the ameer found. A short separation will have little impact. My daughter needs her father as well, and I will not rest until his fate is known," Maaryah forcefully explained.

"As ruler of Te Femma, it is Our supreme duty to see that the city's traditions are upheld. In that way, our unique heritage will be maintained. The sisterhood must follow the traditions if we wish to continue as we have in the past. Consequently, you cannot remain as the commander of the Te Femma

Brigade because that duty separates you from your daughter. As a reward for your faithful service, you will be advanced to the royal rank of toepaur and become an important and well-respected queen's adviser. You will also receive a generous stipend," the queen explained.

"Your Highness, as has been pointed out often, I am not a sister because I'm not a citizen of Te Femma. With all due respect, Your Highness, I already have a royal title and a stipend; I don't need more," Maaryah explained.

"Megatus Maaryah, We will not discuss this further. You will be relieved of command," the queen declared angrily. As the queen prepared to make her final decree concerning the matter, an arbon stepped to the side of the queen's platform and had a short, whispered discussion with the queen. Queen Ezora leaned back on her makeshift throne and said in a loud voice, "All right, let them enter." Idop, Zuni, Dori, and the army's brigade commanders, who had just met with Idop, walked in. The queen scanned the approaching group and focused her stare on the men, a more discrepant group of ferals she had never seen before. Her emerald-green eyes glared with disgust. "Sutrum Megatus Idop, what is this about?"

"Your Highness, we've come to petition you not to relieve Megatus Maaryah. We are at a critical time, now that Ameer Tondo is no longer with us," he paused and added, "at least for the moment." This was in deference to Maaryah's feelings.

Zuni quickly added, "Your Highness, her skill as a commander cannot be matched by any sister. Furthermore, she possesses the inner-power, the same power the ameer has used. I've seen her lift and move a heavy gunstone without touching it."

"Your Highness," Nestess began haltingly, "the Showton has the inner-power, too. We need the ameera more desperately now than ever before." The other ferals rumbled their agreement.

"Your Highness," Idop said, "we will begin the new campaign soon; the final one, I'm sure. The fate of all the freed cities is at stake, including Te Femma. We implore you to allow Maaryah to continue as commander of your brigade."

The queen sat, silently pondering what she'd just learned. After a distressing wait, she spoke, "Your appeal is well received. We certainly don't want Our city threatened again by that beast. Megatus Maaryah, is it true you possess the same power as the ameer?" the queen asked.

"It is true, Your Highness; however, I'm not nearly as powerful as the Messenger. Sutrum Megatus Idop also has a portion of the power, and there are others. Tondo awakened the inner-power of Haro the weaponsmith and Sire Ayascho of the Wilderness, all of whom have had crucial roles in this fight against evil," Maaryah disclosed.

"This revelation changes everything. It appears that deity has set a plan in motion, and We are not One to interfere. Megatus Maaryah, as you have stated, you are not a citizen of Te Femma. Therefore, because you are an outsider, We give you this choice: you may resign and receive the aforementioned honors, or you may continue serving as brigade commander."

Without hesitation, Maaryah emphatically responded, "I choose the brigade!"

"Then, so it shall be," the queen decreed. The men gave a

shout of approval and relief. The queen scowled at the breach of protocol and curtly dismissed everyone.

Maari was playing with Tumper near a corner of Idop's office. She rolled a ball of string across the floor. Tumper fetched it and carried it back to her. Maari's braid was gone, her hair cut short and braided like her mother's. Idop watched the two playing together as Maaryah looked over the plans Tondo had drawn up before leaving on the mission to rescue their daughter.

After reading Tondo's notes and closely examining his hand-drawn map, she looked at Idop and asked, "This looks good to me. I do have one question, though. Where are the gunz? They're not mentioned in the notes, and I don't see them positioned on the map."

"Tondo said he wanted them left in Rendoto. He told me the Showton could easily avoid them now that he knows we have 'em. If they're placed in the center, the Showton will attack the flanks. If we put them on the flanks, he'll attack the center. If we attack, they're useless. He said it was better to leave them behind rather than risk their loss. We'll only need them to knock down city walls," Idop explained.

Maaryah bent over Tondo's map and examined it more closely. After a while, she looked up and said with a smile, "I have an idea."

# CHAPTER 31

# TEACH THEM

Maaryah stood on the Rendoto dock, her heart breaking. The *Anterra* and the *Zerio* were sailing out of the bay, the *Zerio* leading the way. Standing next to Boatmaster Hermanez on the larger boat was the ship's most precious passenger, little Maari. Mother and daughter just had a heart-wrenching parting, neither wanting to say goodbye, but as Maaryah explained in her attempt to console Maari, and herself for that matter, her daughter needed to return to the Blessing of the City. She needed to expend all her energies leading the brigade, crushing the Showton with the hope and expectation of finding Maari's parr, Maaryah's beloved bondmate.

Also aboard the *Zerio* was Queen Ezora. The two ships planned to stop at Te Femma and then sail to the estate, placing Maari in Tenny's loving care, overseen by Lady Idop. The two ships would then sail on to the Ancient City, where Hermanez would make his report to the king, a report that would undoubtedly shake the kingdom to its core: the loss of Ameer Tondo.

Standing next to Maaryah, on either side, were Zuni and Dori. The two had decided between themselves to support their commander, for they understood the ordeal she was going through. She would have preferred to sail home with her daughter, but she had duties to perform and a mission—no, a quest—to complete.

Standing nearby was Arbon Huma. It was apparent she felt out of place and uncomfortable. As the queen was about to board the ship, she ordered the arbon to remain behind and record the brigade's history as it unfolded. Maaryah and her senior lieutenants immediately suspected she was another spy for the queen, and their expressions of acrimony made it clear what they thought of Huma and her assignment. The arbon realized it would take time and some effort to convince the three commanders that she really was only performing the duties of a historian.

From the time the ships departed Rendoto until they returned, three wernts had passed. This voyage was Boatmaster Arbreno's first official assignment as a ship's captain. He had been Hermanez's first officer for many spans. Hermanez had recommended to the ameera that Arbreno be advanced to boatmaster, and Maaryah accepted Hermanez's recommendation without question because she knew little to nothing about seafaring matters. Hermanez had assumed command of the larger and faster boat, the *Zerio*, and Abreno was made boatmaster of the *Anterra*.

Maaryah received word from a military runner of the two ships' arrival, and she breathed a sigh of relief. Undoubtedly, Maari had been delivered safe and sound. Yet, she anxiously awaited Hermanez's full report on the journey and also the king's response to the news concerning Tondo. In the late afternoon, Hermanez and Arbreno were ushered into Maaryah's HQ. As she stood to welcome them, another familiar face entered. It was Master Shergus.

"Boatmasters, welcome back. Has Maari been delivered safely?" Both men nodded, and Maaryah smiled in relief. She continued, "Master Shergus, it's a pleasure to see you again. Do you bring word from the Sutro Seer?" she asked, desperate to hear an encouraging word from the one closest to deity.

"He sends you his blessing," Shergus told her.

An expression of disappointment quickly replaced her smile of relief. "Did he say anything about Tondo?" she asked, her voice almost frantic.

"I'm sorry, ameera, he gave me no words concerning the Messenger; however, he asked me to pass along a gift he has for you," Shergus said.

"A gift? What is it?" she asked. He moved a step closer and placed his hands on her shoulders. Suddenly, she felt a surge of energy passing into her body. It did not stop for the longest time, and when Shergus removed his hands, she swayed and began to collapse. He caught her and, with help from the two boatmasters, eased her into a nearby chair. She sat in silence for a long time, her head in her hands and her elbows resting on her knees.

"We must fetch a physician!" Arbreno exclaimed. Hermanez searched Shergus's face with concerned eyes.

"No need for a physician. She'll recover soon enough. Her inner-power has been bolstered," Shergus told them. Maaryah looked up at Shergus with wondering eyes. "Yes, that is the Sutro Seer's gift to you. You once helped to save a kingdom. Now, you must help save the world. You are the hope of the righteous, the hope of Munnari. You must defeat the evil before us, or all is lost. The Sutro Seer has been given a glimpse of the future, and he has sent me here to safeguard you. I have given him my oath that I will do so even at the cost of my own life," Master Shergus declared. Maaryah was too weak to respond and simply sat staring up at the temple's master swordsman.

After Shergus's words had been pondered by those present, Hermanez chuckled, "I can only imagine the greeting you're going to receive when the other women learn of your assignment. I don't know who to pity more, you or the sisters." Hermanez's chuckle turned into a belly laugh, but Shergus was not amused. Maaryah snickered quietly as her strength began to return.

True to the boatmaster's prediction, Zuni and Dori did not appreciate Master Shergus's assignment; however, something about this feral warned them to tread lightly. His threatening eyes and stern countenance forewarned them that he would not be denied, and if they tried, it would be to their detriment and any others who attempted to interfere with his assigned duty. Privately, Maaryah explained the situation to her senior officers and expressed her annoyance, but she instructed them to accept the master's presence. From that day forth, Shergus was Maaryah's constant companion; however, she drew the line at the bathhouse and bedtime. Nevertheless, Master Shergus was always nearby, his dark eyes ever searching for trouble hidden in plain sight or in shadowy depths.

Maaryah and Idop had spent many days in planning sessions. They had taken Tondo's plan for the army's next encounter with the Showton's army and added their own personal touches to it. They felt they had considered all the variables and were prepared to present the plan to the brigade commanders. Although they felt confident, they remembered Tondo repeating constant quotes he attributed to a great military philosopher from his homeland. He said the great man had written a revered military canon titled Murphy's Laws. Tondo's two most oft-repeated laws from this great philosopher were, 'No plan survives contact with the enemy,' and 'Perfect plans aren't.' These laws were drummed into their memories in nearly every training session he'd held at the estate. There, it had been fun, only a game. Now, the game had turned deadly serious, with the kingdom's future and their families' well-being resting in the balance. Both felt the gravity of their positions, and they were excited and anxious as they awaited the weather change that would usher in a new campaign season.

"It is time," Idop said. "I'll assemble the brigade commanders tomorrow for a council of war. I expect the army to be on the move in no more than a wernt." Maaryah nodded her agreement and glanced over to Master Shergus, who was standing stoically out of the way. She hoped for at least a nod of approval from the temple's representative, but the master remained stolid.

Tondo lay on his belly on the cold stone floor, his eyes closed. His back felt like it was on fire. He had never experienced such acute pain. He could feel the wounds on his back throb with every beat of his heart. He had always thought he could endure such torture with an indomitable spirit; however, he hadn't. Had the Showton demanded his inner-power with the promise of stopping the flogging, he would have surrendered it. He was appalled by his weakness. He felt ashamed and began to sorrow. He had heard about other men from his homeland who had endured much worse treatment than this before breaking. He had learned from his training that every man has a breaking point, but he hadn't expected to reach his so quickly. What was he to do? He wanted to weep like a child, yet he was too proud to allow such a display with the two dungeon dullards undoubtedly nearby.

Tondo steeled himself, opened his eyes, and he saw moldering straw. He started to move, but the slightest movement he made caused his back to recoil in excruciating pain. He abruptly froze in place and lay on the hard, cold stone.

"Hoy, Moeg, our guest has finally awaked," Drueg yelled.

"Ha! It's time I cleansed his wounds. Now that he's awake, he can pleasure in it," Moeg shouted back, followed by a wicked laugh. Tondo soon saw Moeg approaching, carrying a wooden bucket, water slopping out of it as he stepped. Moeg stopped and stood, looking down at his prisoner. "The seshtane ordered your wounds be cleansed. I wanted ya to be awake first, so ya can 'preciate my duty. All in all, I think me and Drueg did a darn good job. Not too bloody since we had to use the knotted tamer; got some nice welts, though. I'm sure this brine will clean out the cuts ya got." With that, Moeg dumped the bucket of salt-laced water onto Tondo's back. Tondo roared in pain and sprang to his knees. Moeg jumped away, swinging the empty wooden bucket in warning. "Don't get no closer, or I'll break this over yer head," he warned.

Tondo grunted and growled as the brine dripped off his agonized back. His red aura erupted but was quickly sucked into the collar around his neck. Although he said nothing, the glare he gave Moeg was unnerving, causing the reprobate to retreat rapidly into the shadows. Tondo's enmity was then turned to Drueg, who also slinked away.

Tondo remained on his knees as the searing pain across his back began slowly to subside to a tolerable level. He quickly realized his despair had been turned into rage. He wanted to kill his two tormentors, and he began imagining ways he could do it. Hate filled his bosom, and his desire for revenge grew with every heartbeat that throbbed across his back. As his malevolence swelled, he realized he had not been fully broken, at least not yet. Through his pain, he accepted that he was a dead man. Maaryah and Idop would soon face the Showton in mortal combat, and he could not allow the Degenerate—the Showton—to gain in power and advantage by taking his tzaah. If he, himself, must die, he would do so with as much honor and self-respect as he could muster.

Tondo finally stood, and it was then he noticed his ankles were manacled and attached to a chain passed through a metal ring secured to the stone floor. He had some freedom of movement but not much. His hands and arms were free, and for the first time, he was able to touch and explore by feel the metal collar around his neck. He gave it a few good tugs, but it seemed very secure. He tugged on the chain and tested the ring anchored in the floor. It, too, was well fixed. He wondered if, over time, he could loosen either or both. If he could, the first targets of his vengeance would fall upon the two sadistic dungeon morons.

Suddenly and unexpectedly, Tondo felt engulfed in an unseen presence. It was shocking but surprisingly non-threatening. A thought came into his mind, an idea as though someone, not himself, was speaking to him, giving him loving advice. The voice simply said, 'Teach them.' The presence was gone as quickly as it had come, leaving him puzzled.

What was that? he wondered silently.

Never before could he recall experiencing such an event. The only thing remotely similar was his encounters with the Tempter, the unseen force that placed evil and wicked thoughts in his mind. The feelings he had then were anger and hate; however, this encounter was one of love, charity, and compassion. Tondo remembered from what he had learned at the Batru village and also from Master Varios, as well, that the Tempter's counterpart in this world was the Whisperer. The Tempter was an agent of Evil, whereas the Whisperer was an agent of Good. What was it the voice had told him?

"Teach them," Tondo said aloud. "Moeg, Drueg, get your arses over here!" Tondo yelled. The two numskulls couldn't believe what they had just heard, their prisoner ordering them to come to him. Like moths drawn to an open flame, they approached; slowly, cautiously. They stopped a safe distance from him and stared. "Alright. The two of you and I need to have a long talk," Tondo began.

"A talk 'bout what?" Moeg asked in an annoyed tone.

"Sit down!" Tondo commanded. The two dolts looked at

each other and then obeyed, remaining a safe distance from their prisoner. Tondo carefully sat and extended his legs, his back still throbbing in fiery pain.

"What ya gonna say?" Drueg asked.

"Oy, let's start by discussing personal cleanliness. You guys need to bathe more often and wash your clothes as often as you can. If you don't, you'll probably come down with some nasty illness that could kill you," Tondo warned. He watched as their eyes widened, and they looked into each other's faces. It appeared he had struck a nerve. "You know someone who got sick, don't you?"

"Ha, Gaft´ did. He used to be here, too, but he got something that made his fingers start rotting off. He was sent away. Don't know what happened to him after that," Drueg explained.

"There you go. Now, listen to me and let's see if I can help you avoid the same fate," Tondo said.

"Ya'd probably love seeing our fingers rot off. What's it to ya, anyway?" Moeg wondered.

"Didn't they tell you? My job is to help people improve their lives. Have you two ever considered a different line of employment?" His two guards responded with only blank stares. "Okay, let's start at the beginning. Fetch a couple of buckets of clean water and some soap, if you got any. Bring back a couple of clean towels if you can find some," he shouted as the two disappeared into the shadows. Tondo had no idea where his plan was going, but at the very least, it had taken his mind off the pain ravaging his back, for a moment anyway.

Attendant Superior Neehoer bore a worried look as he approached the massive doors leading to the Showton's Great Hall. His master had summoned him, and he wondered—actually, he worried—about the call. The Showton had not been himself ever since his meeting with the Tondo. No other but the Dark One witnessed what had happened, and he had not revealed any of the details.

Neehoer moved to Door Attendant Torbo and asked, "What's the master's mood today?"

"Very sullen," Torbo replied. "His boat is long overdue, and this has increased his ire. I would tread carefully if I were you. Punishments are free-flowing this morning."

Neehoer took a deep breath and nodded to the guards. The two enormous wooden doors were swung open, and Attendant Superior Neehoer marched forward, his dark robes flowing around him as he moved. The Showton was sitting on his throne atop his platform. A couple of paces from the platform's stairs, Neehoer dropped to one knee.

"Master, how may I serve you today?" he asked, his head low in a bow.

The Showton's voice rose in volume as he spoke, "This United Kingdom army vexes me. I will put an end to it and make its king suffer for his part in resisting my will. And I must teach that queen from the City of Women what it means to anger me. I now own their loathsome ameer. I'm sure his army is reeling because of it. I will soon crush the others. They cannot withstand my power!" He was nearly shouting by the time he paused. He relaxed a bit. "Neehoer, you may stand. I will leave in two days and go to the northern army. I will personally lead my forces to victory," he declared.

"It will be a great and glorious victory, the greatest of all your conquests," Neehoer proclaimed like the withering toady he was.

"I want you to assemble as many of the remaining armies and garrison units as can be gathered. Reduce the garrisons in the south and recall the armies besieging the cities in the east. After I defeat the Tondo's army, I will take my combined forces, first to retake the City of Women and make them regret their rebellion. After that, I'll invade the United Kingdom and take their king as my prisoner. I'll have him put in a cage and paraded throughout my realm as an example to any who might defy me. After that, he'll be tormented unto death," the Showton declared.

"Yes, master; however, it will take time to assemble the men. They are scattered in many diverse places. I suggest you delay your return to the northern army until the others have been collected. When combined, your army will be invincible," Neehoer asserted.

"I will not wait that long. Now is the time to strike, while they are weak and demoralized," the Showton avowed.

"What of the prisoner?" Neehoer asked.

"I put him in your charge. I want him kept alive. Is that understood?" the Showton barked.

"Yes, Your Excellency; however, wouldn't it be advantageous to slaughter him before the eyes of his army? Wouldn't that drive a stake through his warriors' hearts?"

The Showton thought for a moment, then roared, "His power! His power! I must take his power! There is a greater threat I must yet deal with. A threat much more dangerous than a mortal army. After all his hopes are crushed, he will relinquish his substantial inner strength to me. Need I say more?"

"You are most wise, master," Neehoer cajoled. "I will carry out your orders and see that the prisoner's life is preserved. Is there anything else?"

"I want more zondars readied for my advance into the United Kingdom. I demand their training be completed as quickly as possible. They will lead my assault to the Ancient City, my final campaign," the Showton added.

"I will see to it, master," Neehoer replied.

The Showton leaned back on his throne, grumbling, "Those fools think they can resist me? I'll teach them, and they will suffer for their folly."

# CHAPTER 32

# WHY WE FIGHT

Never before had the residents of Rendoto witnessed such an event. The United Kingdom army was fully assembled, and it far outnumbered the city's population. The people marveled, and their hearts filled with joy. Undoubtedly, the Showton could never defeat such a powerful force, they thought. Those who beheld the spectacle—victims of the Showton's cruelty—began to clamor for his destruction. "His head! His head! His Head!" the throng shouted.

Sutrum Megatus Idop stood before a formation of the kingdom's army, his brigade commanders in a line in front of him. Master Shergus was standing a step behind him and to his left.

Idop raised his right fist high above his head to silence the crowd of onlookers, and slowly the chant subsided. When all was quiet, he began to speak in a loud voice. "Brothers and sisters, today we embark on a new campaign; truly the last one. We fight the forces of Evil who desire to take away our freedom and turn our loved ones and us into slaves. I assure you, this they will never do. You form the greatest and the most powerful army ever assembled. You have been well trained, and you have already shown your mettle in battle. The kingdom expects that everyone will do their duty!"

All warriors, male and female, raised their voices in a cheer that shook the ground and thrilled the Rendoto residents. When all was quiet once again, Idop continued. "Megatus Maaryah, front and center!" he ordered. Maaryah quickly marched to Idop, stopped before him, and saluted. Idop returned her salute and said, "Megatus, your brigade is to lead the advance. Prepare your warriors and lead on."

"Yes, zerr!" Maaryah replied with a salute and a smile. She made an About-Face and marched to where an aide was holding her war-samaran. She mounted and moved to the front of her brigade. "Sisters of Te Femma! We have the honor of leading the final campaign! Prepare to move out!" The sisters gave another cheer, and as they did, Maaryah's mount reared up on its hind legs. Maaryah pulled the Munnari Blade from the scabbard at her side and held it high above her head. It immediately ignited in blue flames. The sisters' cheers increased in volume at the sight. A guttural growl was soon heard coming from the male units. It grew in strength until it exploded in an ear-shattering Victor's Shout as weapons were hoisted high above heads. The Rendoto residents responded with cheers and applause of their own.

Master Shergus leaned forward and spoke into Idop's ear, "This is good, very good! The spirit of the Munnari Blade has accepted its new holder."

The Te Femma Brigade advanced four abreast. The remainder of the army followed in the order Idop had decided upon days earlier. Although the women led the army's advance, Fayeetez's cavalry had been on patrol through the cold and wet season. He had ordered his patrols increased as the weather improved. A large enemy force had been located near Nudart wernts before, and it was kept under constant observation. When Fayeetez informed his commander that it appeared the Showton's army was preparing to move away from Nudart, Idop was ready. He gave Fayeetez orders to find favorable ground for the coming encounter, the battle they all swore would be the last.

Shortly after the Showton arrived at his forward army's winter quarters in the city of Nudart, the order was given to move out. Most men expected to move north, cross the great river, and retake Anderez. Surprisingly, they were moving west, towards either Rendoto in the north or Panemento in the south. It was rumored that the bulk of the United Kingdom's army had spent the wet season garrisoned in the former. The Showton's men became uneasy, for many of them had already seen and felt its power. A rumor was spreading that one of its leaders had been captured by the Sutro Showton, and now their master's plan was to destroy the army that had caused him so much trouble in the past. To most of the conscripts, this was just another march into the hungry maw of Death.

"Trutz, how long did you say you been with this army?" his friend, Perdeeto, asked. He had arrived in Nudart only a couple of wernts before the army moved out.

Perdeeto was a simple, uneducated farmer struggling to feed his woman and four young children daily. When the Showton's men came to his farm the first time, more than five spans ago, they had deemed him too old and his oldest son too young for service in the Showton's army. During the latest cold season, they had returned. This time, it was decided he wasn't too old nor his eldest son too young. Both were conscripted into different armies. The Showton's men also took half of the stores he had set aside for the cold season. He feared for his woman's and three remaining children's welfare. Would they survive until the next crop was planted and harvested? The thought kept him awake at night. He even considered deserting and heading back to his farm. Trutz had stopped him and warned of the consequences should he be caught. He was told the Showton's commanders were ruthless in carrying out discipline. Deserters were always executed in the most gruesome manner as the remainder of the army, mostly fellow conscripts, were forced to watch. The ghastly punishments were meant to deter any other potential deserter by making them witness the severe consequences awaiting such a foolhardy act.

"What ya say?" Trutz asked.

"How long you been in the army?" Perdeeto repeated.

"I've been in this one for three spans. I was on garrison duty in the south for five or six spans before they sent me here. Before that, I was conquering cities in the east. Why do you ask?" Trutz wondered as they tromped along.

"I was just thinking. I want to go home. Will you ever go home?" Perdeeto asked.

"This is my home now, and it's your home, too. Forget the past. It'll be easier if you do," Trutz advised.

"Do you have a family, a woman?" Perdeeto wondered.

"Not anymore, and neither do you." Trutz turned his head

and looked at Perdeeto, marching beside him. "Lose that sad face. You're a warrior in the Showton's army now. Be glad you're fed every day and just follow orders."

"What are we fighting for?" Perdeeto asked.

Trutz chuckled, then said, "We fight for the Sutro Showton's glory. When we go into battle, pray to the gods for a quick death. That's the best we can hope for, and that's why we fight."

Maaryah walked through the brigade's camp, inspecting the pickets and listening to the sisters' idle chatter as they gathered around their fires. The army had already moved three marches southeast of Rendoto. She had received Fayeetez's report that the enemy was moving northwest toward them. She knew it would only be a short time before the two armies met and clashed. The thought both excited and alarmed her. The upcoming encounter with the Showton would be the first without the ameer. Could she, Idop, and the others pull off a victory? She fretted over the thought but would not let her inner fears become outwardly expressed. She had hardened herself, and she always displayed a confident appearance for her warriors to see. Only those closest to her could sense her inner conflict. They knew the pressure she was struggling under. Everyone was looking to her as the ameer's replacement. It was an incredible and frightening expectation. When she felt down, Zuni and Dori would bolster her; however, Master Shergus, her shadow both day and night, wasn't so sympathetic. His comments were as quick and biting as his sword strokes. Once, when she felt particularly overwhelmed, he barked, 'Straighten your back and act like a man!' When he realized what he'd said, they both had a good laugh.

Maaryah moved to one of the inner pickets while Shergus stood a discrete distance away. She began a friendly conversation with the young woman warrior. Maaryah could tell the picket was surprised that her brigade commander would take the time to talk to a lowly soldier. Maaryah was genuinely concerned for each and every sister, and Tondo had trained her always to be cognizant of her warriors' morale.

"How is it going tonight?" Maaryah asked.

"Very well, zerr. No problems on the inside, so far, that is," the picket replied.

The sisters had found it necessary to post pickets both on the outside of their camp, facing the enemy, and on the inside, facing their feral allies. A few uneducated ferals would occasionally sneak over to the sister's area in the dark of night with mischief on their minds. These troublesome fools were quickly taught by the pickets on duty. They were then returned to their own area, bloodied, bruised, and educated.

"Good. What's your name?" Maaryah asked.

"Mendora, zerr," the picket replied.

"Are you from the city, Mendora?"

"No, zerr. My family has a farm well north of the city. The Showton's ferals made an awful mess of it. My two blood-sisters and my brother are helping my mama and papa get it back in order. We lost all of our animals, and it'll take spans to recover our losses."

"It sounds like your family could use you on the farm. Why did you join the brigade?" Maaryah wondered.

"Ma and Pa wanted me to. They don't never wanta go through what the Showton did to us again. We were his slaves for two spans. You can't imagine how terrible that was." Mendora quickly glanced at the slave mark on Maaryah's forehead and lowered her eyes. "I guess you can. Sorry, zerr," she said, a bit ashamed of her last comment.

"Think nothing of it, warrior. We'll never be slaves again, none of us, and neither will our loved ones," Maaryah emphatically declared.

"Zerr, that's why I'm here. That's why we fight!"

# CHAPTER 33

# TERRIBLE TO BEHOLD

Idop and Fayeetez sat on their mounts, surveying the field before them. "Is this what you had in mind?" Fayeetez asked. Idop took his time before responding. In front of them lay a vast open plain, devoid of trees, with only scattered bushes dotting it. In the distance, they could see a hillock with a few short trees on its slopes. Idop rubbed his chin as he wrestled with his weighty decision. "I have three-thousand troopers screening that hill. The Showton's army is two marches away, and if you bring up the brigades quickly, we can hold it," Fayeetez advised.

Idop continued to scan the terrain, and after he had seen enough, he weighed the pros and cons and made his hard decision. "This will do. Pull your men back. We will align a margher from this side of that hill," he told Fayeetez.

"But zerr, the enemy will seize the high ground!" Fayeetez exclaimed.

"Let the Showton have it. Quickly now, withdraw your men and assemble with the rest of the army," Idop ordered.

Fayeetez was shocked. Why would his commander surrender the high ground after ordering him to find it? Nevertheless, he had been given his orders, and he would obey. "By your command, zerr," Fayeetez said with a salute, and Idop returned it. The cavalry commander spurred his mount and took off at a gallop toward the hill, a dozen staff officers and messengers following close behind him.

"What an idiot that one-eyed fool must be," the Showton said aloud to no one in particular. "He surrendered the high ground without a fight. I can survey the whole battlefield from here. This is going to be even easier than I thought." He sat atop his regal tanter on the crest of the hill overlooking the forces of both armies arrayed before him. A couple of dozen staff personnel, attendants, and messengers assembled behind him, awaiting their master's orders. His army stretched across his front in both directions, facing the Army of the United Kingdom more than a margher away.

The Showton noted that his army overlapped his enemy's army on both flanks. From his ideal observation point, it was evident to the Showton that the enemy commander expected him to make a frontal assault because he had placed the two thunder-makers in the center, well behind the frontline, facing his army's leading elements. They had been a real nasty surprise the first time he saw them used, but they wouldn't be this time, the second time. He would simply advance his men, pinning the enemy in place at the front, then his right and left flanks would continue driving forward, enveloping the kingdom's army on both ends. The thunder-makers would have little influence on this battle because they couldn't be repositioned quickly. The Showton believed that with luck, he might even encircle the enemy force and defeat it in detail.

"Behold the wonderful sight!" he shouted. "This victory will be glorious!"

Idop scanned the battlefield from atop the command raster's howdah, Tondo's farseer to his good eye. The male foot brigades formed his front line with Nestess's Teg-ar-mos Brigade in the center. Additional archers had been trained during the cold season, and Idop had created two archer units of about two-thousand men each. He had placed one archer command on each flank, behind the foot units. Fayeetez's mounted force had also been divided into two main bodies, each on a flank. The Te Femma Brigade was positioned directly behind the Teg-ar-mos Brigade in the center. Well behind the Te Femmans, he had placed the two guns. They were set atop a slight rise of the plain. It was a cool, partly cloudy day, with a slight *Zerio* breeze from the southwest. The p´atezas had been rising for the past three segments.

Idop lowered his farseer, took a deep breath, and ordered, "Hornman, sound the Advance to Battle!" The call blasted from the horn's bell, and immediately, orders were shouted up and down the line. The mass of units trudged forward like a plodding beast, all but the guns. As they advanced, the kingdom warriors banged their shields with their assembled metrenas with each step they took.

"The fool is advancing into the teeth of a superior force," the Showton declared. "Sound Advance!" he ordered. A horn blasted, and its call was repeated by other Showton horns. In short order, tens of thousands of warriors began their advance as thundering and fell drum beats set the pace. "Magnificent! Magnificent!" the Showton shouted with glee.

Another horn blast sounded from atop the command raster. The central third of the United Kingdom's army continued to advance. However, a third of the kingdom's army on both flanks slowed their advance until they had bent to forty-five degrees from the center line, forming a flat-faced open-based triangle, thereby making the turning or enfolding of the flanks much more difficult. Fayeetez's mounted troops hovered menacingly at the rear of the flanks, on the right and left of the main line.

Just before the two center lines slammed into each other, a volley of arrows filled the sky and then crashed into the raised shields of Idop's men. This was the first time the United Kingdom faced this type of threat, yet they were prepared for it and suffered little. The lead kingdom line responded by each man flinging his two metrenas with a roar, their deadly shafts sailing in low arcs and avoiding the overhanging Showton pikes, wreaking havoc in the enemy's ranks. The kingdom army's warriors drew their swords, shouted their battle cries, and charged forward.

Nestess's men, in the center, were the first to crash into the enemy line. After only a short pause, they began pushing the Showton's men aside. His orders were to drive a wedge into the middle of the enemy's front, and that he was doing.

The Showton's superior numbers began overlapping Idop's line, and it was quickly apparent to Idop what the Showton's plan was. Fayeetez was ordered to strafe the advancing enemy flanks, picking off many Showton warriors with arrows and slowing the enemy's advance. Also, volley after volley from the kingdom's archers forced the enemy to cover themselves by raising their shields above their heads, protecting themselves from falling death as Fayeetez's cavalry's strafing fired directly into their unprotected front ranks.

The Showton was displeased by what he was witnessing. Why had his cowardly warriors slowed their advance on the flanks? How was it possible for the enemy's center to be driving a wedge into the middle of his line?

"Order Haptane Fentz and Haptane Wat´en on the flanks to re-double their efforts. Tell them I am displeased with their progress," the Showton commanded to an aide.

The aide gave a Showton salute and quickly galloped to the messengers. Shortly after his arrival, two messengers rode off in opposite directions on their way to the flanks.

"I don't like the looks of the center. I may need to reinforce it. Tell the reserve commander to get ready to be committed," the Showton ordered another aide. It wasn't long before the Showton's flanks were advancing again, although at a terrible cost in his warriors' lives.

Maaryah and the sisters waited patiently for Idop's command, and after nearly two segments of fighting, Nestess's men had weakened the Showton's center enough to commit the reserve. A kingdom horn sounded, indicating the Te Femma Brigade was to advance. Maaryah gave the order, and the brigade moved forward, pouring into the wedge made by the Teg-ar-mos Brigade. The sisters tore into the exhausted enemy ranks, and the Showton's line broke. Just as the Te Femma warriors were streaming through the breach, they were met by the Showton's reserve of fresh ferals in the enemy's center. A desperate back-and-forth engagement ensued for the next segment as both armies pummeled each other; however, the superior training, equipment, and motivation of the United Kingdom's warriors became apparent even though outnumbered.

The Te Femma Brigade and several of Nestess's bricks were about to break through the Showton's line when Maaryah looked overhead and saw roiling purple clouds forming. This was the moment both she and Idop were predicting and dreading. Would their ploy work? It had to work. She waited for the expected horn call that would give the answer; she waited and watched as the purple clouds grew more menacing; she waited and watched as the foul and threatening haze began to descend.

"Idop, what are you waiting for? Give the order!" she yelled in frustration over the tumult of battle. She signaled for a messenger, and one quickly rode up to her and saluted. "Go to Sutrum Megatus Idop and tell him, if he doesn't give the order now, the Te Femma and Teg-ar-mos brigades will be crushed!" she cried in a frenzied and stern tone. The messenger saluted and rode away at a gallop.

Maaryah looked up again and watched the purple storm drawing closer. She cursed Idop under her breath. They were all going to die, and even if she ordered a retreat, there wasn't enough time to escape the descending doom. She had to do something and do it fast. She closed her eyes and bowed her head. The power at her center began to burn within her chest, and when she felt she was about to burst, she opened her eyes, raised her head, and lifted her arms high. A sheet of orange flashed from her fingertips and formed a layer of energy that hovered overhead like an orange curtain between her warriors and the purple storm above it. It wasn't long before the roiling purple clouds struck Maaryah's orange barrier, causing a great storm of purple and orange lightning flashing in angry protest of each other. The warriors beneath the raging battle above, friend and foe alike, stopped fighting and gazed in wonder and awe at the frightening display above them. It was terrible to behold.

The Showton couldn't believe what he was experiencing; his power was being successfully resisted. How could this be? Was it the new commander, Idop? Nevesant said he had the inner-power. He said it was white, but this one was orange.

"I'll crush you!" the Showton shouted and dug deeper into his reserve of inner might. "You will not, you cannot, resist me!" He watched as the orange barrier was pushed lower. "I am stronger! Now, I know you are a mere Worlder. You cannot defeat me. I will prevail!" he shouted as the orange barrier dropped even lower.

As confidence in his ultimate victory became assured, he noticed a massive puff of white smoke spewing from one of the thunder-makers. He watched with curiosity as a dark dot flew through the air, passing over his purple cloud. It appeared to move in slow motion, and it seemed to be quickly growing in size. He felt the orange power pushing back with more force, so he returned his focus to the battle raging below. Just as he did, a gunstone crashed into the dirt a short distance in front of him and his mount. The gunstone skipped off the ground once, twice, and slammed into his tanter. The Showton was thrown to the ground and covered in gore. He lay on the ground, wondering what had just happened, and as he regained his senses, he saw blood and chunks of flesh all over his robes. Was it his blood? Was it his flesh? Panic overwhelmed him as terror and revulsion turned his stomach. He rolled onto his side and vomited his ghastly terror. Attendants, aides, and messengers rushed to their stricken master and hovered above him. He looked up just as another gunstone skipped over his head and blasted through the men assembled around him, causing one of them to vaporize in a mist of red as blood and gore splattered everyone.

The Showton looked around and saw the grizzly horror; a severed arm was lying nearby, a leg over there; it was hideous. He wobbled to his feet and checked to see if he was still in one piece; Thank the red moon, I am. He saw a tanter standing a short distance away, dashed to it in panic, mounted, and fled the battlefield.

It was all Maaryah could do to slow the descent of the powerful purple storm above; she knew she couldn't stop it. Just when she thought all was lost, she heard the blast of the first gun, soon followed by another thundering roar—the second gun's report. It was as though a great weight was suddenly lifted from her. The purple storm quickly dissipated, and then it was gone. Her orange shield faded and disappeared. She took a deep breath, slumped in the saddle, and passed out, tumbling from her mount and into Master Shergus's arms.

The Showton fled the battlefield and rushed to his camp far to the rear of his abandoned army. He fretted over his vulnerability even though he possessed the inner-power, he had been weakened by his exertions, and he feared he could be overcome if the one with the orange power overtook him. His new counterpart, Idop, possessed the inner-power, which also worried him. How powerful could he be? In near panic, the Showton decided he must quickly gather some provisions, return to his city, and regroup.

Showton rearguards watched as a lone, mounted man approached at a gallop and were shocked when they realized it was their master, whose robes were covered in blood. The master was acting as though the enemy was about to overtake him. He jumped from his mount and ordered two nearby attendants to fetch enough food and water for travel to Fortress Showtonia. He also ordered them to accompany him. He quickly washed the dirt and blood from his face and arms and changed into a fresh robe. In less than half a segment, the Showton and his two attendants were on the move, heading south toward the safety of his city. A couple of segments later, the camp's rearguards were overwhelmed by the enemy's mounted warriors, and the Showton army base was captured, including a gigantic hoard of Showton riches.

Maaryah's golden-amber eyes slowly opened, and she saw Master Shergus's relieved and warming smile. *That's unusual,* she thought. "What happened? Where am I?" she weakly asked.

Master Shergus stepped back, and Idop's face hovered over her, his unpatched eye searching her face. "You gave us quite a scare," he said.

She tried to sit up, but Zuni put a hand on her shoulder. "Just rest, commander. Just rest for now," Zuni told her. Maaryah looked around and could see she was in a tent. Besides Idop, Zuni, and Shergus, she saw several of her aides standing nearby. She lifted Zuni's hand from her shoulder and sat up, swinging her legs over the side of the cot. After Maaryah settled for a bit, she realized she had the worst head-pounder she'd ever experienced.

"What happened? Did we win?" she painfully asked as she began rubbing her brow.

"We won!" Idop exclaimed joyously. "Your idea to use the guns the way we did worked. Haro's aim was true enough. The gunstones didn't kill the Showton, but he fled. His army unraveled after that. Then, we routed and destroyed it. Fayeetez's men are rounding up its scattered remnants. The biggest problem we have now is caring for the prisoners. Some are begging to join us."

"The sisters, what about the sisters?" Maaryah fret.

"They're doing well, and Dori is seeing to the wounded. All of the sisters worry about your welfare," Zuni told her.

"Tell them I'm all right. I just have a real bad head-pounder." Zuni nodded to one of the aides nearby, and she dashed out to spread the word that their commander was recovering. "Have you learned anything about Tondo? Do you know where he is?" Maaryah asked.

"No, not yet, but we haven't had time to question any of Showton's commanders," Idop said.

Maaryah grabbed him by the jerkin and pulled him closer, "Why did you delay the order to fire the gunz?"

"You're not going to believe this, but the hornman's horn was hit by a stray arrow, knocking it from his grip. It fell to the ground. When he climbed down to retrieve it, the raster stepped on it and smashed it flat. I had to send a messenger," Idop explained. Maaryah's eyes widened, and she released him. He continued, "At least we learned what you're capable of. How did you do that?" he wondered.

"Prayer and desperation," Maaryah simply answered as she started rubbing her forehead again. Master Shergus smiled even more broadly upon hearing her answer. "What about the Showton?" she asked.

"Fayeetez is searching for him. When he's found, he'll bring him to us dead or alive," Idop told her.

"We must take him," Maaryah grumbled. "This war isn't over until we do."

End of Novel Six

# MUNNARI REDEMPTION

## NOVEL SEVEN

After Coleman's capture and imprisonment by the evil Showton, the United Kingdom's army has turned to Maaryah and Idop to carry the burden of leadership in the continuing effort to vanquish the wicked forces of the depraved Showton. The United Kingdom army's recent victory has crushed one of his armies, and its leader is on the run. Can the forces of righteousness catch him before he flees to the safety of his city? Will his followers continue to believe in his omnipotence? Can Coleman survive and escape from his dungeon prison? Will Coleman and Maaryah be reunited in this life?

The epic adventure of the Munnari Chronicles series continues in the seventh novel, *Munnari Redemption*.

# PRONUNCIATION GUIDE

b´ This low-pitched popping sound is made by pursing the lips together, rolling them inward, and releasing them, creating a low-toned pop.

p´ This high-pitched popping sound is made by pursing the lips together, extending them forward, and releasing them, creating a high-toned pop.

t´ This clicking sound is made by placing the tongue against the palate, and pulling it down, making a sharp, clicking sound.

| WORD | PRONUNCIATION |
|---|---|
| Ab´as | ă b´ăs |
| Ada | ā´ dä |
| Adia | ā´ dī ä |
| Adrina | ä drēn´ ä |
| Ayetoz | ā´ ē tōz |
| Agganor | ăg găn ŏr |
| Andent | ăn´ dĕnt |
| Anterra | ăn tĕr´ rä |
| Arbreno | är´ brĕnō |
| Ardo | är dō |
| Areena | ä rē´ n ä |
| argent | är´ jĕnt |
| Atez | ā tĕz |
| Atura | ä too ră |
| Ayascho | ī´ ä shō |
| Bardas | bär´ dăs |
| bataro | bä´ tăr ō |
| Bati | bă´ tē |
| Batru | bă´ troo |
| Bazi | bā´ zē |
| Bazio | bā´ zēō |
| Ben-do-teg | bĕn´ dō tĕg |
| Bento | bĕn tō´ |
| betzoe | bĕt zō´ |
| bhat | bhăt |
| Brand | brănd |

| WORD | PRONUNCIATION |
|---|---|
| Braydo | brā´ dō |
| broesayr | brō sār |
| Buffo | bŭf fō |
| Chashutza | chă shoo´ tzä |
| Chashutzo | chă shoo´ tzō |
| Dada | dä´ dä |
| Danner | dăn´ nĕr |
| Debruntz | dē´ brŭntz |
| Dartez | där tĕz |
| defetane | dĕf´ ĕ tān |
| Demeos | dē´ mē ōs |
| Dendra | dĕn drä |
| detzamar | dĕtz´ ä mär |
| Deveena | dĕ vē´ nä |
| divitz | dīv´ ītz |
| doez | dō´ ĕz |
| Dondi | dŏn´ dē |
| Doros | dō´ rōs |
| Du | dū |
| Duba | doo´ bä |
| Dubo | doo´ bō |
| Dumaz | doo´ măz |
| Dunderno | dŭn´ dĕr nō |
| Duntavo | dŭn´ tăvō |
| Edder | ĕd´ dĕr |
| Endet | ĕn dĕt´ |

| WORD | PRONUNCIATION |
|---|---|
| Eos | ēōs |
| Ezihod | ē zī´ hŏd |
| Eos | ē ōs |
| Fardinza | fär´ dĭnzä |
| Farwune | făr woon |
| Fayeetez | fā ēt´ tĕs |
| Feeder | fē dĕr |
| Fento | fĕn tō´ |
| Fidus | fī´ dŭs |
| Fino | fē´ nō |
| Fredora | frē´ dŏr ä |
| Frunden | frŭn dĕn´ |
| Gaft | găft |
| Gando | găn´ dō |
| Gangorno | găn´ gōr nō |
| gartz | gärtz |
| gee | gē |
| Gheedan | gē´ dăn |
| Gherd | gĕrd |
| gorga | gōr´ gä |
| gravetro | gră´ vĕ trō |
| gravetum | gră´ vĕ tŭm |
| Grazius | gră´ zē ŭs |
| Grebsanto | grĕb săntō |
| greevayr | grē´ sār |
| Grunzen | grŭn zĕn |

| WORD | PRONUNCIATION |
|---|---|
| Gund | gŭnd |
| Gute | gūt |
| ha | hä |
| habaga | hä´ bä gä |
| Hani | hă nē´ |
| Hendetz | hĕn dĕtz´ |
| Hentza | hĕnt zä |
| Harmon | hăr´ mŏn |
| Haro | hä´ rō |
| Hermanez | hĕr´ măn ĕz |
| Henna | hĕn´ nä |
| Hentza | hĕnt zä |
| Hertora | hĕr´ tŏrĭ |
| Hubris | hoo brĭs |
| Huma | hoo mä |
| Hunder | hŭn dĕr |
| Idop | ī´ dŏp |
| Ios | ī ōs |
| Iroesadeen | ī rō´ să dēn |
| Isse | īs sē´ |
| Jeztee | jĕz tē´ |
| Maaryah | mär ī´ ä |
| Magheedo | mä gē´ dō |
| Marna | măr nä |
| Matti-mas | mä tē´ mäs |
| meashe | mē´ shĕ |

| WORD | PRONUNCIATION |
|---|---|
| megato | mĕ gä´ tō |
| megatus | mĕ gä´ tŭs |
| Mendora | mĕn dōrä´ |
| Men-dre-dor | mĕn´ drĕ dōr |
| Mindetta | mĭn dĕt tä |
| Minta | mĭn tä |
| Mintara | mĭn tärä |
| Mordez | mŏr dĕz |
| munna | mŭn´ nä |
| Munnari | mŭn´ nä rē |
| Munnevo | mŭn´ nē vō |
| Munnoga | mŭn´ nō gä |
| Myndron | mĭn drŏn |
| Myron | mī´ rŏn |
| Namad | nä´ mäd |
| Namada | nä´ mäd ä |
| Nedenna | nē´ dĕnnä |
| Neehoer | nē´ hō ĕr |
| Nestess | nĕs´ tĕs |
| Nestor | nĕs´ tōr |
| Nevesant | nĕv ĕ sănt´ |
| Nita | nē tä´ |
| Nitori | nĭ tŏrē´ |
| Nu | nū |
| Nudart | nū därt´ |
| Numo | nūmō |

| WORD | PRONUNCIATION |
|---|---|
| Oetan | ō´ tăn |
| Oeto | ō tō |
| Ootyiah | oo tē´ ä |
| p´atezas | p´ātĕ´ zăs |
| p´oez | p´ōĕz |
| Pahno | päh´ nō |
| Panemento | păn´ nĕ mĕntō |
| Pannera | păn´ nĕr rä |
| Pemmet | pĕm mĕt |
| Pammon | păm´ mŏn |
| Parji | păr jē´ |
| Pendor | pĕn´ dōr |
| Pen-dow-mon | pĕn´ dŏw mŏn |
| Pentina | pĕn tēnä |
| Perdeeto | pĕr dē´ tō |
| Perdiz | pĕr dĭz´ |
| Pershon | pĕr´ shŏn |
| P'on-dre-vitz | pŏn´ drĕ vĭtz |
| Ponti | pŏn tē´ |
| Pontus | pŏn´ tŭs |
| Ponti | pŏn tē´ |
| Pordonzo | pōr dŏnzō |
| Pratina | pră´ tēnä |
| primatza | prĭ mätzä |
| Pundi | pŭn´ dē |
| purrant | pĕr´ rănt |

| WORD | PRONUNCIATION |
|---|---|
| Pydeez | pī´ dēz |
| Radz | rădz |
| rana | ränä |
| Rao | rā´ ō |
| raster | răs´ tĕr |
| Ratorni | ră tŏnē |
| regum | rĕ´ gŭm |
| Remmo | rĕm´ mō |
| Rendoto | rĕn dōtō´ |
| rezus | rē´ zŭs |
| Riazon | rī´ ä zŏn |
| samaran | săm´ ä răn |
| Sassin | să´ sĭn |
| Savas | să´ văs |
| schazu | schä´ zoo |
| Seemo | sē´mō |
| seshtane | sĕsh´ tān |
| sestardi | sĕs tăr´ dē |
| Sevootyiah | sĕv oo tē´ ä |
| Shadi | shă dē´ |
| Shergus | shĕr gŭs´ |
| Showton | shō´ tăn |
| Sofi | sō fē´ |
| Soidentee | soy dĕn´ tē |
| Stasenar | stă´ sĕn ăr |
| Stenz | stĕnz |

| WORD | PRONUNCIATION |
|---|---|
| sutro | soo trō´ |
| T´erio | t´ĕ rē ō |
| taah | tä |
| taahso | tä´ sō |
| Tangundo | tä´ sō |
| tanter | tăn tĕr |
| Tanzi | tăn´zē |
| Teema | tē´ mä |
| Teg-ar-mos | tĕg´ är mŭs |
| Teness | tĕn´ ĕs |
| Tenny | tĕn ē´ |
| tetzae | tĕt´ zā |
| tetzus | tĕt´ zŭs |
| Tezpont | tĕz´ pŏnt |
| Tiro | tĭ´ rō |
| Titus | tī´ tŭs |
| Toba | tōbä |
| Tondo | tŏn´ dō |
| todo | tō dō´ |
| Tono | t´ō nō |
| T´orbin | t´ŏr bĭn |
| Torvenza | tŏr vĕnzä |
| Tretrio | trĕ´ trē ō |
| Tuffen | tŭf fĕn |
| T´uft | tŭft |
| Tumper | tŭm´ pĕr |

| WORD | PRONUNCIATION |
|---|---|
| Tumtuo | tŭm´ too ō |
| tuntro | tŭn´ trō |
| Turvy | tŭr´ vĕ |
| Ty-fen-Ezora | tī fĕn ēzŏrä |
| tzaah | tzä |
| Tzani | tză´ nē |
| Tzeecha | tzē´ chä |
| Tzeechoe | tzē´ chō |
| tzonoe | tzō´ nō |
| Tzorbin | tzŏr´ bĭn |
| Uragah | ŭr ä´ gä |
| Varios | văr ē´ ŏs |
| Vendie | vĕn dē´ |
| Verdeto | vĕr dē´ tō |
| Vetz | vĕtz |
| Vihi | vē´ hē |
| Wandra | wän drä´ |
| Watzen | wätzĕn |
| We | wē |
| wernt | wĕrnt |
| Yaddet | yăd´ dĕt |
| Yos | yōs |
| zanth | zănth |
| Zedo | zē dō |
| Zedona | zĕ´ dōnä |
| Zeffany | zĕf fănē´ |

| WORD | PRONUNCIATION |
|---|---|
| Zerio | zĕ´ rē ō |
| Zet | zĕt |
| Zethus | zĕth´ ŭs |
| Zetz | zĕtz |
| zin | zĭn |
| Zossemo | zŏ sē´ mō |
| Zosse | zŏs´ sĕ |
| Zue | zoo |
| Zuni | zoo´ nē |

# PREVIOUSLY INTRODUCED CHARACTERS

| NAME | ROLE |
|---|---|
| Andarvo | This is King Teg-ar-mos's given name. |
| Atura | Atura is assigned to Coleman by the Batru village chief. He is to become her provider, and she is charged with teaching him world-speak, the native tongue. |
| Ayascho | Ayascho takes an instant dislike for Coleman. During a hunt, their hunt team is attacked by the most fearsome beast in the jungle, a gorga. Coleman notices Ayascho's act of cowardice. Coleman chooses not to expose Ayascho's shame. Ayascho feels he is in Coleman's debt and won't rest until he can reclaim his honor. During their long journey to Anterra, Ayascho and Coleman become friends and allies. He is trained by the priests, becomes literate, and is chosen by Tondo to be a subcommander of the army. After the Munnari War, he is advanced by King Teg-ar-mos to the rank of tetzae, a Sire of the kingdom. He is sent back to his home village by the Sutro Seer on an urgent, undefined mission. He becomes chief of his Batru village and begins forming the Batru Confederation by allying with other villages. |
| Bardas | Bardas is a guard in Titus's detachment. |
| Braydo | King Teg-ar-mos's massive bodyguard. |

| NAME | ROLE |
|---|---|
| Chashutza | Chashutza is the wife of Chashutzo. |
| Chashutzo | Chashutzo is the leader of Coleman's hunt team, who was severely injured during a gorga attack. |
| Coleman | Coleman, an Earthling, who becomes known as Tondo, meaning the visitor, arrives on a distant planet due to a mishap while making an experimental transit from the Earth to the Moon. He soon learns that after his transit, he is imbued with seemingly magical powers. Coleman nourishes the good seeds and chooses to use his increasing power and influence on his new world to benefit others. He prepares the forces of Good for their great struggle against Evil.<br>After freeing the enslaved people on his estate, he rallied the kingdom in the Munnari War, using slave warriors to defeat the invaders. After the victory, the king advances him to the rank of Lord, unites all the kingdoms, and frees all enslaved people in the new domain.<br>Coleman returns to his estate, bonds with Maaryah, and they have a daughter they name Maari. Coleman also eliminates the brigand threat, gaining more influence within the kingdom. |
| Danner | He is an ex-slave freed by Tondo and the younger brother of Edder. He leaves the estate but later returns and becomes a paid laborer. |

| NAME | ROLE |
|---|---|
| Dartez | He is a defetane officer who serves in the Soidentee Army. He was captured during the United Kingdom's first relief of Te Femma, but he escaped and reported back to the Sutro Showton. He was rewarded with a position in the Showton's Invincibles. |
| Deveena | She is a subcommander serving in the Te Femma Stontza and assigned to the Te Femma brigade. |
| Dendra | She is one of the four Te Femma slaves given to Tondo by Queen Ezora. |
| Doros | He is the Tondo Estate manor house manservant. |
| Duba | Duba is Dubo's wife. |
| Dubo | Dubo, a hunter, is gored and killed by a tuntro. Village tradition requires his family to be banished. Coleman argues for ending this wicked tradition. |
| Dumaz | Mama and Papa Dumaz are ancient slaves on the Oetan estate. They prepare Maaryah's slave herd's daily food, flat-cakes. |
| Edder | He is an ex-slave freed by Tondo and the older brother of Danner. He leaves the estate and doesn't return. |
| Eos | He is the Tondo Estate manor house errand boy. |
| Fardinza | She is the senior royal counselor to Queen Ty-fen-Ezora of Te Femma. |
| Fayeetez | He is an ex-slave and a commander of one of Tondo's samaran wings during the Munnari War. He quickly rises in rank and becomes Coleman's esteemed cavalry commander. |

| NAME | ROLE |
| --- | --- |
| Frunden | Megato Frunden commands the crews who manage and fire the United Kingdom army's cannons. |
| Gando | He is one of Tondo's Rangers. |
| Gheedan | Gheedan is a sharp-eyed guard in Titus's detachment. |
| Harmon | He is Maaryah's father and a non-officer leader in the Army of the United Kingdom. |
| Haro | He is an ex-slave freed by Tondo and helper of the estate's blacksmith, Pendor. |
| Hermanez | He is a black man from an island in the middle of the ocean. He assists Master T´erio in building the first successful ship design in the known world. |
| Idop | He is the former commander of the Teg-ar-mos kingdom Pannera, the city guards. He becomes a king's counselor and a good friend to Tondo. He is trained by the priests, and he becomes a subcommander of Tondo's army. After the Munnari War, he is advanced by King Teg-ar-mos to the rank of tetzae, a Sire of the kingdom. Due to a made decision on his part, he and others under his command are captured during the Brigand Campaign, requiring Tondo to initiate a bold and dangerous rescue attempt. Unfortunately, Idop loses an eye at the hands of his cruel captors. |
| Maarea | She was Maaryah's mother. This is also the name given to Tondo's and Maaryah's daughter. |

| NAME | ROLE |
|---|---|
| Maari | She is the daughter of Tondo and Maaryah. She is called Maari for short. She was taken captive by the Showton's manslayers during their attack on the Tondo Estate. |
| Maaryah | Maaryah is a young woman who begins her life as a slave. Through Tondo's intervention, she is freed and is able to reach her full potential. At first, she fears the outlander, but the kindness and respect he offers her changes her fear into love. She manages the Tondo Estate during the Munnari War, and the estate provides the food stocks that allow the kingdom to hold out while Tondo builds his army.<br>After the Munnari War, Tondo returns to the estate and reveals that he comes from another world. They soon bond, raising Maaryah to the rank of Dame. Maaryah gives birth to a daughter they name Maari. |
| Mintara | She is the bondmate of Izeon, the Tondo Estate's senior boss. |
| Myron | Myron is a merchant from Anterra, the Ancient City. Coleman learns he is more than 600 years old. |
| Namad | Namad is the tracker in Coleman's hunt team and Nita's father. |
| Namada | Namada is Namad's wife and Nita's mother. |
| Nedenna | She is the senior commander serving in the Te Femma Stontza, the city guard. |

| NAME | ROLE |
|---|---|
| Neehoer | He is a toady in the service of the Sutro Showtan. He designs and oversees the construction of his new master's palace and castle. He is raised to the position of Attendant Superior. |
| Nestess | He is a commander of one of Tondo's foot warrior wings during the Munnari War. Due to his steadfast defense of the line, Tondo often refers to him as Stonewall. He becomes a brigade commander in the kingdom's growing army. |
| Nestor | Nestor was the foreman of the Oetan Estate. He relished inflicting pain and suffering on the estate's slaves. He leaves the Tondo Estate, but he never forgets the one slave he could never break, Maaryah. |
| Nevesant | Nevesant is a young orphaned delinquent who first notices the strange-looking Tangendo. He comes to revere the outsider. As Tangendo's power and wickedness grow, Nevesant mimics his revered master. When Tangundo declares himself to be the Sutro Showtan, Nevesant is chosen as the leader of his manslayers, and he is given thc title as the Suto Showtan's Dark One. |
| Nita | Nita is Namad's daughter. In a moment of weakness, she steals Tzeecha's necklace. Village law demands that she be banished, a sure death sentence. Coleman argues for a more reasonable punishment. Ayascho is attracted to Nita. |
| Numo | He is a young man, branded as a thief, taken in by Tondo. He becomes the estate's thrice handler. |

| NAME | ROLE |
|---|---|
| Ootyiah | Ootyiah is Oetan's daughter, and she is considered to be the most beautiful young woman in the kingdom. |
| Otean | Oetan had been granted stewardship by the king of the Oetan Estate. He is the master of all estate slaves, including Maaryah. He was killed by brigands. |
| Pahno | He is a temple priest of the attendant rank. He serves Master Shergus and Master Varios while they are training Coleman, Idop, and Ayascho. |
| Pammon | He is the Tondo Estate scholar and schoolteacher. |
| Pendor | He is the Tondo Estate blacksmith. |
| Ponti | Ponti is a dim-witted slave on the Oetan Estate. |
| Pontus | Pontus is a guard in Titus's detachment. |
| Rao | Rao is a guard in Titus's detachment. |
| Riazon | The Riazon's are Lord and Dame bondmates of the old Teg-ar-mos kingdom and now the United Kingdom. |
| Sassin | He is one of Tangundo's outlaws, a follower of Munnevo. After Tangundo's power grows, Sassin is ordered to create the Invincibles, the Sutro Showton's most elite and ruthless warriors. |
| Seemo | He is a young man who is the Tondo Estate samaran handler. |
| Sevootyiah | She is Lady Otan and former mistress of the Otan estate. She is also the mother of Ootyiah, Queen Teg-ar-mos. She bonds with Sire Idop and becomes a Lady of the kingdom. |

| NAME | ROLE |
| --- | --- |
| Shadi | Shadi is the scent-man in Coleman's hunt team. |
| Shergus | Shergus, a master priest serving the Temple of the Unnamed God, is the greatest swordsman in the kingdom. He is sent by the Sutro Seer to train Coleman, Idop, and Ayascho. |
| Sofi | She is a queen's escort assigned to Idop during his and Tondo's diplomatic mission to the besieged Te Femma. She is banished by Queen Ezora and sent by Tondo to his estate. |
| Soidentee | He is a senior commander of warriors of the Ben-do-teg Kingdom. After the king is killed by Tangendo, he changes loyalties to his new and brutal tyrant. |
| Sutro Seer | The senior religious leader and follower of the Great Unnamed God. |
| Taahso | Taahso is the shaman of the Batru village that befriends Coleman. He possesses magical powers that intrigue Coleman and leads him to discover similar powers within himself. |
| Tangundo | Another off-worlder, whose name is unpronounceable, arrives on the planet shortly before Coleman does. This off-worlder initially is named Tangundo, meaning outsider. Because he has a hairy face, the local populace considers him a beast-man, and they force him into the perpetual mist where an unspeakable horror lives. He survives that encounter and befriends the young orphan boy Nevesant. He begins to nourish the evil seeds within himself. |

| NAME | ROLE |
|---|---|
| Teg-ar-mos | King Teg-ar-mos is the ruler of the kingdom where the Ancient City and the Temple of the Unnamed God are located. He is petitioned by the temple's Sutro Seer to send a detachment of city guards into the Wilderness to fetch the unusual outlander, Coleman. After the outlander resuscitates the prince, the king grants Coleman stewardship of a huge estate. |
| Teness | Teness is a guard in Titus's detachment. |
| T´erio | He is a priest of the master rank, and he is considered the best carpenter in the kingdom. With Hermanez's assistance and following Tondo's design, they build the first successful ship in the known world. |
| Titus | Sestardi Titus is a non-officer who leads a detachment of Anterra city guards to fetch the unusual outlander Myron the merchant discovered in the Wilderness. |
| Torbetza | He is a young baron of the United Kingdom. He manages Zedona's musical performances, and the couple has announced they will bond. |
| Torvenza | He is an elderly baron of the United Kingdom. He controls and provides most of the entertainment in the old kingdom of Teg-ar-mos. He is also the father of Baron Torbetza. |
| Turpetz | He is a megato officer who serves in the United Kingdom Army. He commands the 1st Messenger Detachment. |
| Tzeecha | Tzeecha is the wife of Tzeechoe. |

| NAME | ROLE |
|---|---|
| Tzeechoe | \Tzeechoe becomes Coleman's village mentor and close friend, teaching him the skills he must know in order to survive in the Wilderness. |
| Varios | Varios, a master priest serving the Temple of the Unnamed God, is the greatest scholar in the kingdom. He is sent by the Sutro Seer to train Coleman, Idop, and Ayascho. |
| Wandra | She is the bondmate of Pammon, the Tondo Estate scholar and teacher. |
| Yaddet | He is the Tondo Brothers brick commander assigned to protect the Tondo Estate. |
| Zedona | She is a queen's escort assigned to Tondo during his and Idop's diplomatic mission to the besieged Te Femma. She is banished by Queen Ezora and sent by Tondo to his estate. She becomes a renowned musical performer in the United Kingdom. She and Baron Torbetza plan to bond. |
| Zoseemo | Zoseemo is a young slave owned by Myron, the merchant. He is the first slave Coleman meets. Coleman is shocked to learn that the youthful-looking slave is more than seventy spans old. |
| Zuni | She is a subcommander serving in the Te Femma Stontza and assigned to the Te Femma brigade. |

# GLOSSARY OF TERMS

**Novels One through Six**

| DEFINITIONS/TERMS |
|---|
| ***Anterran Calendar and Daily Time*** |
| A typical span is four-hundred days. Every third span is a leap-span, which is four-hundred and one days. |
| ***Apto*** |
| ***Detzamar*** |
| This is a non-officer rank in the Te Femma Stontza, the city guard. |
| Also referred to as detz, a period of 40 days. There are four wernts in a detzamar, and there are ten detzamars in a span. Detzamars have the following names:<br>1. Ant — 6. Du-Ant<br>2. Zue — 7. Du-Zue<br>3. Dzaah — 8. Du-Dzaah<br>4. Tuz — 9. Du-Tuz<br>5. Mot — 10. Du-Mot |
| |
| ***Anterran daily time*** |
| An Anterran day is twenty-two segments, equivalent to twenty-two hours. A segment is ten intervals long, equivalent to sixty minutes. An interval is equivalent to six minutes. |
| ***Anterran measures of distance*** |
| march ≈ 15-20 miles<br>margher ≈ 1 mile<br>rad ≈ 100 yards<br>radett ≈ 100 feet<br>radi ≈ 1 foot<br>radneva ≈ 2 inches |

## DEFINITIONS/TERMS

### *Anterran Military Ranks*

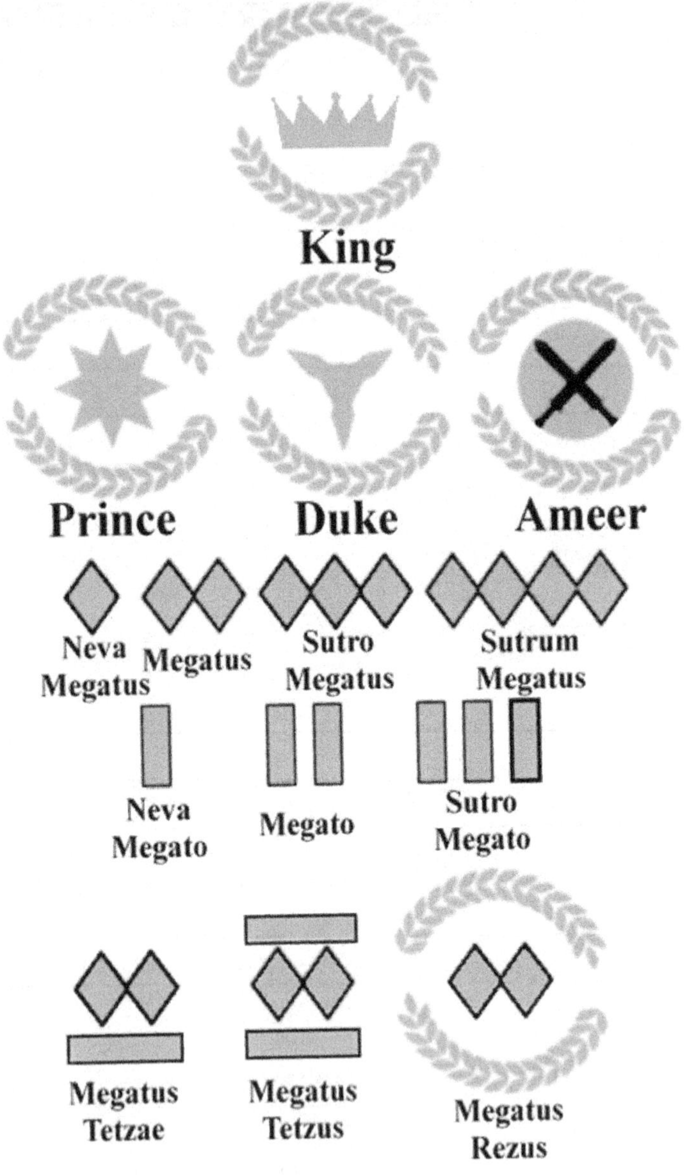

# DEFINITIONS/TERMS

## *United Kingdom Military Ranks*

OFFICER RANKS

Wreaths and Bars

REZUS: **Military rank inside a split wreath**

TETZUZ: **Military rank with a zanth horizontal bar above and below**

TEXAE: **Military rank with a zanth horizontal bar below**

KING: **(Commander-in-Chief): a crown symbol surrounded by a wreath**

PRINCE: **One large eight-pointed zanth star surrounded by a wreath**

DUKE: **Three-pointed zanth star surrounded by a wreath**

AMEER: **Royal Adjutant of the Army and the commander of all military forces; a zanth circle with crossed swords surrounded by a wreath**

SUTRUM MEGATUS: **An Army commander of around 20,000+ warriors; four zanth diamonds**

SUTRO MEGATUS: **A division commander of around 10,000-20,000 warriors; three zanth diamonds**

MEGATUS: **A brigade commander of around 5,000-10,000 warriors; two zanth diamonds**

NEVA MEGATUS: **A sub-brigade commander of around 1,500-2,000 warriors; one zanth diamond**

SUTRO MEGATO: **A wing commander of around 1,000-1,500 warriors; three vertical zanth bars**

MEGATO: **A troop commander of around 200-300 warriors; two vertical zanth bars**

NEVA MEGATO: **A brick commander of around 50 warriors; one vertical zanth bar**

## *Non-Officer Ranks*

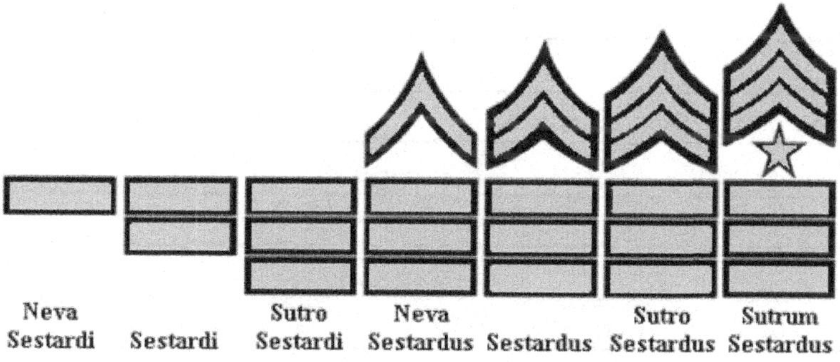

| DEFINITIONS/TERMS |
|---|
| **SUTRUM SESTARDUS: a senior non-officer above brigade level division or army; three blue stripes plus three blue chevrons and a blue star under the chevrons**<br>**SUTRO SESTARDUS: a brigade's senior non-officer; three blue stripes plus three blue chevrons**<br>**SESTARDUS: a sub-brigade's senior non-officer; three blue stripes plus two blue chevrons**<br>**NEVA SESTARDUS: a wing's senior non-officer; three blue stripes plus one blue chevron**<br>**SUTRO SESTARDI: a troop's senior non-officer; three blue stripes**<br>**SESTARDI: a brick's senior non-officer; two blue stripes**<br>**NEVA SESTARDI: a rank's non-officer; one blue strip** |
| ***Arbon*** |
| This the title of a queen's adviser from Te Femma. |
| ***Arjent*** |
| The standard monetary unit of Anterran commoners and the lower-classes, cast from eez (copper). One-hundred arjents equal one bhat. |
| ***Batru*** |
| The native villager's god; also, the name used by the villagers to refer to their tribe |
| ***Bhat*** |
| The standard monetary unit of the Anterran gentry, cast from zin (silver). |
| ***Creeper*** |
| An insect; also, slang for a pest. |
| ***Broesayr*** |
| This is a male spouse of Te Femma. |
| ***Cross-over*** |
| To pass away; to die |

| DEFINITIONS/TERMS |
|---|
| ***Derpentza*** |
| This is a lower-ranking officer of the Te Femma Stontza, the city guard. |
| ***Defetane*** |
| A junior officer rank in the Ben-do-teg Kingdom |
| ***Detzamar*** |
| A 40-day period; refer to Anterran calendar and daily time |
| ***Divitz*** |
| Cotton |
| ***Drund*** |
| Farwune city guards. |
| ***Eez*** |
| Copper |
| ***Gant*** |
| A diluted wine-like drink |
| ***Gartz*** |
| The world-speak rendering of glass. |
| ***Gizz*** |
| The world-speak rendering of kiss |
| ***Godstone*** |
| The world-speak rendering of loadstone. |
| ***Gorn*** |
| The world-speak rendering of corn. |
| ***Gorner*** |
| The standard currency of Te Femma. 1 gorner equates to 1.5 bhat. |

| DEFINITIONS/TERMS |
| --- |
| ***Gravetro*** |
| A metal similar to low-grade iron |
| ***Gravetum*** |
| A metal similar to iron, having the color of brass |
| ***Grevair*** |
| This is a female spouse of Te Femma. |
| ***Gristening*** |
| The world-speak rending of christening; a ceremony in which a new ship or boat is named and launched. |
| ***Groundshake*** |
| An earthquake |
| ***Gumpass*** |
| The world-speak rendering of compass |
| ***Gunz*** |
| Cannon |
| ***Ha*** |
| World-speak for yes; also, an exclamation similar to okay, oh, or well |
| ***Haptane*** |
| A senior officer rank in the Ben-do-teg Kingdom. |
| ***Hoy*** |
| A world-speak exclamation of surprise or despair |
| ***Meashe*** |
| Food; meal |
| ***Megato*** |
| A junior Pannera officer |
| ***Megatus*** |
| A senior Pannera officer |

| DEFINITIONS/TERMS |
| --- |
| ***Munnoga-touched*** |
| A person who has become insane or is deluded |
| ***Oy*** |
| A world-speak exclamation of surprise similar to oh or ah |
| ***P'atezas*** |
| The planet's source of light and life; equivalent to the Earth's sun |
| ***Panerra*** |
| The Anterra city guards |
| ***P'oez*** |
| Honored slayer of prey |
| ***Priest Ranks*** |
| Sutrum Seer Myndron<br>Sutro Seer<br>Sutro Adept (aka 'master')<br>Adept<br>Tutor<br>Attendant<br>Neophyte |
| ***Primatza*** |
| This is the senior rank of the Te Femma Stontza, the city guard. |
| ***Purrant*** |
| This is a person of authority appointed by a king to oversee local affairs. |
| ***Rana*** |
| This is the royal rank of senior advisor to the queen of Te Femma. |
| ***Regum*** |
| A monetary unit primarily used by the Anterran gentry, cast from zanth (gold). One-hundred bhat equals one regum |

| DEFINITIONS/TERMS |
|---|
| ***Rockman*** |
| A slinger |
| ***Sandwitz*** |
| The world-speak rendering of *sandwich.* |
| ***Seshtane*** |
| This is a non-officer rank in the Ben-do-teg kingdom. |
| ***Sister/ Sisterhood*** |
| Female citizens of Te Femma refer to themselves as sisters and members of the city's sisterhood. |
| ***Span*** |
| This is the duration of the planet's orbit around its star, which takes 400.33 days. One day is added to every third span at the end of the detzamar of Ant. |
| ***Sub*** |
| A derogatory term used by Te Femman sisters when referring to non-citizen women; a woman who subservient to a male. |
| ***Sutro*** |
| Greater; senior, superior |
| ***Tamer*** |
| This is a scourge with multiple leather cords attached to a wooden or leather handle. A heavy-tamer has pieces of bones woven into the strands. A knotted-tamer has knots tied in several places along each strand's length. |
| ***Tanter*** |
| This is a stocky mount with spiral horns, primarily used by mounted Showton warriors. |
| ***Tezpont*** |
| The head of a hammer. The World-speak rendering of West Point; the Anterran army's military school for officer training. |

| DEFINITIONS/TERMS |
|---|
| ***Tza*** |
| The inner-power; see tzaah |
| ***Tzaah*** |
| The inner-power, also known as taah |
| ***Vestang*** |
| This is a world-speak profanity and disparaging remark. It means snake-legs, something non-existent and/or useless. |
| ***Weak-ground*** |
| Quicksand |
| ***Wernt*** |
| A wernt is a period of ten days. Days have the following names:<br>1. Nu — 6. Du-Nu<br>2. Tu — 7. Du-Tu<br>3. We — 8. Du-We<br>4. Gute — 9. Du-Gute<br>5. Zet — 10. Du-Zet |
| ***Wur-gor*** |
| The world-speak rendering of *worker.* |
| ***Zanth*** |
| Gold |
| ***Zerio*** |
| The southwesterly wind |
| ***Zerr*** |
| The world-speak rending of sir |
| ***Zin*** |
| Silver |
| ***Zondar*** |
| A Showton war-beast. |

The Coleman Travel Map
Caver's Mountain
Batru's Eye Crater
Magheedo Mountains
Wasteland
Magheedo Plain
The Wilderness
Otterina
Terratia
Anterra
The Ancient City
Coleman's Batru Village

The Three Cities
Magheedo Mountains
Magheedo Plains
Magheedo Marshland
Terratia
Anterra
Otterina

The Tondo Estate
Penno Estate
Tondo Estate

The Munnari War
Battle Area
Teg-ar-mos
Wall

Cities of the
Great Gulf
Magheedo
Mountains
Slave
Camp
Magheedo
Plain
Great
Gulf
Salt Mines
Te Femma
Otterina
Terratia
Anterra
The Ancient
City

The Southlands
Te Femma
Anderez
Rendoto
Nudart
Panemento
Fortress Showtonia

Made in the USA
Monee, IL
04 November 2026

67387475R10223